CONTEXTS
AND
DIALOGUE

The Society for Asian and Comparative Philosophy Monograph Series was started in 1974. Works are published in the series that deal with any area of Asian philosophy, or any other field of philosophy examined from a comparative perspective. The aim of the series is to make available scholarly works that exceed article length, but may be too specialized for the general reading public, and to make these works available in inexpensive editions without sacrificing the orthography of non-Western languages.

Monograph No. 21
SOCIETY FOR ASIAN
AND COMPARATIVE PHILOSOPHY

CONTEXTS
Yogācāra Buddhism and Modern
AND
Psychology on the Subliminal Mind
DIALOGUE

TAO JIANG

UNIVERSITY
OF HAWAI'I
PRESS
HONOLULU

Library of Congress Cataloging-in-Publication Data

Jiang, Tao, 1969–

Contexts and dialogue : Yogacara Buddhism and modern

psychology on the subliminal mind / Tao Jiang.

p. cm. —(Monograph no. 21, Society for Asian and Comparative Philosophy)

Includes bibliographical references and index.

ISBN-13: 978-0-8248-3106-6 (pbk. : alk. paper)

ISBN-10: 0-8248-3106-3 (pbk.: alk. paper)

1. Alayavijñana. 2. Buddhism—Psychology. I. Title. II. Series:

Monograph . . . of the Society for Asian Comparative Philosophy ; 21.

BQ7496.J53 2006

294.3'3615–dc22

2006013715

University of Hawai'i Press books are printed on

acid-free paper and meet the guidelines for permanence

and durability of the Council on Library Resources

Designed by Cameron Poulter

Printed by Versa Press, Inc.

To my parents

CONTENTS

ACKNOWLEDGMENTS

Many people made it possible for me to complete this book, and in the limited space I have here I can do little justice to what is owed them. During my graduate years at Temple University, Shigenori Nagatomo, an inspiring philosopher and teacher, was instrumental in leading me into the world of comparative philosophy. His command of philosophical traditions, East and West, has greatly stimulated my own philosophical endeavors. His inexhaustible patience with me and unwavering confidence in my project and my ability to carry it out were crucial to my fruitful years as a graduate student under his supervision. I will always remember the lively exchanges we had in his Japanese reading classes as well as at his dinner table.

I am also grateful to have had the opportunity to learn from J. N. Mohanty during my years at Temple. His presentation of the ideas of Kant, Hegel, Husserl, Heidegger, and classical Indian philosophy was unparalleled. He has had a major impact on the way I approach philosophy. I would like to express my appreciation to Ellen Zhang, who constantly pushed me to think more critically about the Chinese and Buddhist philosophical traditions, both inside and outside the classroom.

Several other teachers made my life at Temple memorable. Barbara Thornbury of the Critical Languages Center was a great support to me, both in my Japanese study and other academic pursuits. Louis Mangione and John Means of the Critical Languages Center also extended a helping hand when I needed it. Kathleen Uno of the Department of History offered me valuable insights into historiography, particularly in the study of modern Japanese history. The late Charles Wei-hsun Fu was a stimulating teacher whose lectures, personality, and confidence in me I will always cherish. My appreciation also goes to Rosane Rocher of the University of Pennsylvania, whose brilliant exposition of Sanskrit and other Indo-European languages provided me with a completely new perspective on how human languages work. Nathan Sivin of the University of Pennsylvania kindly invited me to his classes on Taoism and traditional Chinese medicine, which opened my eyes to many dimensions of ancient Chinese medical practices of which I was largely ignorant.

The friends I made in graduate school, both inside and outside the religion department, were all amazing people, and in many different ways they taught, supported, challenged, and nurtured me through the program. A special appreciation goes to Amy Weigand, who had the courage and the patience to proofread an earlier version of this work.

I would like to thank my colleagues and friends at Southern Illinois University Carbondale for the memorable four years I spent there. Regular encounters with Thomas Alexander and Stephen Tyman were crucial to sustaining my effort to approach Buddhism and comparative philosophy more critically. Their nurturing care over the years made my life at Carbondale a wonderful experience. Discussions with Anthony Steinbock helped me clarify my thesis in Chapter Five. Our chats after a movie were always refreshing and stimulating. My often heated debates with Randall Auxier challenged me to further my study of philosophy. Robert Hahn was very helpful in showing me how to navigate academia. Larry Hickman, Pat Manfredi, George Schedler, and Kenneth Stikkers were all very generous with their help and encouragement. My close friendship with Sara Beardsworth and Andrew Youpa will always be near to my heart. Our conversations every Friday night at the Chicago Underground restaurant are among my most cherished memories. My student Travis Smith was a great help in early on weeding out errors in the manuscript. Department secretaries Richard Black, Jeletta Brant, Francis Stanley, and the late Christian Martin as well as many graduate students all helped to make my four years at Carbondale memorable.

Thomas Kasulis and Kenneth Inada were gracious enough to read an early version of this work. Their perceptive comments were very important in the revision process. The insights of two anonymous reviewers are also much appreciated.

Rutgers University Research Council provided a generous subvention for the production of this book. The author expresses appreciation to the University Seminars at Columbia University for their help in publication. Material in this work was presented to the University Seminar on Buddhist Studies. The Office of Research Development and Administration, Southern Illinois University Carbondale, also offered financial support. A Yin Shun Foundation fellowship allowed me to devote my time and energy to writing.

I would like to thank John Schroeder, editor of the Monographs on Asian and Comparative Philosophy, for including my book in the series, and Keith Leber, editor at the University of Hawai'i Press, for his invaluable assistance in producing the final work. I am also grateful to copy editor Stephanie Chun for her perfectionist professionalism in weeding out problems in the manuscript. A slightly different version of Chapter Two was published as "*Ālayavijñāna* and the Problematic of Continuity in the *Cheng Weishi Lun*" in *Journal of Indian Philosophy* 33:3. A shortened version of Chapter Four appeared as "The Storehouse Consciousness and the Unconscious: A Comparative Study of Xuan Zang and Freud on the Subliminal Mind" in *Journal of the American Academy of Religion* 72:1. A revised version of Chapter Five was published as "Accessibility of the Subliminal Mind: Transcendence vs. Immanence" in *Continental Philosophy Review* 38:3–4.

Last, but not least, I would like to thank my parents for their loving affection and unwarranted pride in their son. This book is dedicated to them as a small token of my gratitude and love.

INTRODUCTION

One major attraction of Buddhism to the contemporary world is its therapeutic value, which is derived from its penetrating insights into the human psyche and many of its practices. As David Loy observes, "Buddhism's main point of entry into Western culture is now Western psychology, especially psychotherapy" (2). This is evidenced by the fact that "Buddhism . . . is increasingly being looked on, not just as a religion, but as a system for understanding and promoting personal growth, and as such it is seen as offering a much more positive idea of the nature of mental health, and a much richer repertoire of methods for attaining a sense of mental balance, well-being, and personal fulfillment" (Clarke 1997, 151). Since Carl Jung's pioneering engagement with various strands of Eastern thought and the fruitful dialogues between psychologists Erich Fromm, Karen Horney, and Zen Buddhist D. T. Suzuki in the early decades of the twentieth century, many modern psychologists, especially those engaged in various forms of Buddhist practice, have greeted Buddhism with open arms (Claxton, 7). James Coleman even compares the role psychotherapy is playing in the introduction of Buddhism to the West to that of Taoism in bringing Buddhist thought to China two thousand years ago (228–229). Consequently, the psychological approach to Buddhism constitutes a major component of modern Western writing on Buddhism in both popular literature and scholarly works by therapists.

The psychological approach to Buddhism is a multifaceted phenomenon. Mark Finn has identified three general attitudes of modern psychologists toward Buddhism:

> The first, or classical, view equates meditative experience and regression, with only the question being whether the experience is adap-

tive or not. The second view, represented by Transpersonal psychology, has argued that meditation represents an advanced state of psychological experience not contained by psychoanalytic categories and requiring new models of human possibility. A third view has been more impressed by the parallels between Buddhist and psychoanalytic therapeutics. (162)

The first view is represented by Sigmund Freud himself, who regards meditative experience as a regressive "oceanic" feeling characterized by "a sensation of 'eternity,' a feeling as of something limitless, unbounded" (1961a, 11), and the feeling of "oneness with the universe" (21). According to Freud, such an experience seeks "the restoration of limitless narcissism" (20) and a consolation of "infantile helplessness" (21). Freud was ambivalent about this oceanic feeling because he himself did not experience it and such a feeling is hard to deal with scientifically. This attitude is indicative of a time when there was a general misunderstanding or simple ignorance of Buddhism on the part of modern psychologists. As William Parsons summarizes, "[T]he oceanic feeling is but the psychoanalytic version of the perennialist claim that mysticism is 'one and the same everywhere,' and the occasional regression to the preverbal, pre-Oedipal 'memory' of unity, motivated by the need to withdraw from a harsh and unforgiving reality, is the explanation behind the transient, ineffable experience of oneness with the universe" (35–36). Curiously though, "the equation of meditation with preverbal, symbiotic union or regressive oneness with the mother has gone virtually unchallenged within the psychoanalytic community. The most recent qualifications of this model have focused only on whether these experiences can be interpreted as adult adaptive ones, rather than purely regressive or defensive flights from reality" (Epstein 1998, 120).

The second view is represented by Jack Engler, who advocates a developmental model to reconcile the conflict between the psychoanalytic practice of trying to strengthen the ego and the Buddhist teaching to transcend it (1984, 27). He argues that psychoanalysis and Buddhism deal with different phases of personal development: "It seems that our Western traditions have mapped out the early stages of that development and the Buddhist traditions have mapped out later or more advanced stages in which 'decentering' from the egocentrism of early development culminates in selfless altruism. And neither tradition knows much about the other. They're talking about the same continuum of development, but about different segments of it" (1998, 112). Engler has famously stated that *"you have to be somebody before you can be nobody"* (1984, 31, original italics). "This has not been clearly understood either by Buddhists or by Western psychologists who tend to see the two traditions as either complementary or competing, but in either case without a clear awareness of the profound differences in their respective methods, aims and outcomes, and the problems they seek to remedy" (1998, 116).

The third view is represented by Carl Jung, Mark Epstein, John Suler, Marvin Levine, Harvey Aronson, and others who put Buddhist theories on par with psychoanalytic theories and see parallels between them. Some, like Epstein, Suler, and Levine, adopt terminologies in modern psychology to interpret Buddhist concepts, while others, like Jung and Aronson, are more cautious in maintaining the different objectives and orientations of theories involved while drawing inspiration from Buddhist theories and practices.

The first view, though still visibly present, no longer represents the dominant attitude of modern psychologists toward Buddhism. In the last several decades, great strides have been made in Buddhist studies in the West, and Buddism has been exerting a growing influence on Western society. The second and the third views are more recent developments. They represent the increasing maturity and sophistication shown by modern psychologists in their study of Buddhism and the growing recognition of the value of such an approach among psychologists.

The psychological approach to Buddhism, however, is both invaluable and potentially dangerous, as Frederick Streng points out:

Cross-cultural comparisons in therapies for true self-awareness . . . are intellectually exciting and fraught with problems. Such studies are exciting in that they seek to locate and elucidate perennial problems in human self-awareness and in the understanding of one's social and physical environment. Comparisons can provide heuristic devices for probing different cultural imagery and definitions and for constructing analytic tools to examine the coherence and assumptions found in general claims about human experience. By specifying similarities and differences one can clarify issues that may provide the basis for new constructive formulations of recurrent human efforts at understanding and life enhancement. At their best they help to distinguish structural elements from incidental form, the typical from the culturally accidental.

The dangers arise from oversimplification of important distinctions in vocabulary, assumptions, and structural approaches. The difficulties in determining "original" meanings, in assuming the relative importance of concepts in a more comprehensive structure of understanding, and in intuiting the intention of (especially religious or salvific) claims are legion. (233–234)

Indeed, despite the apparent merit of the psychological approach to Buddhism and its immediate relevance to the contemporary world, such an approach (especially by those who take the third view but of course not all of them) runs the risk of oversimplifying Buddhist theories; ignoring its historical, cultural, and religious contexts; and disregarding its paradigmatic assumptions. That is, some modern psychologists as well as scholars of Buddhism with training in psychology are eager to interpret Buddhism through the lens of modern psychology. For example, psychologist Mark Epstein, in his *Thoughts Without a Thinker: Psychotherapy from a Buddhist Perspective*, tries to "translate" Buddhist ideas into the psychoanalytic framework and terminology with this justification: "In our culture, it is the language of psychoanalysis, developed by Freud and carefully nurtured by generations of psychotherapists over the past century, that has seeped into the general public awareness. It is in this language that the insights of the Buddha must be presented to Westerners" (1995, 7). For Epstein, Buddhism is a form of depth psychology and "the Buddha may well have been the original psychoanalyst, or, at least, the first to use the mode of analytic inquiry that Freud was later to codify and develop" (9). Buddhist scholar and Jungian psychologist Mokusen Miyuki, in his articles "A Jungian Approach to the Pure Land Practice of *Nien-fo*" and "Self-Realization in the Ten Oxherding Pictures," attempts to challenge "the prevailing psychological view of Eastern religions as aiming at the 'dissolution,' or at the least the 'depotentiation,' of the ego" (1992, 181) and argues instead that many Buddhist practices also aid "the individual to strengthen, rather than dissolve, the ego through the integration of unconscious contents" (ibid.). Psychologist John Suler, in his *Contemporary Psychoanalysis and Eastern Thought*, also interprets Buddhism through the lens of psychological theories, even though he does recognize the drawbacks of using modern psychology to interpret Buddhism in that it ignores the differences between the two (13–14). Marvin Levine simply regards Buddhism as a form of positive psychology, which is a recent Western psychological movement that "focuses on transforming ordinary living into a richer, more enhanced, more mature happiness" (xv).

As Joy Manné's critique of Epstein points out, such a practice "does not respect the immense cultural difference between the Buddha's times and our own" (117) and simply assumes that the Buddhist theories "were highly developed philosophical systems that in many cases espoused similar psychological concepts" (ibid.) without developing a convincing case for making such an assumption. This claim is made in spite of Epstein's own acknowledgment that "no psychological language *as we know it* existed in the Buddha's time—no talk of narcissism, no grandiosity, no abandonment depression or mirroring" (1995, 63–64, original italics).

Epstein's recognition of the vast difference between the vocabularies employed by Buddhism and modern psychology, together with the historical, cultural, and religious contexts existing between the two, partially explains the reluctance on the part of Buddhologists to engage Buddhism with modern psychology. They are aware of the difficulties of many Buddhist concepts and their historical, social, religious, and philosophical contexts, which constitute an intimidating obstacle to understanding them and comparing them with psychological concepts developed in the modern West. Also many Buddhologists, who are often trained specialists in a narrowly defined academic field or subfield, lack sufficient knowledge of psychology. As the psychologist and Buddhist practitioner Jack Engler laments, neither Buddhist nor modern psychology knows much about the other (1998, 112). Psychoanalyst Jeffrey Rubin echoes such a sentiment in his observation that a genuine dialogue between the two has rarely occurred (2003, 388).

Obviously, this mutual ignorance has to be rectified first before any genuine dialogue between modern psychology and Buddhism can take place. What is encouraging is that Buddhologists—for example, De Silva (1973), Kalupahana (1987), and Waldron (1990, 2003)— are making strides in engaging modern psychology from the Buddhist side. Unfortunately, most of the attempts by Buddhologists are dogged by modern psychological frameworks and paradigms, although not as obviously as the work of many psychologists in this regard. That is, even in the writing of Buddhologists comparing modern psychology and Buddhist theories, the former is, explicitly or implicitly, taken as the norm against which the latter are measured or with which parallels are made without any careful reflection on why certain ones are drawn but not others. This leaves us with the impression that whatever modern psychological theory the Buddhologist happens to be familiar with—be it that of William James, Sigmund Freud, or Carl Jung—that is where the parallels are drawn. Consequently, a particular interpretation of Buddhist theories may resemble a Jamesian, Freudian, or Jungian psychology, depending, very significantly, on which psychological system is being used in the comparison. Furthermore, several of the major differences between some Buddhist and modern psychological theories are reconciled either through reconfiguration of the theories involved or by downplaying such differences without sufficient justification. Even though the accidental nature of drawing particular parallels between modern psychology and Buddhism is hard to avoid, if possible at all, there needs to be a more methodic reflection on the very comparative context within which these parallels are made.

This book is written with the above concerns in mind. It is a reflection on both Buddhism and modern psychology that uses each as a mirror to examine the other's assumptions to make the ongoing dialogue between Buddhism and modern psychology a more conscientious and fruitful one. Its primary objective is not to work out specific schemes by which Buddhism and modern psychology can be integrated. Consequently, I will not be concerned with questions regarding which theory may fare better in coping with a particular issue. Put differently, the motivation of this book is not to find a neutral ground or language so that the two systems can be accommodated or integrated within a new framework. Rather, it is to treat the theories involved as they are within their own contexts first and then examine the very presuppositions behind the formulations when they are brought into a new context of a face-to-face dialogical setting. This new setting is meant to recontextualize both Buddhism and modern psychology vis-à-vis each other to reveal certain paradigmatic assumptions embedded in the original contexts of Buddhist and modern psychological theories. Any effort to integrate the two has to be conducted in the full awareness of the assumptions both systems carry with them. It is my hope that this project will help to promote creative imaginations within both traditions in reformulating and regenerating themselves and drawing inspiration from the other as an initial step toward possible future integration. A rushed integration of the two without a proper understanding and appreciation of the underlying assumptions of the theories involved may compromise their own integrity and original appeals.

At the outset of this dialogue, it is important to realize that, during the last fifty years or so, both modern psychology and Western understanding of Buddhism have gone through many changes:

> Western Psychology has undergone successive and simultaneous revolutions in cognitive psychology, systems theory, neuropsychology, evolutionary psychobiology, artificial intelligence, biological psychiatry, attachment theory, object relations theory, self psychology, traumatology, humanistic psychology, and transpersonal psychology. Western Buddhism has, at the same time, been transformed by the arrival of successive waves of Buddhist teachers from within the Japanese, Korean, and Vietnamese Zen traditions, the Burmese lay meditation and Thai forest monastery traditions, and from the Tibetan Diaspora. In addition, the West has seen the arrival of a significant number of Asian immigrants who have brought other practice forms (e.g., Pure Land and *Nichiren* Buddhism) along with them. (Segall, 1–2)

As a result of the self-transformation of modern psychology and its increasing appreciation of Buddhism in its multifaceted character, the psychological approach to Buddhism has become much more sophisticated and complex. Due to this complexity, a comprehensive study of the psychological approach to Buddhism within the confines of a single work is all but impossible. Therefore, in order to have a systematic and methodic but manageable treatment of the encounter between Buddhism and modern psychology, I have chosen the Yogācāra Buddhist notion of *ālayavijñāna* and the concept of the unconscious in modern psychoanalysis as the interlocutors of the dialogue.

Ālayavijñāna and the Unconscious

Yogācāra Buddhism presents the most systematic and the most detailed version of the Buddhist theory of mind/consciousness or Buddhist psychology within the Buddhist tradition. It started in fourth-century India and became one of the two major Mahāyāna Buddhist schools, the other being Madhyamika, established by Nāgārjuna in the second century. The most prominent representatives of Yogācāra

Buddhism include Maitreya, Asaṅga, and Vasubandhu. This school, in its various strands, pushes Mahāyāna Buddhism to its climatic conclusion by engaging in an extensive discussion on the nature and activities of our mental life and its potential for transformation from delusion to enlightenment. It has exerted a profound impact on the overall development of Buddhist philosophical deliberations and meditative practices. Although Yogācāra is not quite a "living" tradition in the way Zen Buddhism or Theravāda Buddhism is today (it is not associated with any monastic community), it is very much alive in some Asian Buddhist scholastic traditions, especially in Japan, and remains a source of inspiration for contemporary Buddhist practitioners as well as Buddhist scholars. Even in China, where Yogācāra did not survive as a continuing scholastic tradition, the early twentieth century witnessed its revival. Several prominent scholars both within and without the Buddhist tradition, such as Xiong Shili, Zhang Binglin, and Ouyang Jingwu among others, turned to Yogācāra in their effort to deal with intellectual challenges from the West precisely because of the sophistication of the Yogācāra system. Furthermore, the philosophical and psychological insights exhibited by Yogācāra have gained real traction among modern Western Buddhist scholars who in turn have influenced the way Buddhism has been received in the West, where most of the dialogue between Buddhism and modern psychology has been taking place. Therefore, an engagement between Buddhism and modern psychology cannot afford to disregard the contribution of Yogācāra Buddhism.

Ālayavijñāna, usually translated as the storehouse consciousness,[1] is a key concept in the Yogācāra system. It is a subliminal reservoir of memories, habits, tendencies, and future possibilities. The subliminal nature of *ālayavijñāna* renders it susceptible to being interpreted as the Buddhist version of the unconscious. On the other hand, the notion of the unconscious looms large in modern psychology as well as in popular parlance. As John Suler rightly points out, "One of the single most important insights of psychoanalysis is the realization of the unconscious" (1–2).

Due to the eminence of the unconscious in modern psychology and its powerful influence in the West and the rest of the world as well as Buddhism's overwhelming concern for the mind and mental activities, since the early days of the encounter between modern psychology and Buddhism there has been an underlying desire to find a Buddhist version of the unconscious. Francisco Varela records a vivid moment in the search for a Buddhist unconscious by a modern psychologist:

> Joyce McDougall did not lose a moment in launching a question that was clearly burning for her, and for many of us: "I would like to ask Your Holiness if the Freudian concept of the unconscious has any corresponding ideas in Tibetan philosophy?" (265)

This moment captures one underlying impulse of modern psychology in its encounter with Buddhism, namely the search for corresponding concepts, especially core concepts, across cultural systems. Psychologist Elbert Russell recounted his own expectation in his encounter with the Indian tradition during the 1950s: "It was inconceivable to me that a people, a substantial portion of whom had spent thousands of years involved with the inner world, could not have discovered centuries ago what Freud and other psychoanalytic theorists had only discovered during this last century [namely, the unconscious]" (51). However, Russell's search for an Eastern notion of the unconscious was destined to be frustrated from the start. In his article on Eastern and Western approaches to the unconscious he notes, "Western psychodynamic concepts will be used as criteria for determining what understanding of the unconscious is found in the literature of Eastern psychological systems" (53). He lists four criteria derived from the modern psychoanalytic system. After surveying some literature on Eastern traditions, he concludes that "the Eastern psychologies have yielded very little in the way of an understanding of the unconscious or its dynamics" (57). Russell goes on to argue that "the Eastern meditation systems focus on higher states of consciousness, while the Western psychotherapies generally deal with the unconscious" (61).

We should point out that Russell's study of Asian sources in his search for an Eastern theory of the unconscious is by no means exhaustive. Padmasiri De Silva, in his comparative studies of Buddhist and Freud's theories, does identify several candidates for the Buddhist version of the unconscious: *bhavaṅga, anuśaya, āsava, saṅkāra, saṃvatta nika viññāṇa, bhavasota,* and *viññāṇasota* (1973, 50). However, no other concept is more ideal in this regard than *ālayavijñāna,* which has been postulated, developed, and systematically elaborated by the Yogācārins (Waldron 2003, 91). The subliminal nature of *ālayavijñāna* makes it a natural choice for a Buddhist equivalent of the unconscious, both personal and collective (Smart, 58).

In some respects, the Western interpretation of *ālayavijñāna* is the culmination of the search for a Buddhist notion of the unconscious. In other words, the immense popularity of the notion of the unconscious schematized in modern psychology tends to color modern scholarship on *ālayavijñāna* in varying degrees. The fact that the question "Is there a Buddhist or Eastern notion of the unconscious?" has been raised at all points to the wide currency of the notion of the unconscious in modern psychology.

To be fair, modern scholarship on *ālayavijñāna* (e.g., the work of Lambert Schmithausen and William Waldron) has made great progress in understanding and appreciating the concept within its own cultural, historical, religious, and philosophical contexts. It has come a long way in better comprehending this key Yogācāra idea. There has clearly been a turn of the tide from the earlier approach to *ālayavijñāna,* which attempted to make it resemble the modern notion of the unconscious as much as possible, to an in-depth study of the concept itself within its own context. To help us better appreciate the change that has taken place in the West's encounter with *ālayavijñāna,* I have schematized the evolution of the modern psychological approach to *ālayavijñāna* into three "stages" in terms of the questions that have been posed to it. The stages are not meant to be strictly chronological. Rather, they provide us with different contexts within which modern interpretations of *ālayavijñāna* have been experimented. There is, more often than not, overlapping among these stages, or contexts. Sorting them in this manner will facilitate our understanding of how modern Western scholarship has evolved in its approach to *ālayavijñāna* through a series of contexts and questions.

In the first stage of encountering *ālayavijñāna,* the underlying question that is raised or implied tends to be: What is the Buddhist notion of the unconscious (De Silva 1973, 49; Smart, 58)? Padmasiri De Silva observes that Jung's "notion of the 'collective unconscious,' shrouded as it is in speculative theories, bears some kinship to the *ālayavijñāna* concept of later Buddhism, whereas the Freudian Unconscious, rooted in a scientific and empirical framework, resembles the concept of the Unconscious in early Buddhism" (1973, 65). According to De Silva, by virtue of such associations with Freud and Jung, the early Buddhist notion of the "unconscious," like the Freudian unconscious, is more scientific and empirical, whereas the

Yogācāra notion of *ālayavijñāna,* like the Jungian unconscious, is more speculative and obscure. Chapter titles in De Silva's work, such as "The Early Buddhist Concept of the Unconscious in the Light of the Freudian Theory of the Unconscious," are very suggestive of the underlying frame of reference that takes Freud's theory of the unconscious as the norm against which Buddhist theories are measured, even though the latter might fare better on particular issues (1973, 74–75). The question "What is the Buddhist version of the unconscious" is an imposition by modern scholars so that the answers are already framed within the context of the responses to such an underlying question.

At the second stage the question evolves into: What issues are raised within the Buddhist tradition that give *ālayavijñāna* its current shape? In other words, what problems are the postulation of *ālayavijñāna* designed to address? What questions do the Yogācārins ask themselves in conceptualizing *ālayavijñāna*? No concept arises out of a vacuum. All conceptual formulations are raised to address certain specific concerns of a cultural tradition at a particular historical juncture when facing particular challenges to particular audiences. Hence, instead of asking how much *ālayavijñāna* resembles the modern notion of the unconscious, efforts have been made (e.g., Schmithausen, Waldron 2003), to examine the kinds of questions the Yogācārins themselves are raising at the time of formulating *ālayavijñāna* and why they are raising such questions. As a consequence of this reorientation in interpreting *ālayavijñāna,* the following question is raised: Is the notion of *ālayavijñāna* adequate in addressing the challenges that it is formulated to answer? Obviously the questions raised at the second stage are an advance over the first because the former tries to study *ālayavijñāna* on its own terms, within its own context, instead of being framed as a response to questions raised by the concerns and interests of a modern interpreter.

However, even after studying *ālayvijñāna* in its own context, when scholars draw parallels with the modern notion of the unconscious, their efforts are still colored by the latter. That is, the modern notion of the unconscious remains the norm against which *ālayavijñāna* is measured, albeit implicitly in some cases. This marks the third stage in the Western encounter with *ālayavijñāna*. Hence, the following question tends to be raised: How much does *ālayavijñāna* resemble the Freudian and/or Jungian notions of the unconscious?[2] When dif-

ferences are found between the two, interpreters either try to min-
imize them through a reconfiguration of the theories involved or
assume that *ālayavijñāna* represents a less advanced formulation in
that it falls short of the modern notion of the unconscious because
it does not account for certain common modern psychological phenomena (e.g., repression). Of course, scholars are generally careful
not to pronounce the inadequacy of the Yogācāra formulation of
ālayavijñāna when comparing it with the notion of the unconscious
in modern psychology. Nevertheless, they spare no effort to make
the storehouse consciousness look like the unconscious as much as
possible. Let us take a look at William Waldron's comparative study
in this connection.

Waldron's dissertation, "The Ālayavijñāna in the Context of
Indian Buddhist Thought: The Yogācāra Conception of an Unconscious," is a fine piece of scholarship tracing the development of
ālayavijñāna within the context of Indian Buddhism. As such, it can
be deemed a continuation of Lambert Schmithausen's seminal work
*Ālayavijñāna: On the Origin and the Early Development of a Cen-
tral Concept of Yogācāra Philosophy*. At the end of Waldron's dissertation, he compares *ālayavijñāna* with the modern notion of the
unconscious.[3] Despite his careful contextualization and meticulous
argument, which generate many insightful observations, Waldron
ultimately falls prey to his eagerness to make *ālayavijñāna* as akin
to the notion of the unconscious in modern psychology as possible.
Accordingly, the differences between the two are "based more upon
the great gulf of divergent terminology than on overall design and
conception and when the ideas behind their technical vocabularies
are examined a bit the divergences, though still real, turn out to be
considerably smaller than first appears" (1990, 438).[4]

Nowhere is Waldron's effort to make *ālayavijñāna* look like the
modern notion of the unconscious more pronounced than in his
endeavor to account for the lack of the conception of repression in
the formulation of *ālayavijñāna*: "[I]n the Buddhist tradition there
is nothing quite like the concept of repression. But there is an
approach to it; it is 'homologizable'" (442). Waldron appeals to the
general Buddhist teaching of the frustrating and ignorant nature of
existence as a way to account for an implicit idea of repression in
Yogācāra Buddhism. This is not to dispute the value of Waldron's
effort to bring Yogācāra Buddhism and depth psychology together.
However, the fact that he feels the need to justify the lack of an

explicit account of repression in the Buddhist theory of the subliminal consciousness points to an underlying frame of reference on Waldron's part that takes modern psychology as the norm against which the Yogācāra theory is measured. His effort to put forth *ālayavijñāna* as a viable formulation of the unconscious from a Buddhist perspective, admirable as it is, cannot escape the shadow of modern psychology in terms of how the discussion is framed. Hence, a new approach to engage *ālayavijñāna* and the unconscious is called for and that is what the present work will strive to do.

I propose that if we are to get out of the framework set by modern psychology in discussing *ālayavijñāna*, we need to change the way we question it. The new overarching question I am posing to *ālayavijñāna*, and to the unconscious, is this: What do the differences between *ālayavijñāna* and the unconscious tell us about the presuppositions of the modern psychological notion of the unconscious and the Yogācāra notion of *ālayavijñāna*? Put differently, instead of using the modern notion of the unconscious as the norm to approach the Yogācāra Buddhist notion of *ālayavijñāna*, I use both concepts as mirrors to reflect each other. That is, I am not taking either the Yogācāra notion of *ālayavijñāna* or the modern notion of the unconscious as the norm against which the other is measured. Rather, I switch between them so as to look at the modern notion of the unconscious from the Yogācāra Buddhist perspective and at *ālayavijñāna* from modern psychological perspectives represented by Freud and Jung. My purpose is not to reconcile the differences between them. Instead I use those very differences to expose certain taken-for-granted presuppositions of both that come to light using this approach. In this way, we will not supplant the earlier "Eurocentric" attitude to the study of the subliminal mind with an "Orientocentric" one.[5]

A New Context: Orientalism and Dialogue

Since the publication of Edward Said's *Orientalism* in the late 1970s, the asymmetrical power relationship in the dialogical discourse between the West and the East has been brought to the forefront of cross-cultural studies: "Orientalism is a style of thought based upon an ontological and epistemological distinction made between 'the Orient' and (most of the time) 'the Occident'" (Said, 2). It is "a Western style for dominating, restructuring, and having authority over the Orient" (3). Said's powerful critique of the Western construction of the "Orient" in the West's search for self-definition and the domination over the Orient reveals a deeply troubling condition—namely power and domination—underlying all academic discourses that involve the East and the West.

However, as J. J. Clarke points out, Said's presentation of Orientalism, while potent and justified, is guilty of being too narrow and reductionistic (1997, 27). It does not offer a complete picture of Orientalism:

> European hegemony over Asia represents a necessary but not a sufficient condition for orientalism. . . . Orientalism . . . cannot simply be identified with the ruling imperialistic ideology, for in the Western context it represents a counter-movement, a subversive entelechy, albeit not a unified or consciously organized one, which in various ways has often tended to subvert rather than to confirm the discursive structures of imperial power. (9)

Accordingly, Said's picture of Orientalism reduces it to European hegemony alone without paying due attention to the other aspect of Orientalism that is subversive to the very imperial power Said critiques. Clarke argues for an alternative to Said's picture of Orientalism, pointing out two affirmative Orientalist themes in the relationship between East and West:

> The first theme is the search for parallels between Eastern and Western thought, leading to the postulation of a universal religion or philosophy underlying all cultural differences, which in turn can be linked to the concept of the oneness of mankind. The second theme concerns the critique of Western civilization, of its decadence and narrowness, and the mounting of a challenge to the uniqueness of the Christian message, of the belief in progress and in European superiority. The East has . . . provided the West with a mirror with which to scrutinise itself, an external point of reference with which to conduct its agonising obsession with self-examination and self-criticism. (1994, 36)

My book somewhat echoes the second theme in facilitating the self-examination and self-criticism of modern psychology through the lens provided by the Yogācāra Buddhist theory of the subliminal mind, *ālayavijñāna*, and vice versa. It focuses on how modern psychology and Yogācāra Buddhism can shed light on each other's formulation of the subliminal mind. It will first discuss both the

Yogācāra concept of *ālayavijñāna* and the modern notion of the unconscious within their respective contexts. By bringing them together I will introduce a new context within which the idea of the subliminal mind can be discussed to reflect presuppositions, which are not so readily exposed if left to themselves and their own contexts.

My work is therefore a comparative study of Yogācāra Buddhism and modern psychology on their radically different formulations of the subliminal mind. On the Yogācāra side, I use seventh-century Chinese Yogācāra Buddhist Xuan Zang's formulation in his celebrated *Cheng Weishi Lun* (*Vijñaptimātratāsiddhi-śāstra*, *The Treatise on the Establishment of the Doctrine of Consciousness-Only*). I chose Xuan Zang because his treatment of *ālayavijñāna* has not yet been adequately studied in modern scholarship on the subject despite his prominence within the Buddhist tradition. One goal of this book is to make known Xuan Zang's contribution to the conceptualization of *ālayavijñāna*. On the side of modern psychology, I involve Sigmund Freud and Carl Jung, both of whom are known as psychologists of the unconscious and whose works laid the foundation and continue to serve as sources of inspiration. As we shall see, the engagement between Buddhism and modern psychology on the formulation of the subliminal mind will produce refreshing insights into the well-critiqued notion of the unconscious within Western intellectual discourse.

I will start by asking the following questions: What is the context within which Yogācārins like Xuan Zang are working and, given that context, what issues are they concerned with in the conceptualization of *ālayavijñāna*? In other words, what kinds of questions does Xuan Zang himself raise? How well are these questions addressed theoretically in his deliberation of *ālayavijñāna*? The same questions will be asked of Freud and Jung: What is the context within which they are working, and, given that context, what issues do they address in their conceptualizations of the unconscious?

The next series of questions involves the new dialogical context into which I am bringing Xuan Zang, Freud, and Jung: Where does the modern notion of the unconscious, formulated by Freud and Jung, differ from the Yogācāra notion of the storehouse consciousness? Why are there such differences and how are they carried out in terms of the principles behind their formulations? This is the crucial stage of my inquiry. I will focus on the what, why, and how of the theories involved in the dialogue. Specifically, the what refers to the content of the theory, the why its objective, and the how its method. The overall assumption here is that these aspects, namely, the content, the objective, and the method, are interrelated and they all contribute to the merits as well as the limitations of a given theory. Through the new dialogical context, we will come to the realization that the modern notion of the subliminal mind vis-à-vis the unconscious is vastly different from the Yogācāra notion of the subliminal mind vis-à-vis *ālayavijñāna*. I will examine what those differences are in terms of their contents, why the differences exist in terms of their objectives, and how their methods of theorization contribute to their differences.

On a larger scale, this is an attempt to expose how philosophical arguments—broadly defined here—are constructed, refined, and defended within the context of different cultural orientations and how a new context of dialogical inquiry into these arguments can help to reveal such different paradigms with respect to their assumptions, insights, and limitations. Despite its increasing popularity, a comparative study of distinct conceptual systems across cultural boundaries is a risky endeavor because there is the danger of doing disservice to the systems involved; my project—a cross-cultural dialogue bringing together classical Yogācāra Buddhism and modern psychology—is by no means an exception in this regard. However, such a risk is worth taking because the motivation of most, if not all, scholarly approaches to a classical work is colored by modern perspectives and concerns in any case, irrespective of whether such perspectives or concerns are explicitly dealt with or not. It is therefore better to thematize these very factors coloring our approach to a classical work rather than simply leave them operative without any clear reflection on them.

My approach is different from the typical traditional comparative one that tends to postulate parallels and draw analogies between different theoretical frameworks across cultural boundaries. A unique feature of the approach I have adopted in this book "involves mediating Western philosophical concepts through Eastern ideas rather than, as has traditionally been the case, the other way around" (Clarke 1997, 125). In fact, such a mediation goes both ways in this work, namely mediating modern psychological concepts of the unconscious through the Yogācāra Buddhist notion of *ālaya-vijñāna* as well as the other way around.

In order to conduct this dialogical inquiry into different formulations of the subliminal consciousness, I will treat the dialogue as a new context that brings them together. If the prevailing issue that drives the formulation of the subliminal mind within the original contexts is the truthfulness of such a concept, the issue that arises in the new dialogical context is reoriented toward probing into the perspective within which such a truth claim can be justified. It is my hope that this dialogical inquiry into the conception of the subliminal consciousness will shed new light on a notion that is well known in modern intellectual discourse as well as popular parlance. Since it was made known by Sigmund Freud in the early twentieth century, the notion of the unconscious has been thoroughly critiqued from perspectives of various disciplines within the Western intellectual world. What I am hoping to accomplish in this book is to investigate this seminal concept from the perspective of comparative thought by bringing it into a much broader context of intercultural dialogue. I will argue that many of the underpinnings of a key concept—in this case the subliminal mind—that operate within a given theoretical paradigm—here Yogācāra Buddhism and psychoanalysis, respectively—and the mode of reasoning by which it is conceptualized can be revealed by introducing it into a new context of cross-cultural comparative study and dialogue. To be more specific, my inquiry will show that the three theories have vastly different thematic contents formulated to address different audiences and their concerns. Furthermore, I will demonstrate how Xuan Zang, Freud, and Jung intend their theories to be used by thematizing different modes of access to the subliminal mind allowed in their systems, and I will argue that such a difference in these modes is due to the different roles the principles of transcendence and immanence play in the three conceptualizations of the subliminal mind.

Given the magnitude of the study, I have neither the ambition nor the ability to make this research exhaustive or definitive. Neither is it my intention to judge the validity of the theories involved. This inquiry is only meant to be a tentative step toward shedding light on the way our theoretical efforts are colored by interpretive objectives and the modes of reasoning we resort to, thus offering a new way to look at a well-critiqued notion, the unconscious. It is my position that the primary purpose of a comparative approach to philosophical systems across cultural, historical, and social boundaries is not to solve each other's problems, even though it does not necessarily preclude that. Rather, it is a powerful way to bring awareness to certain implicit assumptions a theory makes and, therefore, to shed new light on that theory, however well known and thoroughly critiqued within an intellectual tradition it may be. I hope that the insights gained from a mutually challenging dialogue will help us become more aware of these presuppositions so that we may find ways to transcend their limitations without compromising the integrity and appeal of the original formulations or to move toward a possible future integration.

Summary of the Chapters

I begin with the Yogācāra Buddhist concept of *ālayavijñāna*. Chapter One examines the origination and the rationale of *ālayavijñāna* by spelling out certain key problematics in some of the pre-Yogācāra Buddhist discourse, whose solutions call for the postulation of a concept like *ālayavijñāna*. The Yogācārins are trying to deal with a set of problematics and doctrinal conflicts that their Buddhist predecessors are unable to solve, such as the conflicts between the doctrines of *karma* and *anātman*, between continuity and momentariness, between succession and causality. Yogācāra offers the most complex Buddhist examination of consciousness, employing analytical scrupulousness and encyclopedic inclusion of earlier Buddhist theories, in an effort to smooth out these doctrinal conflicts. However, as Buddhists, the Yogācārins' theoretical endeavors are circumscribed by the accepted doctrinal orthodoxies, the most important of which is the taboo on substantialization and reification. That is, they have to find ways to reconcile the above-mentioned doctrinal conflicts without resorting to any form of reification or substantialization, as prescribed by the Mahāyāna Buddhist principle of *śūnyāta*, or emptiness. They achieve this goal by postulating a subliminal layer of the mind, what is known as the storehouse consciousness, or *ālayavijñāna*, which is both momentary and continuous, and as such effectively accounts for continuity while avoiding the pitfall of reification.

Chapter Two offers a detailed analysis of *ālayavijñāna* in its more mature formulation as presented by Xuan Zang in his *Cheng Weishi Lun*. The conceptualization of *ālayavijñāna* lies at the very foundation of Yogācāra's demonstration of the possibility of Buddhist enlightenment. The issues covered are: What is the nature, structure, and function of *ālayavijñāna*? What is its relationship with other forms of consciousness in the traditional Buddhist discourse?

What is achieved in the Yogācāra postulation of the concept of *ālayavijñāna*?

In Chapter Three, I will deal with the context within which the notion of the unconscious is theorized by Freud and Jung, respectively, highlighting the connections as well as the distinctions between the two formulations. This is done with an eye on the subsequent dialogical inquiry of the three theories of the subliminal mind that is carried out in the next two chapters. Assuming that many readers already have some knowledge of Freud and Jung, my discussion of them will be less extensive compared with my treatment of *ālayavijñāna*.

The next two chapters are devoted to the discussion of the subliminal mind in the new context of dialogical and comparative discourse. My comparison will focus on three questions: what, why, and how. That is, what are the major differences between the three theories of the subliminal mind? Why are they different? How are such differences formulated? Chapter Four deals with the what and the why aspects of the comparative study. I will look at the three theories from the perspective of the individual and collective dimensions of the subliminal consciousness and the dynamics between these two dimensions within each theory itself. We will see that the differences between the three are, in large part, due to the fact that Xuan Zang, Freud, and Jung, in their respective formulations, are trying to accomplish vastly different objectives, appealing to very different audiences and their concerns. Three radically different pictures of what a human being is and/or should be, as implied by the three theories, will emerge.

Ultimately, my inquiry will lead to the question: What does the difference in the formulations of the subliminal mind tell us about a "typical" person reflected in modern psychological formulations in contrast with one reflected in the Yogācāra formulation? It will become clear to us that both are constructs, socially, historically, and culturally conditioned. That is, the theories of the subliminal mind, on the one hand, are conditioned by their contexts, while, on the other hand, they help to shape that very condition to a greater or lesser extent.

Chapter Five examines the "how" component of the comparative study. It deals with the question of how different modes of reasoning contribute to their differences. I will focus on the different modes of access to the subliminal consciousness that the three theories allow within their frameworks. Xuan Zang allows a direct access to the subliminal consciousness whereas Freud and Jung only allow an indirect access. Such differences have to do, at least partially, with how they intend their theories to be used: Direct access to the storehouse consciousness is a necessary condition for a Buddhist practitioner to reach enlightenment according to Xuan Zang's Yogācāra theory; in contrast, the denial of direct access in Freud's and Jung's theories saves room for psychoanalysts in treating their patients. I will examine this from the perspective of the different roles played by the principles of transcendence and immanence and see how transcendence and immanence have greatly shaped the modes of access to the subliminal mind in the three theories.

I will conclude by reflecting on the emerging new world as the ultimate new context for our dialogical inquiry. Even though the cross-cultural dialogical discourse might have been dogged by Western power and domination, as Said has acutely observed, we need to be reminded that such an observation is itself the result of the ongoing Orientalist discourse Said has critiqued. Therefore, instead of throwing out the baby with the bathwater, we should be encouraged by the fact that the Orientalist discourse has promoted some mutual understanding between cultures as well as enhancing the self-understanding of a culture in the face of another while being mindful of the risk involved.

I
THE ORIGIN
OF THE CONCEPT OF
ĀLAYAVIJÑĀNA

RELIGIOUS DOCTRINES are a complex web of teachings whose sources are far from being singular or homogeneous. If a religious tradition has a founder, whether actual or alleged, the received teachings of the founder become the foundation upon which the orthodoxy evolves. However, when the founder addresses questions from disciples directly, various explanations are given on different occasions within different contexts to different audiences addressing different concerns. When the founder dies, his disciples are left with the task of assembling his teachings to preserve them for future generations. Because different teachings target different audiences in their lived situations, apparent inconsistencies emerge when such concrete contexts are left out in the pursuit of abstract doctrinal formulations. With the teacher gone, the contexts of many of the teachings go with him, and his disciples have to deal with these inconsistencies. Although some of them can be explained away through a study of the contexts of the teachings, others are harder to clarify by appealing to the contexts alone. This latter kind of inconsistency is usually indicative of tensions among some foundational doctrines within the religious tradition. Such tensions constitute a major source of creativity, often leading to the development of various doctrinal systems.

In the context of Buddhism, the rise of Abhidharma literature in early Buddhism, which is meant to classify and analyze the fundamental teachings of the Buddha, reflects the Buddhist effort to overcome a variety of tensions in these teachings. Yogācāra Buddhism, which started around the fourth century C.E., inherits the Abhidharma's systematic pursuit of a body of coherent and cogent Buddhist doctrines. As William Waldron points out, "[I]t was within the historical and conceptual context of Abhidharma scholasticism that the Yogācāra school arose, and within whose terms the notion of the ālayavijñāna was expressed" (2003, 47). In this chapter we will explore one fundamental tension within the Buddha's teachings that Abhidharma Buddhists attempt to overcome. This will set the stage for our discussion, in Chapter Two, of the continual effort by Yogācāra to grapple with this critical problem in its theoretical endeavors with the postulation of ālayavijñāna at the center.

The tension in question is between identity and change, reflected in the difficulty in conceptualizing continuity. On the one hand, for there to be continuity in change, there needs to be something—identity—that is continuously changing; on the other hand, if there is identity, change is either impossible (identity itself cannot change otherwise it would be lost) or regarded as the attribute of unchanging substance or identity; hence change is only apparent/illusory but ultimately unreal. Such a tension is played out in the Buddhist struggle to provide a coherent account of the Buddha's core teachings of anātman (no-self), karma, anitya (impermanence), and pratītya-samutpāda (dependent origination). In other words, can anātman be reconciled with karma if there is no underlying bearer of karma? Can the impermanence of existence account for the continuity and coherence of our experience of the world as depicted by dependent origination? We will see how various schools of Abhidharma Buddhism, prior to or contemporaneous with the Yogācāra School, attempt to cope with this tension so that Yogācāra's effort, culminated in the formulation of ālayavijñāna, can be understood within a proper context.

In providing a philosophical account of the origin of the concept of ālayavijñāna, this chapter is written with one primary objective in mind: to reveal the rationale for the postulation of a concept like ālayavijñāna within the Buddhist tradition. This will provide a proper context for our detailed discussion of the formulation of ālayavijñāna in Chapter Two, thus laying the foundation for the comparative study of Yogācāra and modern psychoanalysis and their respective conceptualizations of the subliminal mind later in the book.

Given this book's intended audience (Buddhist specialists as well as non-specialists), its dialogical and comparative nature, and the existence of several fine scholarly works on some of the issues examined,[1] our investigation of the origin of ālayavijñāna will not be exhaustive; neither is an exhaustive investigation desirable for our purpose here. I will focus my attention on the theoretical endeavors that anticipate the formulation of *ālayavijñāna*. In doing so, I will provide the religious and philosophical ambiance within which a concept like *ālayavijñāna* is called for. At the end of the chapter, I will trace the early development of the notion of *ālayavijñāna* as conceived by Yogācārins. Let us start with the Buddha's teaching of *anātman*, or no-self.

Anātman

Arguably, the doctrine of *anātman* (Pāli: *anatta*) is *the* defining teaching of the Buddha.[2] So much so that Vasubandhu in his *Abhidharmakośabhāṣyam* declares that "[t]here is no liberation outside of this teaching [Buddhism], because other doctrines are corrupted by a false conception of a soul" (1313).[3] In other words, the teaching of *anātman* is taken to be the decisive element, when compared with non-Buddhist teachings, in achieving enlightenment according to most Buddhist schools, with the apparent exception of Pudgalavādins (Personalists).[4]

Despite its prominence, the meaning of *anātman* is not without ambiguity.[5] Etymologically, the prefix *an-* can be translated as either "no" or "not." Consequently, *anātman* can be understood as either no-self or not-self, and indeed it has been translated in these two ways (Harvey, 7–8). The translation depends on the interpretation one adopts. When translated as "no-self," which is accepted by most Buddhist scholars, the term suggests that the Buddha categorically denies the existence of a self or soul because that which is negated by the "no" in "no-self" is the self as an entity.[6] However, if we adopt the latter translation, not-self, this suggests that the Buddha only denies what is not a self rather than denying that there is any self at all because the "not" in "not-self" negates whatever is predicated of or attributed to the self. Proponents of this interpretation of *anātman* often cite a passage in the *Saṃyutta Nikāya* (44:10; translated by Bhikkhu Ñāṇamoli, 209–210) wherein the Buddha remains silent when a wandering Vacchagotta inquires about the existence of self. Later the Buddha explains to his disciples that the assertion of the existence of the self leads to eternalism while the assertion of its non-existence leads to annihilationism (Bhikkhu Ñāṇamoli, 209–210).

Historically, the interpretation of *anātman* as not-self comes from an earlier time, and this is evident in the Buddha's own exposition of *anātman* as recorded in the *Sutta Nipāta* and the *Saṃyutta Nikāya*, which are believed to be the earliest records of Buddha's teachings

(Nakamura, 27).[7] In this connection we find, "This is not mine, this is not what I am, this is not my self" (*Saṃyutta Nikāya* 22:59, translated by Bhikkhu Ñāṇamoli, 46–47). The first statement denies the ownership of the aggregates, the second and the third reject the metaphysical entity called "I" or "self" as the owner denied in the first statement.[8]

Steven Collins, in his discussion of the Buddha's teaching of *anatta* (Sk: *anātman*), also approaches *anatta* as not-self in the early Buddhist teachings: "It is precisely the point of not-self that this is *all* that there is to human individuals. . . . There is no central self which animates the impersonal elements" (82) into which personality is analyzed. In the *Anattalakkhaṇa Sutta*, *anatta* vis-à-vis not-self is discussed in terms of the lack of control of the five constituents of personality and in terms of the inappropriateness in regarding what is impermanent and unsatisfactory as self (Bhikkhu Ñāṇamoli, 46–47).

If the Buddha only preaches the doctrine of *anātman* vis-à-vis not-self, this means that the interpretation of *anātman* as no-self, as accepted by most Buddhist scholars, is a later development that is then anachronistically attributed to the Buddha. What is indeed puzzling, as many scholars have observed (e.g., Frauwallner, 125–126; Harvey, 7; Werner, 95), is that the Buddha in the early Suttas never explicitly denies the existence of the self.

Be that as it may, the issue at stake here is this: Is the no-self interpretation of *anātman* compatible with the not-self interpretation of the doctrine? After a meticulous investigation of the early Suttas,[9] Peter Harvey observes:

> [I]t can thus be said that, while an empirical self exists—or rather consists of a changing flow of mental and physical states which neither unchangingly exists nor does not exist—no metaphysical Self can be apprehended. This does not imply that it is real but inapprehensible, as the Buddha of the 'early Suttas' saw views on it as appropriate, *if* it was real. Moreover, even *nibbāna* is not-Self and not related to a Self, and the Buddha did not accept that Self exists, or that it even lay beyond existence and non-existence. Indeed, the concept itself is seen as self-contradictory, for 'Self' is dependent on a sense of 'I am,' and this can *only* arise by clinging to the conditioned factors of personality, which are *not*-Self. (33)

There are a number of interesting points in this passage. First, the Buddha's teaching does not reject an empirical self as constitutive of our everyday experience.[10] Only the empirical self accounts for our sense of a self, which is nothing other than an empirical continuum vis-à-vis a series of psychophysical events mistaken as a metaphysical identity. This interpretation of the existence of an empirical self in the Buddha's teaching is also defended by David Kalupahana (1992, 70–77). According to Kalupahana, the Buddha's analyses of the personality as the sum of five aggregates, namely, body or material form *(rūpa)*, feeling or sensation *(vedanā)*, perception *(saññā)*, dispositions *(saṅkhāra)*, and consciousness *(viññāṇa)*; six elements *(cha-dhāth)*, namely, earth *(paṭhavi)*, water *(āpo)*, fire *(tejo)*, air *(vāyu)*, space *(ākāsa)*, and consciousness *(viññāṇa)*; and the twelve factors of "dependent arising" (Pāli: *paṭiccasamuppāda*)—serve two purposes: the rejecting of a metaphysical self and an embracing of an empirical self.[11] In other words, although the Buddha uses these three taxonomies to make the point that there is no unchanging soul over and above those changing elements of a personality, he also uses them to explain our sense of a self, which is nothing other than the empirical continuum of a series of psychophysical events constituted by those elements.

Second, and more interestingly, Harvey points out that the Buddha brushes aside the issue of a metaphysical self due to the incomprehensibility of its putative metaphysical status. It is very tempting to suggest that the Buddha does not actually rule out the possibility of the existence of a metaphysical self and that he only cautions us against our commonsensical understanding of the self that mistakes the empirical continuity as the metaphysical identity. This would be reminiscent of the well-known Kantian antinomy regarding the existence of the soul, which contends that neither the existence nor non-existence of a soul can be proved or disproved because the soul is not a possible object of knowledge. However, instead of following the Kantian way of relegating the metaphysical question of the existence of the soul to a realm in which human rationality falters in the face of the antinomy,[12] the early Suttas (e.g., the *Mahānidāna-sutta* in *Saṃyutta Nikāya*), reveal the self-contradictory nature of the very concept of (the metaphysical) self (Bhikkhu Ñāṇamoli, 46–47) and the pointlessness in speaking of a self apart from experience (Collins, 98–103):

> The self-contradictory Self-concept, then, concerns something which is supposed to be *both* permanent *and* aware of itself as 'I.' But to

get even an illusory sense of I-ness, it must be feeling, or one of the other personality-factors, which work in unison with feeling (or all the factors), but these are all *im*permanent. (Harvey, 32)

All of those characteristics by which the self can be known are impermanent, and therefore any attempt to even conceive of a permanent self is hopelessly self-defeating. Consequently, it is meaningless to either affirm or deny a metaphysical self. This is why the Buddha is silent on the issue of the self. However, this does not mean that we do not even have a sense of self. On the contrary, we do have a sense of self, but it is neither substantive nor eternal. That is, the metaphysical self is not the self we have the sense of. I will revisit this issue throughout this book.

Therefore, it is clear that the two interpretations of the doctrine of *anātman*, not-self and no-self, are indeed compatible. Not only are they compatible with each other, the no-self interpretation is a natural development of the not-self teaching of the Buddha. Put differently, the not-self teaching of the Buddha anticipates the later development of the doctrine of *anātman* as no-self in that the former denies even the conceivability of a metaphysical notion of the self as explicitly brought out by the latter. Hence, the accepted interpretation of *anātman* as no-self should be understood as maintaining that, although it is inconceivable to have a metaphysical concept of the self, it does not reject the empirical sense of the self. It is in this sense that the term "*anātman*" will be subsequently used in this book.

However, there are problems associated with the teaching of *anātman*, as Hindu philosophers very quickly point out:

> One difficulty of this theory, as should be immediately obvious and as was pointed out by most anti-Buddhist philosophers, is that it fails to account for the unity of self-consciousness and for experiences such as memory and recognition. . . . For the Hindu thinkers, the identity of the I is a condition of the possibility of knowledge, of social life and moral relationships, of suffering and enjoyment, of spiritual bondage and release from that bondage, or ignorance and illumination. (Mohanty, 30–31)

The critiques of the Buddhist theory of *anātman* are mainly centered around the following issues, which the *anātman* theory is believed to be ill-equipped to deal with: the unity of self-consciousness; the necessary possibilities of memory and recognition; the identity of the subject for the purposes of knowing; and the identity of the person for the purposes of social life, moral responsibilities, suffering, enjoyment, ignorance, enlightenment, transmigration, et cetera. Essentially, all of the issues have to do with the question of "whose": Without a metaphysical self, whose consciousness; whose past, present, and future; whose memory; whose recognition; whose knowledge; whose family; whose friends; whose responsibility; whose suffering; whose enjoyment; whose ignorance; whose enlightenment; and whose transmigration are Buddhists talking about?

Karel Werner has ably demonstrated that "[n]either Hinduism nor Buddhism posits an abiding, unchanging, purely individual soul inhabiting the personality structure and therefore the Upaniṣadic assertion of the *ātman* and the Buddhist arguable negation of the *atta* do not justify or substantiate the view, still perpetuated in some quarters, that Hinduism believes in a transmigrating soul while Buddhism denies it" (95). In his observation of the early Upaniṣads, what transmigrates is the subtle body with *ātman* as the controlling but uninvolved power; in Buddhism it is the mental body, *nāmakāya*, that structures the personality that transmigrates (73–97). Consequently, the above accusation against Buddhists that they—in the absence of the recognition of a metaphysical self such as the Upaniṣadic notion of *ātman*—cannot account for "the possibility of knowledge, of social life and moral relationships, of suffering and enjoyment, of spiritual bondage and release from that bondage, or ignorance and illumination" (Mohanty, 31) is somewhat misplaced because even within the systems of the Upaniṣadic tradition the metaphysical self, *ātman,* does not perform such functions as a unifying *and* participating subject or agent.

In this connection, it is interesting to call attention to the fact that similar concerns have indeed tempted certain Buddhists to seek solutions in the direction of a substantive self. An obvious example is Pudgalavādins (Personalists), who, like Vātsīputrīyas and the Sāmmitīyas within the Buddhist tradition, advocate the existence of "something called a *pudgala,* ('person[hood]') *from an ultimate point of view, as a real thing*" (Williams & Tribe, 125, original italics). The *pudgala* is regarded as neither identical to the aggregates nor different from them. Such a view is forcefully refuted by Vasubandhu in the last chapter of his *Abhidharmakośabhāṣyam.* However, as Paul Williams and Anthony Tribe observe, Pudgalavādins are struggling with genuine philosophical problems here:

The Vātsīputrīya-Sāmmitīya tradition may have had a particular interest in Vinaya matters, in which case their concern with personhood
could have been significant in terms of an interest in moral responsibility. It is indeed persons who engage in moral acts, and attain
enlightenment. For moral responsibility there has to be some sense
in which the *same person* receives reward or punishment as the one
who did the original deed. It is persons who have experiences of love
and hate. All this, as Pudgalavāda sources make clear, has to be taken
as given. (126–127, original italics)[13]

Nevertheless, the Pudgalavādins' effort is rejected by the majority
of Buddhists because it violates the orthodox teaching of *anātman*.
In the course of pursuing more satisfying solutions to the problem
of "whose," Buddhists embark on a truly radical path.

What makes mainstream Buddhist solutions radical is that they
reject the very legitimacy of questions concerning "whose." These
inquiries arise only within the linguistic convention and as such it
is not necessarily reflective of the reality, whatever that may be. In
fact, Buddhists, in recognizing the thoroughly conventional nature
of language, are seeking to challenge the very way of thinking behind
the linguistic structure that gives rise to the question of "whose." I
will use the theory of *karma,* due to its immediate relevance to the
origination of the concept of *ālayavijñāna,* to illustrate how the above
issues concerning "whose" can be addressed.

Karma and Anātman

Karma means action that gives rise to the world, according to
Vasubandhu's *Abhidharmakośabhāṣyam*. But what is action? "It
is volition and that which is produced through volition" (551). In
keeping with this definition, there are two types of action, namely,
volition and the action it produces. Furthermore, the *Abhidharmakośabhāṣyam* argues that volition is mental action, and that which
arises from volition, willed action, is made up of bodily and speech
actions. In other words, volition and willed action give birth to three
kinds of action: mental, bodily, and speech.[14] The *Abhidharmakośabhāṣyam* holds that these three account for, respectively, the original cause, the support, and the nature of action. To be more specific,
all actions have their origins in the mind, the body provides a physical support for all actions, and speech is the ultimate action by its
nature (552).[15] The uniqueness of the Buddhist theory of *karma* is

its steering clear of the physicalist interpretation embraced by the Jainas and its emphasis on the mind in the generation of *karma*.

The main theoretical function of *karma* in classical Indian spiritual traditions, both orthodox Hindu schools and heterodox Buddhist and Jain schools, is to account for the cycle of transmigration. One of the most controversial issues in this connection is the alleged inconsistency between the theory of *anātman* and that of *karma*, both of which have been accepted by Buddhists. Given the Buddhist endorsement of both *anātman* and *karma*, who is it that performs actions and enjoys the results? How can the no-self, *anātman*, reap the results of "her" own action? Who is responsible for the actions, and who is going through the transmigration? Without a self as a responsible agent, there would be nobody who transmigrates. The issue at stake is the bearer of action. Although Buddhists can deny that there is a substantive self that transmigrates, they still need to account for the karmic continuity that is not limited to a single life-span: I will refer to this as reincarnation as opposed to transmigration, which implies a substantive self that transmigrates from one life to another.

The reason that *anātman* is taken to be incapable of accounting for reincarnation is due to the fact that *anātman* tends to be interpreted negatively—as rejecting any sense of self whatsoever. As we have seen previously, *anātman* does not deny the possibility of *any* self but only the substantiality of such a self or a metaphysical self. In fact the notion of *anātman* actually opens up the possibility for an empirical, individual, and dynamic self that is manifested as the continuum of a series of psychophysical events constituted by the five aggregates or the twelve links of dependent origination. The notion of *ātman* does not account for such a self at all.

This explains, at least partially, why Buddhists reject the notion of *ātman* while accepting the theory of *karma*. As Genjun Sasaki argues, *anatta/anātman* "is nothing other than *kamma* [Sk: *karma*] in its nature" (34). In other words, "the conceptions of both *kamma* and *anatta* refer to one and the same fact, differently viewed" (40). The bearer of *karma*, if we are to look for one, should be located within, not without, *karma* or action itself. Such an interpretation proposes that there is no need to posit a subject or agent separate from *karma* because such an agent *qua* the karmic continuum is obviously not an unchanging entity, and it can be understood as nothing other than *anātman*. This echoes our previous discussion that the teaching of *anātman* allows for an empirical self, and such a self is thoroughly karmic in nature.

This explanation effectively solves the above dilemma for Buddhists concerning the relationship between *karma* and *anātman* because it demonstrates that *karma* is *anātman* and *anātman* is *karma*.[16] For Buddhists actions and their bearer are identical, and any attempt to separate one from the other would result in the reification of the agent as the permanent and unchanging self, or eternalism as it is referred to in Buddhist literature. In other words, action, in its bodily, mental, and verbal expressions, *is* the person and there is no person hiding behind her actions.[17]

One major consequence of Buddhists' rejection of the notion of a substantive self is that they are able to turn their attention to a more primordial question concerning the ground upon which our sense of identity arises in the first place. This rejection is significant in that it brings to the fore the issue of continuity, which remains largely concealed by the notion of a substantive self. When the metaphysics of identity is thrown out, the challenge posed to Buddhists is how to account for continuity without appealing to substance. Granted that the self is nothing but a series of continuous momentary psychophysical events due to the instantaneity of all that are constitutive of the self and that our postulation of an eternal self is the result of mistaking continuity as identity, Buddhists still need to answer a crucial question: Can they account for continuity?

One clear difficulty in this regard within the early Buddhist framework is, as William Waldron observes, "the incompatibility of the continuity of effect within a strictly momentary analysis of mind, or, in terms of cognition, how any past effects can remain to influence present cognition and knowledge" (1990, 9). How can Buddhists explain continuity within their framework, which only acknowledges the momentariness of the psychophysical events that constitute the empirical self? Without continuity, the momentariness of *dharma* alone is hopelessly inadequate in explaining the possibility of any meaningful experience.[18] Put differently, without accumulation of some sort (including memory, habit, etc.), moment-to-moment events cannot themselves provide anything that assembles those momentary episodes into a coherent structure, thus nullifying the very possibility of experience. This thorny problem concerns the issues of momentariness and continuity, and for this we need to turn to the two leading non-Mahāyāna Buddhist philo-

sophical schools, Sarvāstivāda and Sautrāntika. Both exerted important influences on the development of the Yogācāra School in setting
the parameters for the Yogācāra's effort in tackling this issue, as noted
by Erich Frauwallner: "Of the Mahāyāna schools, it was especially
that of the Yogācāra which attempted to develop its doctrines into
a system modeled on those of the Hīnayāna schools" (131). Sarvāstivāda and Sautrāntika are two of the most prominent Hīnayāna
schools.[19]

Momentariness and Continuity:
Sarvāstivāda versus Sautrāntika

The theory of the momentary nature of conditioned *dharma*s,
despite its orthodox status in Buddhist philosophical discourse, did
not appear at the beginning of Buddhism in the Buddha's recorded
teachings. As Alexander von Rospatt notes, "It does not fit the prac-
tically oriented teachings of early Buddhism and clearly bears the
mark of later doctrinal elaboration" (15). The starting point of this
theory is the Buddhist teaching of impermanence and change of the
empirical world, and its precise formulation is arrived at gradually
(Stcherbasky, 109; Rospatt, 153).[20] In Rospatt's words, "[J]ust as
the momentariness of mental entities follows from the denial of a
permanent Self and from the observation of the fleeting nature of
mental events, so the momentariness of all forms of entities follows
from the denial of a substance underlying change and from the con-
viction that things always change" (11). In other words, the perceived
momentariness of mental entities paves the way for the establishment of the doctrine that all conditioned entities are momentary,
given the Buddhist teaching of the non-substantiality of all entities,
mental as well as physical. Th. Stcherbatsky nicely summarizes the
Buddhist teaching of momentariness:

> The theory of Universal Momentariness implies that every duration
> in time consists of point-instants following one another, every exten-
> sion in space consists of point-instants arising in contiguity and simul-
> taneously, every motion consists of these point-instants arising in
> contiguity and in succession. There is therefore no Time, no Space
> and no Motion over and above the point-instants of which these imag-
> ined entities are constructed by our imagination. (84)

The momentary point-instant is the primary *dharma* that is ultimately
real—in the sense that it is irreducible to any entity more basic than

it—and the compounded entity observable in the empirical world is only secondary and derivative, according to the Abhidharmikas. This point-instant is timeless, spaceless, and motionless "in the sense of having no duration, no extension and no movement[;] it is a mathematical point-instant, the moment of an action's efficiency" (87), and efficiency, not substance, defines existence in Buddhism (89). In Rospatt's observation, this point-instant, *kṣaṇa*, "may in some contexts be understood as a precisely defined unit of time (e.g., 1/75th of a second), while in others it may (at least in certain compounds) refer to the momentary entity itself" (94). I will not dwell on the development of the theory of momentariness in early Buddhism because it does not directly pertain to our discussion here. What concerns me is not so much how a compound entity can be analyzed into a series of discrete momentary entities, but rather the other way around, namely, how discrete momentary entities can become a compound entity *qua* a continuum. Hence the question before us is the question of continuity vis-à-vis momentariness.

As noted at the end of the last section, early Buddhist philosophers struggled to reconcile the doctrine of momentariness with that of continuity entailed by the theory of *karma*. With the rejection of a substantive self, what is it that continues from one moment to the next? If nothing continues, how can *karma* work? Apparently, within such a theoretical framework, there is a discrepancy between what William Waldron calls the synchronic analysis and the diachronic analysis of *dharma*s: "the relations between the diverse *dharma*s within each single mind-moment, [and] the causal relations between succeeding moments" (1990, 150). According to Abhidharma Buddhists, all phenomena are transient and momentary; when the effect is born, the cause should have already perished. However, if the cause has indeed ceased to exist at the moment the effect is born, the effect cannot be caused in the strict sense because that which has perished does not have any causal power. As Waldron summarizes, "[T]*his exclusive validity accorded to the synchronic analysis of momentary mental processes threatened to render that very analysis religiously vacuous by undermining the validity of its overall soteriological context—the diachronic dimension of samsaric continuity and its ultimate cessation*" (2003, 56, original italics). In other words, for Buddhist religious practices to be meaningful their effects must be preserved in some way so that the spiritual goal of liberation from suffering is possible.

The problem for Buddhists is this: Is it possible to account for continuity without positing some persisting entity? This may be called "the problematic of continuity" in Buddhist philosophical discourse. Continuity presupposes change. Without change continuity would be meaningless because it simply becomes identity. Any meaningful sense of continuity has to be continuity in change, or continuous change.

What then is this continuous change? Historically, continuity has been conceived of in three ways. First, a continuous change may be a continuing alteration of the state of being of one and the same object. In other words, change is predicated upon a substance; it is the change *of* something without which even the concept of change is impossible and that something is the substratum that grounds change or subsumes change as its attribute. In this case, change is change of properties of an unchanging substance (e.g., the duration of a desk from its creation to destruction). The second scenario, unique to Buddhists, is to "formulate a theory of immediate contiguity *(samanantara)* and grant causal efficiency *(arthakriyā-kāritva* or *paccayatā)* to the immediate preceding *dhammā*" (Kalupahana 1975, 72–73). Lastly, continuity is conceived in such a way that it rejects the idea that time consists of a series of instantaneous moments. In this conception of continuity, a moment is not instantaneous, but rather it contains the structure of the immediate past, the present and the immediate future within itself.[21] In other words, a moment is itself conceived as a continuum that is a horizon containing what immediately precedes and immediately follows instead of as a discrete instant. As we will see, the first view is adopted by Sarvāstivāda,[22] the second by Sautrāntika, and all three views, with important modifications, are adopted by Yogācāra. In its advanced stages, Yogācāra postulates a grounding but changing consciousness, *ālayavijñāna,* consisting of forever changing seeds whose subliminal existence warrants a contiguity between succeeding dharmic moments. I will briefly examine the positions of the two non-Mahāyāna schools relevant to the emergence of a concept like the *ālayavijñāna* formulated by Yogācārins.[23]

Let us start with Sarvāstivāda. This is one of the earliest Buddhist philosophical schools of great prominence, famous for its doctrine that things in three stages of time (i.e., past, present and future) all exist. By advocating this rather counterintuitive position, Sarvāstivādins hope to accomplish two objectives: to account for all objects of consciousness and to lay to rest the problem that if all things are momentary, causality will not be possible. In the case of the first objective, Sarvāstivādins take the view that:

> A consciousness can arise given an object, but not if an object is not present. If past and future things do not exist, there would be consciousness without an object; thus there is no consciousness without an object. (*Abhidharmkośabhaṣyam*, 807)

In other words, a consciousness must have an object, and the object must be present when the consciousness of it arises. The reason Sarvāstivādins assume such a position is due to their dogma, which strictly stipulates the concomitance of an object, sense organ, and consciousness in the production of a valid cognition (Mimaki, 81). This is a causal account of cognition in that the object causes the sense organ to produce the cognition of that object. Sarvāstivādins contend that in the case of past or future objects, the fact that we can have a valid cognition of them itself warrants their existence as real objects. Put differently, instead of arguing that the cognition of a past or future object leads to the postulation of the existence of that object, Sarvāstivādins take the opposite stance that it is the existence of that past or future object that causes the cognition of it. This means that, to use contemporary philosophical terminologies, Sarvāstivādins reject any intentional analysis of consciousness while maintaining a strictly causal analysis.[24]

Even though Sarvāstivādins may have a point in maintaining that an object of consciousness has to exist in some sense—for example, exist as a past object to be recollected or as a future object to be anticipated—such an existence is clearly not a real existence if the real existence is defined vis-à-vis the present. What is particular about an object of the past or the future is that its very existence cannot be separated from the recollecting consciousness in the case of the past and the anticipating consciousness in the case of the future. Both past and future objects can be understood as intentional but not as real because real objects are present objects that alone have causal efficacy, independent of consciousness. The position that Sarvāstivādins advocate is a strict causal account of valid cognition, stipulating that there has to be a real object that causes the consciousness of it by affecting the corresponding sense organ. It is realism in its extreme form.

Secondly, by resorting to the teaching that *dharma*s in all three stages of time exist, Sarvāstivādins hope to render the problematic of continuity irrelevant in that this enables them to claim that because a *dharma* exists all the time, it can always produce an effect as its cause. This theoretical move effectively bypasses the dilemma between momentariness and continuity.

Two questions should immediately become apparent regarding the Sarvāstivāda position: First, if things exist in all three stages of time, how does this square with the fundamental Buddhist position of the impermanence of conditioned *dharma*?[25] Second, how can they account for the difference in the three stages of time if existence is not the criterion that differentiates them? As we have seen previously, the dilemma for Buddhists concerning the problematic of continuity is their advocacy of the impermanence of *dharma*. If Sarvāstivādins advocate that things in all three stages of time exist, they have, or at least appear to have, rejected this fundamental principle of Buddhism. Consequently, the Buddhist position is, instead of being defended, abandoned. On the other hand, if things in all three stages of time exist, how do they differ? What makes the past past, the present present, and the future future? How does something in the past differ from something in the present or future? Furthermore, if *dharma*s always exist, the effects should likewise exist all the time. Why then can't they generate effects all the time? Indeed, if the effects always exist, the issue of the arising and perishing of *dharma*s and their effects would not exist.

In their defense against the first charge, Sarvāstivādins argue that although *dharma*s exist all the time, they are not eternal because they are conditioned and only unconditioned *dharma*s exist eternally (*Abhidharmakośabhaṣyam*, 806).[26] Although Sarvāstivādins are obviously aware of the precarious situation they put themselves in by advocating such a position, they have chosen to stay with it. But their defense is rather weak, to say the least.[27]

However, it is the second question, namely the difference between past, present, and future, that preoccupies most of the efforts of Sarvāstivādins.[28] After some rounds of struggle, Sarvāstivādins settle on the concept of efficacy:

> The answer given was that this difference is based on the efficacy (*kāritram*) of the things, which is not yet present in the future, appears in the present and has disappeared again in the past. This explanation sufficed for a time and was unproblematic as long as efficacy

was defined simply as activity (*vyāpāraḥ*). . . . In the meantime, a doctrine had been created which assumed in the case of things in the different stages of time a changing property (*bhāvaḥ*) in addition to their unchanging essence (*svabhāva*), which was neither different nor not different from the essence of the things. Then efficacy was equated with this property. (Frauwallner, 206)

In other words, what differentiates things in the three stages of time is the efficacy of their causal power. What was efficacious in the past, is in the present, and will be in the future. A past *dharma* is defined by its no-longer efficacious causal power, a present *dharma* by its efficacious causal power, and a future *dharma* by its not-yet efficacious causal power. This efficacy is regarded as a changing property of the unchanging essence of things from which it is neither different nor non-different.

In defending their position in this way, Sarvāstivādins must answer this question: By separating efficacy of a *dharma* from the *dharma* itself in classifying the former as a changing property and the latter as unchanging, aren't they advocating a substantialist stance with regard to the *dharma* that blatantly violates the fundamental Buddhist position of impermanence? This is indeed very significant because "for the first time in the history of Buddhist thought, the Sarvāstivādins accepted a bifurcation of elements as having substance and characteristics" (Kalupahana 1975, 63). As we have just seen, the Sarvāstivādins' answer that these *dharma*s are not unconditioned *dharma*s, hence not eternal, is not convincing.

Another question is this: What determines how the property of efficacy works in relation to the *dharma*s? In other words, why is it that sometimes the *dharma* is efficacious and sometimes not? What determines the timing of its efficacy? Sarvāstivādins deal with this question by linking the timing of efficacy with the human mind through which the status of a *dharma*, be it past, present or future, is determined:

What determines the presence of a dharma at a certain moment in a certain mental stream *(santāna)* is the presence or absence of the *prāpti*, the "possession," of that dharma at the moment when that "possession" drops into one's own mental stream. This is to say, rather tautologously, that it is present when it has "possession" of that dharma. The *prāpti* itself, however, is a dharma non-associated with the mind *(citta-viprayukta-saṃskārā)*, the contrary of the relation of the mental dharmas *(caitta)* with mind, and thus not in contradiction with the quality of that mind-moment. (Waldron 1990, 190–191)

In other words, Sarvāstivādins think that *dharma*s exist all the time, and it is our mind, through the function of a *dharma* called "possession," that determines whether it is past, present, or future. Thus a *dharma* is efficacious when its efficacy is possessed by "possession." This dharmic entity is not associated with the mind because if it were *dharma*s of past, present, and future would be always efficacious, thus nullifying the very purpose of postulating the entity "possession." Obviously, what Sarvāstivādins have done in explaining the difference between the *dharma*s in three stages of time is to introduce another *dharma*, the *dharma* of possession, which eventually determines whether the other *dharma*s are causally efficacious or not. The postulation of this *dharma*, possession *(prāpti)*,[29] however, is apparently an ad hoc explanation of the efficacy of a *dharma* because it cannot really explain how this possession works without resorting to either tautology, as Waldron points out in the passage quoted above, or infinite postulation of other *dharma*s (e.g., the possession of possession of *dharma*).[30]

Although the theory of efficacy is designed to differentiate things in the past, present, and future, it can also be regarded as an effort to keep Sarvāstivādins committed to the Buddhist doctrine of momentariness in that the efficacy only lasts a moment, the present. But the separation of attributes from substance leaves Sarvāstivādins vulnerable to the charge, as we have already seen, that they postulate an unchanging essence of things in direct violation of the impermanence doctrine generally accepted in Buddhism. No wonder Sarvāstivāda is regarded by many other Buddhist schools as heretical (Kalupahana 1975, 149).

By now it should be clear that the solution proposed by Sarvāstivādins—that things in all three stages of time exist—is hardly satisfying because it gives rise to too many complications that are unacceptable within the confines of already accepted Buddhist orthodoxy.

Having briefly examined the merits and the difficulties of Sarvāstivāda's attempt to reconcile traditional Buddhist doctrines with a viable theory of continuity, let us now turn to Sautrāntika. The emergence of the Sautrāntika School is the result of a series of critiques of its predecessor, the Sarvāstivāda School,[31] especially the latter's position on separating substance from attributes. Their rejection is based on the orthodox Buddhist ground that the state of being of an object *is* itself that object and there is nothing that exists apart from its states of being as a separate entity. Apparently, Sautrāntikas do not differentiate substance from attributes or properties but rather regard them as the same. To them, the separation of the two is the result of intellectual abstraction with no experiential correlates.[32] Clearly, Sautrāntikas take the second view on continuity that we mentioned previously (Kalupahana 1975, 73) to accommodate both the momentariness of *dharma*s and continuity between those moments.

Sautrāntika prides itself as a defender of the *sūtra*s in Buddhist philosophical discourse; "Sautrāntika" means "the school of the *sūtra*s."[33] In defending the traditional Buddhist teaching of impermanence *(anitya)*, Sautrāntikas held the view that the external world has "only an instantaneous existence and . . . argued that its existence could be recognized only through inference" (Hirakawa, 119).[34] Sautrāntikas recognize only two moments of a *dharma*, nascent *(utpāda)* and cessant *(vyaya)*, and reject the static moment *(sthiti-kṣaṇa)* (Kalupahana 1975, 151). Thus a *dharma* perishes instantaneously the very moment it comes into being, without lasting even a moment. This is clearly a sharp departure from the Sarvāstivāda position that things in all three stages of time exist, which as we have seen runs the inherent risk of falling into an essentialist position. On the other hand, the Sautrāntika position pushes the traditional Buddhist doctrine of impermanence to its logical conclusion by advocating that a *dharma* perishes instantaneously. In this way, Sautrāntikas inevitably have to take up the thorny problematic their predecessors have tried and failed to solve, namely, how to reconcile the conflict between momentariness and continuity without sacrificing fundamental Buddhist positions such as impermanence—something Sarvāstivādins appear to have done without acknowledging it. Sautrāntikas refuse to accept a grounding substratum as Sarvāstivādins have done. Instead, they stipulate two immediately succeeding moments as congruous and render the preceding one causally efficacious, although congruity itself does not necessarily mean causality. Essentially, the problem comes down to this, as nicely summed up by G. C. Pande:

> Motion and change become intelligible only when the notion of a continuum as an identity in difference is superimposed on separate moments. But there is no separate reality corresponding to the notion of the continuum. Since what is real is only momentary, it

cannot really move or change. . . . Causality then becomes simple temporal succession. In the absence of any influence or activity between cause and effect, how can there be dependence between them or invariance in their succession? If causality were to be real it would be impossible to explain the relationship of cause and effect as one of either identity or difference. (206)

What is especially noteworthy in Pande's observation is that some Buddhists, especially Sautrāntikas in our case, replace causality with temporal succession. In other words, according to some Buddhists, a temporal continuum by itself sufficiently constitutes a continuous change without positing something persisting through. However, in order to establish a causal relationship that presupposes a continuous change, there has to be some necessary connection, something more than just a temporal succession between the cause and the effect, in that the latter is *caused* by the former. But what is this causal relationship? How can a causal relationship be established without a grounding substratum or something persisting through from the cause to the effect? Without a causal relationship, there can only be a succession of moments. If so, the relationship between the preceding moment and the succeeding one is contingent rather than necessary.

To account for the missing link between the cause and the effect within the Buddhist system, Sautrāntikas postulate the concept of seed, *bīja*. It represents their attempt to overcome the difficulties that Sarvāstivādins encounter in their effort to reconcile the traditional Buddhist doctrines with a viable theory of continuity.

In the *Abhidharmakośabhāṣyam*, a seed is defined as follows:

> *Kāmarāgānuśaya* means "*anuśaya* of *kāmarāga*." But the *anuśaya* is neither associated with the mind nor disassociated from it: for it is not a separate thing *(dravya)*. What is called *anuśaya* is the *kleśa* [affliction] itself in a state of sleep, whereas the *paryavasthāva* is the *kleśa* in an awakened state. The sleeping *kleśa* is the non-manifested *kleśa*, in the state of being a seed; the awakened *kleśa* is the manifested *kleśa*, the *kleśa* in action. And by "seed" one should understand a certain capacity to produce the *kleśa*, a power belonging to the person engendered by the previous *kleśa*. (770)

Here Sautrāntikas are differentiating two kinds of *kleśa* (affliction)— *anuśaya* and *paryavasthāva*—a distinction not recognized by Sarvāstivādins. The former is *kleśa* in the latent state, the latter in the manifest state. The former is identified with the seed and the latter is described as a manifestation of the former. In this context, "seed" is defined as "a certain capacity to produce the *kleśa*, a power belonging to the person engendered by the previous *kleśa*." In other words, it is a capacity, not an efficacy. As such, it is only potentially efficacious. Because a *dharma* is defined by its causal efficacy according to Buddhists, a mere capacity, or potential efficacy, cannot qualify it as a *dharma*. As a result, although we might want to think that seeds actually exist, their existence is not a dharmic existence. That is, they exist nominally or as a designation *(prajñapti)* that is neither existing nor non-existing.

In making a distinction between *anuśaya* and *paryavasthāva*, Sautrāntikas hope to solve the following dilemma:

> If the *akuśala-mūlas* [roots of evil volitions] are not annihilated till the attainment of arhatship and if they are incompatible with the *kuśala-mūlas* [roots of good volitions], how are we to explain the operation of *kuśala-mūlas* or of *kuśala* volitions in a mundane *(alukika)* existence? Being incompatible they cannot operate simultaneously. Nor can they operate successively, for succession demands a certain element of homogeneity between the preceding and succeeding moment. If a *kuśala-citta* were to follow an *akuśala-citta*, then it will depend for its nature on a heterogeneous cause. This will amount to an admission of the unacceptable position that good springs out of evil or vice versa. (Jaini, 238)

Simply put, the above dilemma is this: In the mundane state that generally characterizes our existence, both evil and good volitions operate, and their relationship clearly can be neither that of simultaneity nor that of succession. They cannot be simultaneous due to their incompatibility or successive due to their heterogeneity. Sarvāstivādins, as expected, appeal to their doctrine of possession, *prāpti,* to get out of the trap. Sautrāntikas reject *prāpti* on the grounds that this doctrine, as we have seen, leads to infinite regress. Rather, they try to solve the problem by formulating the theory of seed. There are three kinds of seeds: seeds of evil *(akuśala-dharma-bīja),* seeds of good *(kuśala-dharma-bīja),* and seeds of indeterminate characteristic:

> The Sautrāntikas maintained that the *anuśayas* as well as the *kuśala* elements *(bījas)* co-exist side by side in the form of subtle seeds, but only one of them operates at one time. When the *anuśayas* operate

(i.e., become *paryavasthānas*), the mind is *akuśala*. When the seeds of *kuśala* operate the mind is *kuśala*. (Jaini, 240)

By relegating the otherwise incompatible elements to mere potentiality in the form of subtle seeds, Sautrāntikas are able to work out the inherent conflict of the two elements due to their lack of efficacy in the dormant state, while maintaining the doctrine of non-contradiction within one dharmic moment and our common sense.

As a consequence of establishing the theory of seeds, Sautrāntikas are better equipped to solve the problem of continuity. That is, even though a *dharma* perishes in the same moment it is born according to the Sautrāntika interpretation of the Buddhist doctrine of impermanence, its effect does not have to be manifested in its immediate successor. Rather, the effect will take a back seat and remain a seed, dormant for some time, accumulating its potency and waiting for the right conditions for it to come to fruition. In this way, both momentariness and continuity can be theoretically accommodated. In terms of the manifested *dharma*, it perishes instantaneously; in terms of continuity, it is retained by the dormant seeds to be manifested later. Because one is manifested and the other is latent, their coexistence is not hindered by their homogeneity. More importantly, the seeds, working behind the scenes as it were, provide a critical connecting link between cause and effect within the boundary of Buddhist orthodoxy without relying on a persisting entity; seeds are not dharmic entities due to their inefficaciousness, but rather a designation for propensities and proclivities of our mental life.

However, the postulation of seeds has given rise to other questions that essentially concern the status of seeds "during two states of deep meditation, the attainment of 'unconsciousness' and the attainment of cessation, in both of which there is complete cessation of all mental activities. Since the seeds themselves are carried along in or with the *citta*, or more precisely, the *vijñāna*, the continuity of the seeds is also brought to a standstill in these meditative practices" (Waldron 1990, 211). The problem is that if, as some Buddhist scriptures describe, in the two deep meditative states all mental activities are brought to a halt, how is it possible for the meditator to emerge from such states? As Paul Griffiths points out, the standard Sautrāntika view on this is as follows:

The consciousness that emerges from the attainment of cessation has as its immediately antecedent and similar condition the physical body of the practitioner in the attainment of cessation. This is possible because, according to the Sautrāntika theoreticians, mind and body, the physical and the mental, 'mutually seed one another'—that is, each is capable of planting seeds in the others, seeds which may lie dormant until the proper time for their maturation occurs. (64)

In other words, Sautrāntikas regard the physical body as capable of holding seeds of the mental activity, which in turn provide the immediately antecedent condition for the meditator's mind to emerge out of the deep meditation states wherein all mental activity is supposed to have ceased. However, this view is clearly problematic for the following reason:

The Sautrāntikas also wish to preserve the necessity of an immediately antecedent and similar condition for the emergent consciousness, but by allotting that function to the 'seeded' physical body they are forced to loosen, almost to the point of disregarding, the requirement that the relevant condition be 'similar.' For it is difficult to see even a 'seeded' physical body, a continuum of physical events, as being generically the same kind of thing as a continuum of mental events. (65)

In order for the meditator to come out of the cessation states, two conditions are required: the operation of sense organs and the immediately antecedent mental activity (Waldron 1990, 213). The first condition concerns bodily support, the second mental support. The meditator still retains her body, but she does not have mental activity as the immediate antecedent on which her emerging post-meditative mental state can rely because it is interrupted in those meditative states. Bodily support cannot give rise to mental activities, as Sautrāntikas claim; the two are perceived as heterogeneous and as such they cannot be in a cause-effect relationship.[35] Consequently, this difficulty appears to threaten the very purpose for which seeds are postulated in the first case, namely to account for continuity in the course of instantaneous change.

To find a solution to this difficulty, Sautrāntikas have tried to formulate an undercurrent of seeds into a new kind of consciousness (Waldron 1990, 216) that is subtle and difficult to detect, thus it is different from the forms of consciousness (*vijñāna*) hitherto known in Buddhist, or even general Indian, philosophical discourse.[36] Sautrāntikas claim that the two states of deep meditation are free of all other mental activities except the subtle form of mind that is still functioning without being detected, thus providing the meditator with the crucial *mental* support to emerge from the cessation states. This formulation comes very close to the Yogācāra conception of *ālayavijñāna*, but it is in the hands of Yogācāra Buddhists that we witness a full and systematic development of the concept of a subliminal mind, *ālayavijñāna*, that incorporates Sautrāntika's insight regarding the subliminal activities in the form of seeds. And this is the topic to which I now turn.

Early Development of *Ālayavijñāna*

After examining some Buddhist endeavors predating the conceptualization of *ālayavijñāna* to smooth out the inconsistencies and difficulties regarding the orthodox Buddhist doctrines of *karma* and impermanence (continuity and change), let us now move to the conception of *ālayavijñāna* formulated by Yogācāra Buddhists in their effort to carry on their predecessors' work. As William Waldron rightly observes, early Buddhists share similar presuppositions expressed in similar terminology, and they are troubled by similar problems; what is different are their solutions (1990, 141). In a nutshell, the similar problem before them is how to reconcile the tension between two central Buddhist doctrines, impermanence and *karma,* with the former advocating momentariness and the latter continuity.[37] This is an issue of continuity in the course of instantaneous change, what I have called the "problematic of continuity" in Buddhist philosophical discourse. Based on the theoretical advances made by their predecessors, such as the Sarvāstivādins and the Sautrāntikas, Yogācārins have developed a more cogent and sophisticated theory to tackle this problem. This is the celebrated theory of *ālayavijñāna*. As Paul Griffiths aptly observes, the Yogācāra notion of *ālayavijñāna* is an "intellectual construct designed to account for problems of continuity in Buddhist theories of personal identity" (96), and it has "substantial and interesting effects upon the soteriology of the Yogācāra theorists" (ibid.).

Lambert Schmithausen has written hitherto the most comprehensive and thorough investigation on the early development of this concept in his *Ālayavijñāna: On the Origin and the Early Development of a Central Concept of Yogācāra Philosophy*. My discussion here is primarily based on his eminent book with the aim of making the ongoing presentation of the origin of the concept complete, thus laying the groundwork for an exploration of the role played by *ālayavijñāna* in the work of a later Yogācārin, Xuan Zang. I will limit my presentation here to the very beginning of the conceptualization of *ālayavijñāna* with an eye on its relationship to earlier efforts to tackle similar problems. The later development will be left to Chapter Two, where the concept of *ālayavijñāna* will be dealt with in greater detail.

The issues concerning us at this point are how and where the conceptualization of *ālayavijñāna* actually begins. What are the salient characteristics of *ālayavijñāna* in its earliest schematization as opposed to its later development? In order to trace the origin of the conceptualization of *ālayavijñāna*, Schmithausen sets an ambitious goal to locate the initial passage where the concept originally appears in existent Yogācāra literature. Before launching the effort to look for the initial passage, if there is one to be found, Schmithausen lays down two requirements for identifying such a passage: It has to have a justifiable motive to introduce a new type of *vijñāna* different from the six traditional *vijñāna*s, and the choice of the name *ālayavijñāna* also has to be reasonable (15). He finds one passage in the Basic Section of the *Yogācārabhūmi*:

> When [a person] has entered [absorption into] Cessation (*nirodha* [*samāpatti*]), his mind and mental [factors] have ceased; how, then, is it that [his] mind *(vijñāna)* has not withdrawn from [his] body? — [Answer: No problem;] for [in] his [case] *ālayavijñāna* has not ceased [to be present] in the material sense-faculties, which are unimpaired: [*ālayavijñāna*] which comprises (/possesses/has received) the Seeds of the forthcoming [forms of] mind *(pravṛttivijñāna)*, so that they are bound to re-arise in the future (i.e., after emerging from absorption). (Quoted in Schmithausen, 18)

This passage appears to have met the two conditions set by Schmithausen. The subject matter that this passage deals with is the issue of the mind during a deep meditative state, *nirodha-samāpatti*. As we saw earlier in this chapter, during such a meditative state all mental activities are brought to a halt. That is to say, there is an interruption of the otherwise continuous mental activities. Consequently, when the meditator emerges from such a state, she would have no mental antecedent as the support. Without this the emergence itself would not even be possible because the emerging consciousness has to be given rise to by its immediate mental antecedent as its mental support in addition to the bodily support I discussed earlier. Apparently the traditional six types of *vijñāna* are not able to offer this support. What Yogācārins have done is to propose another form of mind that is subtle and subliminal with the hope that it will both keep the integrity of the Buddhist teaching that in *nirodha-samāpatti* there are no mental activities and provide a continuity between the mundane state of the mind of the meditator before and after it is interrupted by deep meditation. However, in asserting that during a deep meditative state like *nirodha-samāpatti* there still exists a subliminal form of mind in the state of unmanifested seeds, Yogācāra Buddhists have essentially revised the description concerning mental activities during such a state from no mental activities to no *detectable* mental activities. This leaves room for the postulation of a concept like *ālayavijñāna*, and indeed even renders such an effort imperative.

Moreover, the above passage also justifies the use of the word "*ālayavijñāna*"; "in it, this term would be most appropriate if taken to mean 'the (or, if the term is new, perhaps better: a) [form of] mind [that is characterized by] sticking [in the material sense-faculties],' in the sense of being hidden in them—a meaning which moreover would contrast perfectly with the term '*pravṛttivijñāna*,' i.e., mind as it comes forth or manifests itself in a [cognitive] act" (Schmithausen, 22). In other words, *ālayavijñāna* as formulated here is a form of mind that is hidden in the material sense faculties as opposed to the mind that manifests itself in a cognitive act, *pravṛttivijñāna*, like the other *vijñāna*s.

There are a number of points worthy of our attention once the hypothesis of this being the initial passage is accepted. First, it is obvious from this initial passage, as well as from our previous investigations, that the new *vijñāna* is originally formulated primarily with an eye on the problematic of continuity.[38] Because the mental continuum is interrupted during the deep meditative state, some form of continuity has to be worked out. The Sarvāstivādin pan-realist answer has almost insurmountable theoretical difficulties as we have seen. The Sautrāntika theory of *bīja* is appealing, but because the seeds are themselves not a form of mind but simply associated with the mind and the mental activities are interrupted in the given circumstances, they should also in turn cease their activities and thus become incapable of providing mental support to the re-emergence of mental activities for the meditator from the deep meditative state. Consequently, a new form of mind, subtle and undetected, is called for. Indeed, the initial passage seems to have provided a link between the Sautrāntika theory of seeds and a more developed form of *ālaya-vijñāna* in that the passage does nothing more than to "hypostatize the Seeds of mind lying hidden in corporeal matter to a new form of mind proper, this new form of mind hardly, or, at best, but dimly, acquiring as yet an essence of its own, not to speak of the character of a veritable *vijñāna*" (Schmithausen, 30).

This brings us to the next noteworthy point in the initial passage, namely, *ālayavijñāna* is explicitly taught to be embodied in the material sense faculties. That is, the *ālayavijñāna* as it initially appears in Yogācāra literature has a distinctly corporeal character to it. Instead of subsuming the material sense faculties under it, it sticks in them. Interestingly enough, in this initial passage there is no mention of its being the basis of personal existence or being mistaken for the Self, functions that will come into play later on.

In order for *ālayavijñāna* to assume the prominent position it comes to occupy later in the Yogācāra theoretical edifice, this primarily corporeal nature of *ālayavijñāna* would have to be transformed. Instead of sticking in the material sense faculties, it would become their foundation. This happens in the *Pravṛtti Portion* of the *Yogācārabhūmi* (Schmithausen, 51).

In the initial passage, there is no indication as to whether this new form of consciousness is good, bad, or neutral. Furthermore, the issue of the occurrence of *ālayavijñāna* in ordinary states other than the *nirodha-samāpatti* has not yet become an explicit one (32). All these issues will become important when *ālayavijñāna* starts to assume other roles in addition to its maintaining continuity for a meditator who goes through deep meditation. I will deal with these issues in Chapter Two.

What is striking—if we look back on the historical development of Buddhist attempts to solve the problematic of continuity, from the pan-realist Sarvāstivādins to the somewhat constitutionist Sautrāntikas,[39] and eventually to the metaphysical idealist Yogācārins[40]— is that Buddhists appear to have increasingly resorted to human subjectivity in finding a solution. Consequently, although I agree with Schmithausen that "the Initial Passage does not show any trace of idealism or spiritualism" (32) and that "the origin of the *ālaya-*

vijñāna theory does not seem to have any material connection with the origin of the doctrine of *vijñaptimātratā* [cognition only]" (33), its further advancement in the hands of Yogācārins, its eventual incorporation into the grand Yogācāra system, and the central role it has come to play within that system fit rather nicely into the general trend of idealization in the development of Buddhist doctrines, culminating in the Yogācāra School itself. In this respect, it is interesting to note that scholars have generally distinguished two schools of Yogācāra, the "classical" and the "new." The classical school is represented by the early Yogācārins such as Maitreya, Asaṅga, Vasubandhu, Paramārtha, and Sthiramati, and the new school by Dharmapāla and Xuan Zang. The new school is considered more idealistic in its orientation.[41] This means that even within the Yogācāra School, the idealization trend continues. In the next chapter we will see how Xuan Zang's formulation of *ālayavijñāna* reflects this trend.

2

ĀLAYAVIJÑĀNA
IN THE
CHENG WEISHI LUN

A BUDDHIST THEORY OF THE

SUBLIMINAL MIND

IN THE LAST CHAPTER, I briefly traced the origin of the concept of *ālayavijñāna*. I investigated the rationale behind the Yogācāra postulation of *ālayavijñāna* as a new form of consciousness, *vijñāna*, which is initially designed to provide support for the meditator during two meditative states wherein mental activities are supposed to have stopped. However, once formulated, the development of *ālayavijñāna* takes a course of its own, and the concept is expanded to accommodate other doctrinal needs of Buddhism, the most important of which is to account for our sense of self and our cognition of external objects.

In this chapter, we will look into the concept of *ālayavijñāna* in its more developed form as presented in the *Cheng Weishi Lun* (*Vijñaptimātratāsiddhi-śāstra, The Treatise on the Establishment of the Doctrine of Consciousness-Only,* hereafter *CWSL*).[1] The authorship of *CWSL* is traditionally attributed to Xuan Zang, the famous seventh-century Chinese Buddhist pilgrim and translator. He traveled to India between 629 and 645 and brought back to China numerous Buddhist scriptures. Many of his Chinese translations of Indian Buddhist scriptures have been widely accepted as the most authoritative. The *CWSL* is one of two texts by Xuan Zang that is not a translation.[2] It was composed as an extended commentary on Vasubandhu's *Thirty Verses* (*Triṃśikā*), a key text in Yogācāra Buddhism, and incorporated commentaries on the *Triṃśikā* by prominent Indian Yogācāra Buddhists, of which only Sthiramati's survives today in Sanskrit.[3] The text sides with Dharmapāla's commentary and uses it as the ultimate authority in the interpretation of *Triṃśikā*.[4]

In *Triṃśikā* Vasubandhu presents a comprehensive picture of different layers of the mind and their interactions that constitute our mental life. Given the orthodox Buddhist doctrine of impermanence that applies to both the self and external objects, Buddhists reject any substantive identity. As we have seen in Chapter One, this rejection brings to the fore the problem of continuity, which is hidden behind identity. What makes continuity attractive to Buddhists is that it is *mistakable* as identity. Accordingly, they argue that identity is the result of misidentification of continuity. That is, continuity is mistaken as identity. Now the task facing Buddhists is how to account for continuity without appealing to identity. This is what I have called the "problematic of continuity" in Buddhist philosophical discourse. The formulation of *ālayavijñāna* is precisely an effort in that direction.

We have discussed three ways continuity has been conceived historically.[5] First, continuity is change of properties of an unchanging substance. Second, continuity is nothing but an immediate contiguity, with the immediately preceding moment being the efficient cause of the immediately succeeding moment. Lastly, the conceptualization of continuity involves a rejection of the momentariness of an instant and instead sees a horizon consisting of the immediate past, the present, and the immediate future within each instant. As we have seen, Sarvāstivāda adopts the first way and Sautrāntika the second. All three ways, with certain nuanced but important modifications, are adopted by Xuan Zang. His strategy consists of three steps. First, he adopts the Madhyamaka Buddhist position that all existents are empty of any intrinsic nature;[6] he interprets this to mean that a being does not have any metaphysical identity but is itself a continuum of momentary entities. Second, he attempts to reduce the continuity of external objects to the continuity of conscious activities; this is the culmination of the idealist tendency of Buddhism. Third, once the primacy of consciousness is established, he then moves to the theorization of the possibility of enlightenment as a continuous process from the deluded state of consciousness to the enlightened one. Apparently, the second step holds the key to a viable account of continuity for the Buddhist and in this chapter I will focus on precisely this second step. I will evaluate Xuan Zang's effort to account for continuity vis-à-vis his presentation of *ālayavijñāna*. We will see that *ālayavijñāna* is conceived as a grounding but changing consciousness, consisting of ever-changing seeds whose subliminal existence warrants a congruity between successive dharmic moments. I will focus on this question: Does *ālayavijñāna* as presented in the *CWSL* eventually solve the problematic of continuity within Buddhist discourse, and if so, how?

The Primacy of Consciousness

In order to argue for continuity within the dormain of consciousness, Xuan Zang has to establish its primacy first. His strategy is to challenge the reification of the two aspects of a cognitive experience, namely, mind and its object. He considers mental process and its object to be two aspects of the same cognitive experience;[7] neither one is independent of the other. However, the mutual dependency of mental activities and external objects alone does not establish the primacy of the former over the latter. That is, Xuan Zang still has to justify his approach, which prioritizes the mental-aspect over the object-aspect. Hence, he needs to make the argument that an object is not independent of the cognitive structure through which it is cognized and verified.

According to Xuan Zang, there are ultimately two kinds of beings, *dharma* and *ātman*,[8] which correspond to the two realms of existences, external and internal. *Dharma* refers to the external and *ātman* the internal. Let us take a look at how he makes the argument that the real existence of the two is irrelevant to his philosophical endeavor. Xuan Zang defines the way the two terms are used thusly: "'*Ātman*' (Ch: *wo*) means ownership and domination whereas '*dharma*' (Ch: *fa*) means norms and grasping" (8). He contends that *ātman* and *dharma* are the result of the misidentification of a continuum as identity or substance. It is with this observation that Vasubandhu begins his *Triṃśikā*:

> *ātmadharmopacāro hi vividho yaḥ pravartate/*
> *vijñānapariṇāme 'sau pariṇāmaḥ sa ca tridhā/*
> *vipāko mananākhyaś ca vijñaptir viṣayasya ca*

> For the various metaphorical usage of "self" (*ātman*) and "objects" (*dharma*) is employed on the basis of the transformation of consciousness. And that transformation is threefold: retribution, intellection, and perception of the sense field.

There are a number of points worthy of our attention here. First of all, Vasubandhu points out that self (*ātman*) and objects (*dharma*) are nothing but metaphors. As such, they have no reference to real self-contained entities. Then what are the referents of *ātman* and *dharma?* According to Vasubandhu, *ātman* and *dharma* correlate to no reality beyond the realm of the mind. Instead, our sense of *ātman* and *dharma* is nothing but the result of the transformation of consciousness.[9] This transformation is threefold: the five sense consciousnesses together with the sixth, or sense-centered, consciousness (*manovijñāna*) that discriminates and cognizes physical objects; the seventh, or thought-centered, consciousness (*manas*), that wills and reasons on a self-centered basis; and the eighth, or store-house, consciousness (*ālayavijñāna*).

At first sight, the claim that both *ātman* and *dharma* are the results of the transformation of consciousness easily associates it with the position of a metaphysical idealist, if metaphysical idealism can be roughly understood as a view that holds the ultimate reality to be mental or spiritual, or mind-dependent.[10] Is Xuan Zang's Yogācāra Buddhism a form of metaphysical idealism? Let us look at how he accounts for the self and the external world by appealing to the trans-formation of consciousness.

Xuan Zang begins by investigating our cognition. An examina-tion of our cognition would reveal a distinct structure:

> When a defiled consciousness itself is born, it is manifested in two apparent characteristics [Sk: *lakṣaṇas*; Ch: *xiang*]: as the appropri-ated [Sk: *ālambana*; Ch: *suo yuan*] and the appropriating [Sk: *sālam-bana*; Ch: *neng yuan*]. . . . As an apparent object, the appropriated explains the perceived aspect of consciousness [Sk: *nimittabhāga*; Ch: *xiang feng*]. As an apparent subject, the appropriating explains the perceiving aspect [Sk: *darśanabhāga*; Ch: *jian feng*]. (138)

To put it simply, there is a dual structure in all of our—obviously defiled—cognitive activities, namely the perceiving aspect, *darśa-nabhāga,* and the perceived aspect, *nimittabhāga.*

As Shunkyō Katsumata (245) acutely observes, Xuan Zang makes this case by adopting Dharmapāla's controversial commentary of verse seventeen of Vasubandhu's *Triṃśikā* because it is not clear whether *Triṃśikā* can be read in such a way if we are to be faithful to the literal meaning of the text.

vijñānapariṇāmo 'yaṃ vikalpo yad vikalpyate/
tena tan nāsti tenedaṃ sarvaṃ vijñaptimātrakam

The transformation of this consciousness is imagination.
That which is imagined does not exist.
Therefore all is cognition-only.

However, as Katsumata points out (245), in Xuan Zang's commentary that follows Dharmapāla's explanation, this verse is interpreted as stating that the transformation of consciousness is the result of its being bifurcated into the discriminating and the discriminated. Because neither of the two exists outside of consciousness, there can be nothing but consciousness. This interpretation

> argues for the transformation of consciousnesses by pointing to the perceiving and the perceived aspects of the eight consciousnesses and their concomitant mental activities (*citta* and *caitta*s), and as a result, the perceiving aspect of the transforming consciousness becomes the discriminating aspect and the perceived aspect the discriminated. Therefore, because the self and entities do not exist apart from the bifurcation of the transforming consciousness, it is said that all is consciousness. (Katsumata, 246)

This is an important departure from Vasubandhu's text and a key development of the Yogācāra teaching by Dharmapāla and Xuan Zang. What is significant is that to Xuan Zang this dual structure is intrinsic to consciousness. That is to say that consciousness has an inherent structure to it, or, to use the traditional terminology in Indian philosophical discourse, consciousness is formed *(sākāra)* and it is not formless *(nirākāra)*. The *CWSL* defends the position this way:

> If the mind and its concomitant mental activities (*citta* and *caitta*s) did not have in themselves the characteristics of the appropriated, they would not be able to appropriate their own objects. Otherwise they would be able to appropriate indiscriminately all objects because they would appropriate their own objects as the objects of others and appropriate the objects of others as their own. (138)

What is being argued here is that if consciousness does not have the perceived aspect within itself, it would be impossible for consciousness either to perceive anything as its own object or to perceive discriminately. Two issues are at stake in this connection. First, how is it possible for consciousness to perceive its *own* object? If consciousness is formless, and all the forms, namely its content, would come from without (because what is external to consciousness is publicly available, it cannot become the private object of consciousness), without the private object, consciousness would not have its *own* object. If, however, consciousness has an inherent form, such a problem can be easily resolved because in that case the form vis-à-vis the object/content is intrinsic to itself. Second, if consciousness is formless, how can it perceive objects discriminately instead of indiscriminately perceiving all objects? Why does it perceive some objects instead of others at one point or another? This is especially problematic when any apparent external object is absent.

As is well known, Hindu realists, such as Nyāya philosophers, argue that consciousness is formless and all distinction is derived from outside of consciousness. But there are at least two difficulties associated with the realist position, namely how to account for misperception and dream experience; in both of these cases there are no corresponding external objects. Without going into the complexities of the arguments,[11] it should be clear that formlessness or receptivity is at least not sufficient in explaining consciousness. Realists take the view that consciousness is formless, hence receptive, whereas Yogācārins think that consciousness has an intrinsic structure to it, hence it is formed. The realist theory of the receptivity of consciousness, such as Nyāya's, has an easier time explaining the collectivity of experience because according to it, the foundation of the collectivity is from without, therefore independent of consciousness. However, it has a much harder time explaining misperception, dreams, and the personal nature of cognitive experience. The idealist theory of formed consciousness, such as Yogācāra's, has just the opposite advantages and disadvantages. It is admittedly more successful in explaining the private aspect of our cognition, but how can an essentially private cognition become publicly available in the Yogācāra theory? I will deal with this issue later in the chapter.

On the subjective aspect of consciousness Xuan Zang argues:

> If the mind and its concomitant mental activities did not have in themselves the characteristics of the appropriating, they, like space, would not be able to appropriate any object. Otherwise we would have to say that space itself can appropriate objects. (138)

This point is less controversial because, after all, the distinguishing characteristic of consciousness is its subjectivity and cognitive ability. However, what is of special interest to us here is that Xuan Zang takes the subjectivity of consciousness as just one of its components; both subjectivity and objectivity are intrinsic to the structure of consciousness: "Therefore the mind and its concomitant mental activities must have two aspects, the perceived aspect *(nimittabhāga)* and the perceiving aspect *(darśanabhāga)*" (Xuan Zang, 138).

However, there is still a problem with this view:

> That which *nimittabhāga* and *darśanbhāga* depend on is itself called the "thing." This is the "self-corroboratory" aspect, *svasaṃvittibhāga*. If this *bhāga* did not exist, there would be no recollection of the mind and its concomitant mental activities (*citta-caittas*), just as there is no memory of situations that have never been experienced. (Xuan Zang, 140)

To put it simply, according to Xuan Zang, each conscious moment has to be aware of itself so that memory or recollection of that moment can be possible. In other words, aside from the aspects of the perceiving and the perceived, there has to be an awareness of *this* perception of the perceived so that this perception can be recollected; otherwise, each perceptive moment would be self-contained. If that were the case, successive moments of perceptive experience would be rendered unrelated, resulting in the impossibility of memory and recollection of experiences.

Be this as it may, Xuan Zang has to address the following concern: Is this self-corroboratory aspect also contained within each moment of perceptive experience or does it lie without? If it is outside of each moment of perception, it would resemble some notion of an uninvolved self—or to use Bina Gupta's term, *sākṣin* ("the disinterested witness"),[12] which is the empirical manifestation of the eternal *ātman*. This would mean that some metaphysical concept of self, already rejected by Buddhists, would sneak back into Buddhist discourse. On the other hand, if the self-witnessing division is within each cognitive moment, the succession of moments becomes unaccounted for, hence defeating the very purpose of its postulation in explaining the possibility of memory and recollection.

In this connection, we find the following statement in the *CWSL*:

> Transformation (*pariṇāma*) of consciousness means that consciousness itself is transformed into two aspects, *nimittabhāga* and *darśanabhāga*. These two aspects originate by depending upon the self-corroboratory aspect (*svasaṃvittibhāga*). (10)

What interests us in the above passage is that the perceiving and the perceived divisions originate from the self-corroboratory division of consciousness. This means that the two functional divisions of the perceiving and the perceived are within the self-corroboratory division of each conscious moment. Consequently, this third self-corroboratory division is apparently not outside of the two functional divisions. But the question remains, how can the momentary self-witness division warrant the continuity of the cognitive experience to account for the possibility of memory and recollection of a particular experience? On the one hand, this self-corroboratory aspect gives rise to the two functional divisions, while on the other hand it retains the effects generated by the cognitive experience of the two functional divisions of each conscious moment. In other words, the self-corroboratory division and the two functional divisions are mutually causal. Apparently, the self-corroboratory division is not simply witnessing the activities of the other two divisions but is also involved itself. The self-corroboratory division is involved in two ways, according to Xuan Zang: It gives rise to the two divisions and receives the seeds as the effects retained from the function of the two divisions. This means that the continuity of consciousness relies on its self-corroboratory division, not the two functional divisions; although the two functional divisions can appear to be continuous, their continuity derives from the continuity of the third division as its manifestations.

Hence, the CWSL concludes that "it is on the basis of these two aspects that *ātman* and *dharma*s are established, because there is no other basis" (10). On the issue of the existence of *dharma,* the external world in this connection, a typical metaphysical idealist position denies the independence of a world apart from our cognition of it. Xuan Zang's claim that *dharma* is the result of the transformation of consciousness appears to be the quintessential metaphysical idealist position. However, the CWSL apparently tries to steer itself clear of the metaphysical question here. Accordingly, after carefully examining the structure of our cognitive experience of an external object, the noncontroversial conclusion is that within each cognitive moment there are an experiencing subject and an experienced object, putting aside the self-corroboratory division for the moment. So far this is acceptable to Xuan Zang, and any step further is to him an unacceptable move because it means to posit the existence of that which is independent of this cognitive structure. Here is how Xuan Zang raises the objection:

How can we tell that there really are no external objects, but only internal consciousness appearing as external objects? It is because the existence of a real *ātman* and real *dharmas* cannot be ascertained. (12)

In fact, Xuan Zang is not denying the possibility of a real *ātman* or real *dharmas* but is simply pointing out that their reality cannot be ascertained independent of consciousness. This means that the perception of an external world does not, by itself, warrant the existence of such a world, and that there is no a priori reason to either affirm or deny, within the parameters of consciousness, the existence of the "real" external world. In fact, Xuan Zang argues that to posit an external world independent of our cognition of it is an unnecessary theoretical complication insofar as the adequacy of explaining our cognition is concerned; and I call this "qualified metaphysical idealism."[13] It is not simply a reflection of the relationship between consciousness and the world, which would be epistemological, but rather how the realm of consciousness becomes the world as we experience it. Therefore, it is a form of metaphysical idealism in the sense that it holds the view that the realm of consciousness *is* the world. It is qualified in the sense that any existence outside the realm of consciousness is neither affirmed nor denied.[14]

This qualified metaphysical idealist position is evidenced by the following remark: "In all of the graspings of *dharmas*, there might or might not be *dharmas* exterior to the mind, but there always are *dharmas* interior to the mind" (Xuan Zang, 88). It is revealing to note that Xuan Zang actually starts by conceding that in certain cases our experience of a physical object may indeed have a corresponding object exterior to the mind. The caveat in this connection is the contingent nature of such a correspondence; as he rightly observes, *not all* experience of an external object has its corresponding object external to the mind. A stock example would be dream experience, wherein the experience of an external object does not have any correspondence beyond the realm of the mind. Obviously in some of our experiences of external objects, their externality is not a necessary condition. This amounts to saying that the externality of objects is only a contingent factor in our experience of physical objects, whereas their internal representation within the realm of consciousness is a necessary component of all our experiences of physical objects. Or to be more exact, our experience of objects is real but their external existence is not necessarily so.

Opponents might argue that unless there is a real external world it would be impossible for the sense of externality to arise in the first place, including in dreams. Such an argument is a typical realist "line" and Xuan Zang, being an idealist (albeit a "qualified metaphysical idealist") cannot accept the realist presupposition in the argument. In any case, Xuan Zang is simply not interested in tracing the origin of our cognition, which would result in a hopelessly circular inquiry into whether it is the real existence of the external world that gives rise to the sense of externality or the other way around.[15] What fascinates him is this question: Why is consciousness able to create an external world in the absence of it? In order to respond to such a question, a thorough inquiry into the nature of consciousness is called for, and this is precisely Xuan Zang's goal. Hence we find the *CWSL* claiming that:

> On the basis of the manifold activities of inner consciousnesses that serve as conditions for one another, the cause and effect are differentiated. The postulation of external conditions is not of any use. (574)

Put simply, external objects are reduced to cognitions in the realm of consciousness and their actual existence is rendered irrelevant within Xuan Zang's Yogācāra paradigm.

To Xuan Zang, the same logic is applicable to both the subject and the object of our experience regarding the positing of their existence. In other words, if the experience of an external world does not warrant the existence of one, the experiencing of a subject cannot, by the same token, be used to justify the existence of a self. Xuan Zang, in keeping his commitment to the Buddhist doctrine of *anātman*, rejects the existence of a self as the owner, as it were, of the experience. His line of defense is similar to the one against the existence of an external world. That is, the existence of a substantive self cannot be ascertained within the parameters of consciousness. Although he agrees that there is a subject/object structure in our cognitive experience, the subject cannot be translated into a self, *ātman*, independent of the cognitive structure because the subject itself also undergoes changes in the course of experience.

In this way, Xuan Zang has successfully established the primacy of consciousness by rendering irrelevant any speculations of real existence outside the cognitive structure of consciousness. What he needs to do next is to explain the relationship among different kinds of consciousnesses and their transformations. The success or failure of his effort depends on whether he is able to address this critical question: Is consciousness alone sufficient to account for our cognitive experience? To this end, Xuan Zang has engaged in a painstakingly detailed analysis centered around a new form of consciousness, *ālaya-vijñāna*. The significance of *ālayavijñāna* in the Yogācāra system lies in the fact that until the postulation of this consciousness, Buddhists did not really have a good and convincing explanation of the apparent continuity of our everyday experience, memory, and sense of self, given the central Mahāyāna Buddhist doctrine of non-substantiality of reality, *śūnyatā*. Let us now turn to the concept of *ālayavijñāna* as presented by Xuan Zang in the *CWSL*.

Ālayavijñāna: A New Form of Consciousness

The early Buddhist model of consciousness consists of five senses (visual, auditory, olfactory, gustatory, and tactile) and the mind, whose object is mental. The Yogācāra theory of consciousness significantly revises and expands this traditional model.[16] It splits the mind in the traditional model into two consciousnesses: *manovijñāna* and *manas*. *Manovijñāna* is called "sense-centered consciousness," and it works in conjunction with the five senses. These six, namely *manovijñāna* and the five senses, constitute one kind of consciousness that "appropriates crude objects" (Xuan Zang, 96). This means that the objects of this group of consciousnesses are "external objects." Any perception of "external objects" requires the co-presence of "such factors as the act of attention (*manaskāras*) of *manovijñāna*, the sense-organs (*indriyas*), (whose attention is directed in accordance with *manovijñāna*), the external objects (*viṣayas*) towards which this attention is directed" (Wei Tat, 479). In other words, the role of *manovijñāna* is to direct the attention of sense organs toward their objects to produce *clear* perceptions of these objects. *Manovijñāna* also has a cogitative or deliberative function, but such a function is crude and unstable and it might be interrupted in certain states.[17] The uninterrupted mind is called *manas*, which "is related to the view of the existence of self" (Xuan Zang, 314). This means that *manas* is responsible for the genesis of the idea of personhood, the essence of a person. Its function is intellection and cogitation: "It is called 'cogitation' or 'deliberation' because it cogitates or deliberates at all times without interruption in contradistinction to the sixth consciousness (*mano-*

vijñāna), which is subject to interruption" (Wei Tat, 97). Compared with *manovijñāna, manas* is fine and subtle in its activities (Xuan Zang, 478). Hence the delusion it generates, namely the idea of self, is much more resistant to being transformed to reach enlightenment. *Manovijñāna* works with the five senses in cognizing "external" physical objects; *manas* works with another consciousness, which is for the first time postulated by Yogācāra as the storehouse consciousness *(ālayavijñāna),* or the eighth consciousness. *Manas* is attached to *ālayavijñāna* and regards it as the inner self (104).

Ālayavijñāna is also known as *vipākavijñāna,* ripening consciousness, or *mūlavijñāna,* root consciousness. "It is the eighth consciousness, the maturing or retributive consciousness (Sk: *vipākavijñāna*; Ch: *yishu shi*) because it has many seeds that are of the nature of ripening in various ways" (96). This consciousness is meant to account for the karmic retribution within the doctrinal boundary of Buddhism in that it stores the karmic seeds until their fruition, and this karmic continuity is one crucial kind of continuity that Buddhists try to explain without reification. The tactic here is to render this retributive consciousness subtle and subliminal; its activities surface only when conditions allow, that is, when karmic retribution is fulfilled. This is a completely different form of consciousness from those in the traditional model in that the traditional forms of consciousness are strictly causal, meaning they are object-dependent in their cognitive activities. *Ālayavijñāna,* by contrast, does not depend upon any specific object and it grounds the other seven consciousnesses, which include *manas* as one kind and *manovijñāna* and the five senses as another.

> These three kinds of consciousness are all called 'consciousnesses that are capable of transformation and manifestation' *(pariṇāmi vijñāna).* The manifestation *(pariṇāma)* of consciousness is of two kinds: manifestation with respect to cause *(hetupariṇāma)* and manifestation with respect to effect (fruit) *(phalapariṇāma).* (Wei Tat, 97)

The manifestation as cause refers to the seeds, *bīja,* stored in *ālayavijñāna,* and the manifestation as effect to the eight consciousnesses. In other words, according to the Yogācāra theory, the seeds give birth to the eight consciousnesses. It is obvious that the conceptualization of *ālayavijñāna* is premised upon the theory of *bīja.* Therefore, let us continue our study of *ālayavijñāna* with a closer examination of the Yogācāra theory of *bīja.*

Xuan Zang's Yogācāra Theory of Bīja

Xuan Zang defines *bīja* thusly in the *CWSL*: "They are those which, found in the root-consciousness *(mūlavijñāna)* as various potential forces, immediately generate their own fruits" (108).[18] One point of interest in the definition of a *bīja* is the stipulation that *bīja*s are in *ālayavijñāna*. This has to do with the relationship between *bīja* and *ālayavijñāna*, which will be crucial in the Yogācāra effort to account for continuity without reification. I will leave this for later in the chapter. What concerns us at this juncture is the point that *bīja* is a potentiality that immediately engenders an actual *dharma*. Being potential, a *bīja* is not actual, compared with the fruit to which it gives birth, a *dharma*, which is actual. Does this mean that a *bīja* does not have a real existence, but only a nominal one? Aware of such possible confusion, Xuan Zang moves to clarify this right away by stating that "the *bīja*s are real entities" and that "those which have only nominal existence are like non-existent entities and cannot be a causal condition, *hetupratyaya*" (ibid.). Apparently, Xuan Zang categorizes entities into two kinds, real and nominal. Both actual and potential are regarded as real by Xuan Zang, but nominal is regarded as merely fictional, hence unreal.

A comparison between Xuan Zang's definition of *bīja* and William Waldron's interpretation of it—which is based on the Abhidharma literature—may shed more light on the struggle Xuan Zang has in defining *bīja* as a potentiality. According to Waldron, *bīja*s are

> not real existents *(dravya)* at all, but simply metaphors for the underlying capacities (*śakti* or *samārthya*), potentials and developments of mind in terms of the life processes of insemination (*paribhāvita*), growth (*vṛddha*) and eventual fructification (*vipāka-phala*: "ripened fruit"). (1994, 220)

It is conceivable that Xuan Zang would dispute at least the wording of Waldron's interpretation of *bīja*s as "not real existents . . . but simply metaphors." Indeed, the *CWSL* tells us that Sthiramati maintains the view that a *bīja* has only a nominal existence. This position is shared by Sautrāntikas, but it is rejected by Xuan Zang (108). Waldron's interpretation somewhat echoes Sthiramati's position on *bīja*s. Apparently, Xuan Zang is struggling to give *bīja*s a higher sense of reality than simply a nominal or metaphorical one.

Hence the distinction Xuan Zang makes is between potentiality and actuality, rather than reality and nominality as is the case with Sthiramati. Accordingly, there are entities that are actually real, like *dharma*s, and others that are potentially real, like *bīja*s.

What kinds of potentials does the postulation of *bīja* register? *Bīja* is also called habit energy or perfuming energy (*vāsanā*), and Xuan Zang lists three kinds of *vāsanā*: "image (*nimitta*), name (*nāma*), and discriminating influence (*vikalpavāsanā*)" (138). The image (*nimitta*) refers to the dual structure of our perceptual activities, and discriminating influence (*vikalpavāsanā*) to the dual structure of our conceptual activities. *Nāma* refers to the linguistic activities that involve naming and conceptualizing.[19] Xuan Zang sums up the seeds by explaining that they are the potential proceeding from the two *grāha*s and the potential producing the two *grāha*s (580). The two *grāha*s refer to the grasping *(grāhaka)* and the grasped *(grāhya)*. This means that all of our conscious activities, be they perceptual, conceptual, or linguistic, share the same dual structure, the grasping and the grasped. Such a discriminatory function of our mental activities produces *bīja*s, and the *bīja*s thus produced also perpetuate this discriminatory function, dragging us back into the transmigratory realm. Therefore we find the *CWSL* declaring:

> The wheel of life and death turns by *karma* and the two *grāha*s. None of them are separate from consciousness, because they are, by nature, *dharma*s of *cittas-caitta*s. (582)

According to the *CWSL*, *bīja*s have six characteristics: They are momentary, constitute a continuous series, belong to a definite moral species, depend on a group of conditions, lead to their own fruits, and are simultaneous with their fruits (126–128). The momentariness of seeds means that they "necessarily vanish right when they are born" (126), which makes them the most active elements capable of generative activity, engendering either succeeding seeds or actual *dharma*s. Their generative activities bring about two results. First is the succession of seeds constituting a continuous series, second the simultaneous support as the ground for actual *dharma*s. Moreover, a seed can only give rise to a fruit, either a succeeding seed or an actual *dharma*, whose nature is similar to that of the seed itself. Otherwise, if a seed can generate a succeeding seed or an actual *dharma* of a different kind, the world would be haphazardly ordered without any regularity. Therefore, for Xuan Zang, a defiled seed can only give rise to a defiled *dharma* and a pure seed to a pure *dharma*. Hence, seeds belong to a definite moral species: defiled, pure, or non-defined. For potential to become actual, there has to be a collaboration of conditions. In addition, "each *bīja* produces its own fruit whose nature is similar to its own. That is, the *bīja* of *rūpa* generates *rūpa*, and the *bīja* of *citta* generates *citta*" (128).

However, what attracts our attention is the characteristic of *bīja*s being simultaneous with their fruits.

> When the *bīja* engenders the actual *dharma*, the cause is simultaneous with the fruit. When the *bīja* engenders a *bīja* which is similar to it, the cause is anterior to the fruit. But we attribute 'causal activity' only to present things, not to future things (not yet born) and past things (already destroyed) which have no specific nature (*svabhāva*, reality). Hence the name of *bīja* is reserved for that *bīja* which engenders the actual *dharma*, not for that which leads to the production of a *bīja* similar to itself. (Wei Tat, 127)

The stipulation that the cause has to be simultaneous with its effect apparently goes against our common sense, which assumes that the cause precedes its effect, as Junshō Tanaka acutely points out:

> Furthermore, when coupled with such mutually contradictory concepts, the simultaneity of cause and effect is not limited to the generation of entities by seeds, nor is it explained merely psychologically with respect to the generation of seeds through the perfuming by entities, even though at first glance it appears to be a psychological phenomenon. This suggests that there has to be a doctrinal explanation. (275)

In other words, there has to be a doctrinal consideration in Xuan Zang's counterintuitive stipulation of the simultaneity between cause and effect. Indeed, in this regard, we find Xuan Zang contending that if the cause precedes its effect, when the effect comes into existence its cause will have been gone. If this were the case, in what sense can we claim that the cause causes the effect because the cause and the causal activity belong to the past, and hence no longer exist? By the same token, if the effect succeeds its cause, when the cause is engaged in the causal activity its effect has not yet emerged.

Such a position on causality is unique to Dharmapāla/Xuan Zang's Yogācāra system, which is not necessarily accepted by other Yogācārins (Fukaura, 1:353–355). Here Xuan Zang clearly has the Sarvāstivāda position on causality in mind. Sarvāstivādins advocate that things in the past, present, and future all exist. By resorting to this doctrine, Sarvāstivādins contend that the cause and the effect are simultaneous because an existent *dharma* can always produce an effect as its cause, hence rendering the problematic of continuity irrelevant. There are numerous problems that make it difficult to defend such a position, the most important of which is its abandonment of the orthodox Buddhist teaching of the non-substantiality of *dharma*. Consequently, this view on the existence of *dharma*s in all three stages of time is rejected by Yogācārins like Xuan Zang. However, Xuan Zang does embrace the Sarvāstivādins' stance that the cause and the effect have to be simultaneous in order for causation to take place, although in his case, the simultaneity of cause and effect is possible only when the cause is a potential and the effect is an actual *dharma*. This means that, to Xuan Zang, causality can take place only in a situation wherein potentiality causes actuality, and the two have to be simultaneous. However, it is no longer causality as we normally understand it, because the conventional understanding of causality does not require the simultaneity of the cause and the effect but their succession; this is not to say, however, that any succession is necessarily causal.

What, then, is the causality that Xuan Zang talks about here when he stipulates that cause and effect have to be simultaneous? If causality necessarily involves the succession of effect after cause, his insistence on the simultaneity of cause and effect actually transforms causality into grounding, with the *dharma* grounded in the *bīja*, the actual grounded in the potential. Simultaneity of the cause and the effect renders the former the ground for the latter. To quote Junshō Tanaka again:

> Because the generation of entities (*dharma*) by seeds (*bīja*) does not require time, it surely has to be viewed as indicating the root of possibilities. In other words, we should not interpret it as the cause that generates seed-carrying entities, but rather as the root [or ground] for the generation of entities. (269)

Because one is potential and the other actual, there is no conflict between the two in order for both to exist at the same time and in the same place with the potential grounding the actual.

After dealing with Xuan Zang's presentation of *bīja*, we are in a position to bring in *ālayavijñāna*. Let us see how *ālayavijñāna* is presented in the *CWSL*.

Ālayavijñāna *in the* Cheng Weishi Lun

What is *ālayavijñāna?* According to the *CWSL,* this concept has three aspects:

1) It is that which stores up *bīja*s (Ch: *neng cang*);
2) It is that which is stored (Ch:. *suo cang*);
3) It is that which is attached to (Ch: *zhi cang*). (104)

Put simply, *ālayavijñāna* is that which stores up seeds that are per-fumed by the defiled *dharma*s, and it is the object of attachment by *manas* resulting in the erroneous notion of *ātman.* Here *ālayavijñāna* is granted a sweeping role in accomplishing the objective of explain-ing everything from within the structure of consciousness without having to appeal to anything outside of that structure. In other words, the formulation of *ālayavijñāna* makes the Yogācāra idealist system, albeit in the qualified sense we talked about earlier, complete by ren-dering consciousness alone sufficient to explain all of our experi-ences. Let us begin our inquiry of Xuan Zang's presentation of *ālayavijñāna* with its relationship to the *bīja.*

Ālayavijñāna and *Bīja*

As the bearer of seeds, *ālayavijñāna* is closely related to *bīja,* but the exact nature of this relationship is difficult to determine. Here Xuan Zang encounters a thorny issue. If *ālayavijñāna* is understood as that which stores up *bīja*s, we are faced with this question: Even though *bīja*s are momentary, as we have discussed, does the postu-lation of *ālayavijñāna* as their storehouse make it a permanent dwelling place for *bīja*s? As Kōitsu Yokoyama rightly observes:

> Now, if we only pay attention to the point that various *dharma*s as fruits are stored in this consciousness, this *ālayavijñāna* becomes that which stores in itself the seeds that are the fruits of various *dharma*s. To use a space metaphor, *ālayavijñāna* is the storing place where *bīja*s as goods are stored. However, *ālayavijñāna* and *bīja* are not mate-rial things like storage or stored goods, but rather something spiritual. Consequently, there arises a complex question in their relationship. (148–149)

If *ālayavijñāna* is a permanent dwelling place for *bīja*s, it would be against the Buddhist doctrine of impermanence. It would also defeat the very purpose in the postulation of *ālayavijñāna,* which

is to account for continuity without accepting any form of substantialization in line with the general Buddhist position against
reification as demonstrated in such core Buddhist concepts like
pratītyasamutpāda (dependent origination), *anitya* (impermanence),
anātman (no-self), and *śūnyatā* (emptiness). This is indeed a key conceptual difficulty in the Yogācāra formulation of *ālayavijñāna*. Xuan
Zang is well aware of the trap in making *ālayavijñāna* into some
kind of permanent entity. In tackling this critical issue regarding the
relationship between *bīja* and *ālayavijñāna*, we find the *CWSL* claiming that

> the *bīja*s are neither identical with nor different from the root-con-
> sciousness *(mūlavijñāna)* and the fruits. This is because only such a
> relationship, between consciousness itself and its activities and
> between the cause vis-à-vis *bīja*s and the fruits vis-à-vis *dharma,* is
> reasonable. (108)

The relationships between *bīja* and *ālayavijñāna* and between the
cause *(hetu)* vis-à-vis a *bīja* and the fruit *(phala)* vis-à-vis an actual
dharma are characterized as neither identical nor different. What is
especially interesting here is the claim Xuan Zang makes that *bīja*
is the activity of *ālayavijñāna*. Moreover, "the *bīja*s depend on the
eighth consciousness itself *(svasaṃvittibhāga)*, but they are only the
perceived aspect *(nimittabhāga)* because the perceiving aspect
(darśanabhāga) always takes them as its objects" (ibid.). *Svasaṃvittibhāga* of the eighth consciousness, namely, the self-corroboratory
aspect of *ālayavijñāna* that is perfumable, refers to its susceptibility
to the influence of other aspects (Wei Tat, 109). This means that *bīja*s
depend on the self-corroboratory division of *ālayavijñāna*. Furthermore, *bīja*s are the *nimittabhāga,* the object-aspect, of the eighth
consciousness because they are always taken by its perception-aspect
as its object. We have seen in our earlier discussion that the perceiving
and the perceived aspects *(nimittabhāga* and *darśanabhāga)* of
ālayavijñāna arise out of its self-corroboratory division. When this
is juxtaposed with Xuan Zang's claim that *bīja* is the activity of
ālayavijñāna, the natural conclusion is that *ālayavijñāna* is more than
the collection of *bīja*s and that *bīja* is only one of its aspects, namely
the perceived aspect. The other aspects of *ālayavijñāna* are its perceiving aspect and its self-corroboratory aspect. This is how *ālayavijñāna* is formulated as a form of consciousness itself, instead of
simply as a collection of seeds.[20]

However, when Xuan Zang argues that *ālayavijñāna* is neither identical with nor different from the *bīja*s, as we have seen above, he is clearly in a dilemma that he is keenly aware of. The two are obviously not the same because the latter is only one aspect of the former. However, Xuan Zang cannot make them different either; that would lead to the substantialization of *ālayavijñāna* against the orthodox Buddhist view that substance is itself the continuum of activities and that there is no substance separate from such a continuum. In order to find his way out of the dilemma, Xuan Zang makes *ālayavijñāna* "neither permanent nor impermanent" (170). The rationale is provided as a commentary on the fourth stanza in Vasubandhu's *Triṃśikā:* "It is in perpetual transformation like a torrent."

> "Perpetual" means that this consciousness has continuously evolved without interruption as a homogeneous series since before the beginning of time, because it is the basis that establishes realms of existence (*dhātu*), directions of reincarnation (*gatis*), and forms of birth (*yoni*), and because it does not lose *bīja*s it holds due to its firm nature.
>
> "Transformation" means that this consciousness arises and perishes instantaneously and mutates from one moment to the next. Due to the constant extinction of cause and generation of fruit, it is never a single entity. Hence it can be perfumed by other consciousnesses to produce *bīja*s.
>
> "Perpetual" states that it is uninterrupted; "transformation" suggests that it is impermanent. (Xuan Zang, 170)

Xuan Zang is trying to achieve two objectives here. One is to make *ālayavijñāna* causally connected with other consciousnesses, hence it is said to be perfumable. The other is to make it a continuous series of activities but not a substance of some sort. The first objective is necessary because otherwise *ālayavijñāna* would be rendered unaffected by activities of the other consciousnesses, resembling the *ātman*. The second objective is needed because otherwise our experience of the world would become chaotic if the foundation of our cognition, *ālayavijñāna*, is discontinuous and haphazard. The first point addresses the self-corroboratory aspect of *ālayavijñāna*. Because it is causally connected with the other two aspects—the perceiving and the perceived—of *ālayavijñāna* as well as the other seven consciousnesses, the self-corroboratory aspect of *ālayavijñāna* would not be regarded as some sort of witnessing consciousness standing apart from and unaffected by the cognitive process (like the Hindu Advaita Vedānta notion of *sākṣin*, which is the empirical manifestation of *ātman*). The second point, on the other hand, makes the activities of *ālayavijñāna* abide by the rule of dependent origination:

> Since before the beginning of time this consciousness has been of the nature that the generation of fruit and the extinction of cause take place instantaneously. It is not impermanent due to the generation of fruit; it is not permanent due to the extinction of cause. To be neither impermanent nor permanent: This is the principle of dependent origination (*pratītyasamutpāda*). Hence it is said that this consciousness is in perpetual transformation like a torrent. (Xuan Zang, 172)

It is not permanent, in the sense that it is itself an activity, not a substance; it is not impermanent, in the sense that the activity is a continuous and uninterrupted process. Xuan Zang here appeals to the central Buddhist doctrine of dependent origination to account for the law regulating the activities of consciousness. In this way, Xuan Zang proves that *ālayavijñāna* is not some permanent dwelling place for *bīja*s or permanent ground for the *dharma*s but rather is itself a continuum of activities.

As Shunkyō Katsumata (225) points out, in the above interpretation Xuan Zang follows Dharmapāla by inserting of the word "perpetual" into Vasubandhu's *Triṃśikā*. The original Sanskrit word in Vasubandhu's text that can imply such a meaning is *srotasā*, which means "as a stream or torrent" (ibid.). Because "perpetual" becomes so important in Dharmapāla/Xuan Zang's commentary, we can clearly see their departure from Vasubandhu, wherein lies their creativity:

> In Dharmapāla's exposition, the principle of dependent origination is articulated as the successive series of *ālayavijñāna* that is neither impermanent nor permanent and is without interruption. Therefore, here, after the theories of causality held by Sarvāstivādins, Saṃmatīyas, Sthaviravādins, Sautrāntikas, and others are tossed out, we can conclude that "the correct doctrine of dependent origination in Mahāyāna Buddhism, which stipulates the succession between cause and effect, is rendered credible." (Katsumata, 227)

This is how Xuan Zang uses *ālayavijñāna* to reinterpret dependent origination without having to postulate any entity that continues from one moment to the next. As a result, *pratītyasamutpāda* becomes the law that governs the activities of *ālayavijñāna*.

Ālayavijñāna *and the Seven Consciousnesses*

Now that Xuan Zang has established the primacy of consciousness over the objective world—if he can demonstrate, first, that the continuum of the conscious activity is the result of its following the causal law and, second, that our experience of externality is the result of the self-externalizing activity of consciousness—he will succeed in explaining continuity within the confinement of the Mahāyāna Buddhist orthodoxy of the non-substantiality of reality.

What is at stake in achieving the first goal is the sorting out of the relationship among the various forms of consciousness, namely the eight consciousnesses. That is, Xuan Zang has to explain that the manifestation of consciousness itself follows the causal law. In order to reach the second goal, he has to explain how the self-externalization of consciousness takes place. Let us begin our inquiry with an examination of the first question, namely how the *CWSL* makes the case that the causal law governs the various dynamics of consciousness.

Causal Relationship among Consciousnesses

First, Xuan Zang argues what causality means in his system:

> This right principle is profound and mysterious beyond words. Such words as cause *(hetu)* and fruit *(phala)* are mere metaphorical postulates. When the phenomenon that the present *dharma* produces its succeeding *dharma* is observed, the succeeding fruit is postulated so as to explain the present cause. When the phenomenon is observed that the generation of the present *dharma* is due to a preceding *dharma*, the past cause is postulated to account for the present fruit. "Metaphorical postulates" means that it is the present consciousness itself that appears as a future effect or a past cause. Thus the rationale of the causal principle is clear. It is far from the two extreme views of permanence and impermanence and is in accordance with the Middle Path. (174)

What is interesting in this passage is that Xuan Zang regards the principle of causality as mysterious and cause and effect as merely metaphorical postulates. He is obviously well aware of the conventional understanding of causality as the succession between cause and effect. However, he claims that the cause and the effect can only be understood metaphorically because they are not simultaneous, as we have discussed previously. The true nature of causality is, according to Xuan Zang, that the present consciousness itself appears as the semblance of a future and a past, of cause and fruit.[21] In other words, there is only the activity of consciousness at each present moment, and past/future and cause/effect are nothing but the self-differentiating activities of consciousness at each present moment.

The natural question, then, seems to be: What is this self-differentiating activity of consciousness? It relates to the different manifestations of consciousness in the Yogācāra system. In this connection, we find Xuan Zang saying:

> Although consciousness can be transformed into infinite forms, what is capable of such transformations is of three kinds only. The first is the ripening consciousness (Sk: *vipāka*; Ch: *yishu*), namely the eighth consciousness, because it holds *bījas* that are of the nature of ripening in varied ways. The second is the deliberative consciousness, namely the seventh consciousness, because it is always engaged in deliberation and speculation. The third is the consciousness that discriminates spheres of objects, namely the first six consciousnesses, because the spheres of objects are crude. The word "and" in the stanza indicates that the six consciousnesses form one group. The above three kinds are all called consciousness that is capable of transformation. (96)

Put simply, the manifestation of consciousness at each moment is simultaneously a threefold process: retribution process, self-cogitation process, and cognitive process of objects other than the self. The three processes are intermingled with each other at each moment:

> The consciousness that perfumes (*darśanabhāga* of a *pravṛttivijñāna*) is born of *bījas*: at the moment of its birth, it is a cause capable of increasing and creating *bījas*. Hence three *dharmas* must be considered: the *bījas* that engender the consciousness, the engendered consciousness that perfumes and creates *bījas*, and the *bījas* created or caused to grow by the perfuming influence of the engendered consciousness. These three revolve in a cycle reciprocally and simultaneously functioning as cause and effect, just as a candle-wick

engenders the flame and the flame engenders the incandescence of the wick. (Wei Tat, 133)[22]

Pravṛttivijñāna refers to the seven consciousnesses, namely the five senses, *manovijñāna,* and *manas.* They are born of *bīja*s, but they also perfume *bīja*s, resulting in either the creation of new *bīja*s or causing the existing ones to grow. These three processes, namely the birth of the seven consciousnesses by *bīja*s, the birth of new *bīja*s as the result of perfuming by the seven consciousnesses, and the growth of existing *bīja*s as the result of perfuming by the seven consciousnesses, move in a cycle, reciprocally and simultaneously functioning as cause and effect.[23] This is what the *CWSL* means when it states that "the transformation (*pariṇāma*) of consciousness is of two kinds: The first is its transformation as cause (*hetupariṇāma*) . . . and the second is its transformation as effect (*phalapariṇāma*)" (96).

However, if the three processes are going on simultaneously at each present moment, how can they account for the past and the future as Xuan Zang claims? A closer look at the threefold process will reveal that although the three are in a simultaneous process, past and future are contained in each present moment. More specifically, the perfuming of *bīja*s by the seven consciousnesses and the engendering of seven consciousnesses by *bīja*s are processes wherein the cause and the effect are simultaneous; the engendering of new *bīja*s by their predecessors is a process wherein the cause and the effect are successive. As Xuan Zang explicitly points out, "In the *bīja*s' generation of similar *bīja*s, the cause and the effect are not simultaneous; in the mutual generation of *bīja*s and *dharma*s, the cause and the effect are simultaneous" (254). Therefore, both the past and the future are contained within the present; let us recall Xuan Zang's claim: "It is the present consciousness itself that appears as a future effect or a past cause" (174). Obviously, Xuan Zang's Yogācāra theory incorporates both the Sarvāstivāda position on the simultaneity of cause and effect and the Sautrāntika view on the succession of *bīja*s. More importantly, by accommodating both views Xuan Zang recognizes a horizon within each moment in that each moment contains the past, the present, and the future within itself. This is how Xuan Zang manages to incorporate the third approach to continuity I discussed at the beginning of this chapter.

However, for Xuan Zang to explain the order in our experience by analyzing the relationship among consciousnesses without appealing to the existence of that which is experienced, he has to answer this question: Is consciousness alone sufficient in explaining our experience? In order to deal with this, the *CWSL* further elaborates the relationship among the eight consciousnesses into four conditioning categories: *hetupratyaya* (condition *qua* cause), *samanantarapratyaya* (condition *qua* antecedent), *ālambanapratyaya* (condition *qua* perceived object), and *adhipatipratyaya* (condition *qua* contributory factor). Let us briefly examine them one by one.

First is *hetupratyaya*, condition *qua* cause, defined by Xuan Zang as the condition under which "the conditioned *dharmas* (*saṃkṛtas*) themselves produce their own effects" (534). This refers to two kinds of causal conditions, namely the *bīja*s and the *dharma*s:

> The *bīja*s with respect to the two following cases are *hetupratyaya*: they can generate succeeding *bīja*s of the same kind and can produce *dharma*s of the same nature simultaneous with them. *Dharma*s refer to the seven transforming consciousnesses (*pravṛttivijñāna*) and their contents. (ibid.)

This *hetupratyaya* is basically a reformulation of our previous discussion of the Yogācāra causality theory. As I pointed out earlier, such a causal theory is unique to Dharmapāla/Xuan Zang's Yogācāra system because it stipulates that cause and effect are simultaneous—except in the case of *bīja*s engendering *bīja*s, wherein there is a succession between cause and effect. Because *bīja*s are only potential, not actual, even though there is a succession between *bīja*s vis-à-vis cause and *bīja*s vis-à-vis effect, it is a succession of potentials, an undetected succession. Nevertheless this still means that true succession can only be succession of *bīja*s, albeit an undetected occurrence. Dharmic moments, namely the seven consciousnesses as a group—because there is no succession among them—are mediated by their own *bīja*s: "[T]he successive transformations of similar *dharma*s are not *hetupratyaya* one for the other, because they are born from their own *bīja*s respectively" (534–536). For Xuan Zang, the conventional understanding of causation is a mediated kind of causation, mediated by *bīja*s. In other words, causation in Xuan Zang's theory looks like this: *dharma* perfumes *bīja*; *bīja* creates a succeeding *bīja* of a similar kind; new *bīja* engenders new *dharma*, whose nature is similar to the *dharma* of the preceding moment. Our conventional understanding of causation does not heed the mediating role played by *bīja*s. Therefore, there is only succession, not direct causation, between *dharma*s mediated by *bīja*s. Seibun Fukaura (1:354) compares the generation of *dharma*s by *bīja*s to the casting of shadows by objects. Just like the causal relationship between objects and their shadows and their simultaneous existence, *bīja*s and *dharma*s coexist simultaneously despite the causal relationship between the two.

The *dharma* of the preceding moment is, according to the *CWSL*, *samanantarapratyaya* (condition *qua* antecedent) of *dharma* of the succeeding moment. This is the second condition Xuan Zang lists, meaning that "the eight consciousnesses and their concomitant mental activities form a group in the preceding moment and pass into the succeeding group of similar kinds without any mediation" (536). Apparently "the eight consciousnesses are not *samanantarapratyaya* between themselves because several species of consciousness coexist" (Wei Tat, 537). In other words, this condition concerns the succession between *dharma*s, not those that are simultaneous with one another, as in the case of *hetupratyaya,* condition *qua* cause. The eight consciousnesses as a group at the present moment are the *samanantarapratyaya* of the eight consciousnesses of the succeeding moment. This is apparently the conventional understanding of causation in that there is a successive relationship between the cause and the effect.

Interestingly, however, impure *dharma*s can be *samanantarapratyaya* of pure *dharma*s (Xuan Zang, 538); because the impure cannot be the cause of the pure, Xuan Zang needs something else to explain the succession of the pure after the impure, namely the pure *dharma* from the *dharmadhātu*. This line of thought is a clear indication that the theorization definitely has the possibility of enlightenment in mind. Xuan Zang has to maintain the view that the pure can succeed the impure, or else there would be no possibility for enlightenment because we are all currently in the impure state. However, he also wants to maintain the homogeneity between successive dharmic moments, otherwise there would be disorder and chaos in our experience. This would lead to the unintelligibility of the world as we experience it, regardless of whether it exists independently of consciousness or not. Consequently, Xuan Zang makes a distinction between succession and causality. Because there is only a relationship of succession between two dharmic moments, even when they are heterogeneous, the law of causality that guarantees the order of our cognition—hence of the world as we experience it—is not violated as long as there is a causal relationship between successive *bīja*s whose relationship with their respective *dharma* is also causal.

The third condition is *ālambanapratyaya*, condition *qua* perceived object, referring to "the *dharma*s upon which the mind and its concomitant activities, which perceive those *dharma*s as such, depend" (542). This condition apparently accounts for the objective grounding of our cognition and it holds the key to the success or failure of Xuan Zang's effort to explain the adequacy of cognition by appealing to the transformation of consciousness alone. He distinguishes two kinds of *ālambanapratyaya*, close (Ch: *qin*) and remote (Ch: *shu*):

> If a *dharma* is not separated from the appropriating consciousness and it is cogitated by *darśanabhāga* and taken as its inner support, we can tell that it is the close *ālambanapratyaya*. If a *dharma*, though separated from the appropriating consciousness, is the material capable of generating that which *darśanabhāga* cogitates and takes as its inner support, we can tell that it is the remote *ālambanapratyaya*. (542–544)

In Seibun Fukaura's words, "the close *ālambanapratyaya* is that which mental *dharma*s depend on directly" (1:375), and "the remote *ālambanapratyaya*, as the material that mental *dharma*s depend on indirectly, is manifested as the *nimittabhāga* that *darśanabhāga* relies on" (1:376). In other words, the remote *ālambanapratyaya* is an entity that is capable of producing the close *ālambanapratyaya* within that consciousness upon which *darśanabhāga*, the perceiving aspect, finds its support as its *nimittabhāga*, the perceived aspect. The remote *ālambanapratyaya* here refers to a dimension in our perceptual experience of an object that is not personal. Xuan Zang, in differentiating two kinds of *ālambanapratyaya*, recognizes that there are two dimensions of the perceived. The close one is the personal dimension of the perceived whereas the remote one is the non-personal dimension. The remote "generates" the close.

Xuan Zang realizes that a viable idealist theory of cognition must account for the collectivity of our experience. However, because he is a metaphysical idealist, albeit in the qualified sense mentioned earlier, his effort to explain the collectivity of our experience has to seek that collective dimension *within* the parameters of consciousness and differentiate it from the personal dimension. There is no meaningful external world within his system to which he can appeal in explaining the collective dimension of our experience. This is the primary reason for the postulation of the remote *ālambanapratyaya*, which can account for the collectivity of our experience without going outside the realm of consciousness.

Within the domain of consciousness, what belongs to the collective dimension and what to the private dimension? In this connection, we find that

> one can experience the body and land belonging to another person because the content of the other's eighth consciousness resulting from its transformation is the basis of the contents of one's own consciousness. On the other hand, one's own *bīja*s or *indriya*s are not experienced by others because the evolving eighth consciousness of the other is not the same as one's own evolving eighth consciousness.[24] This is because not all sentient beings' *bīja*s are of the same number. Therefore it should be said that we cannot ascertain whether or not the remote *ālambanapratyaya* exists in the eighth consciousness in all cases of existents. (Xuan Zang, 544)

Xuan Zang is making an unequivocal distinction between the personal dimension and the collective dimension of our experience. The first point made in the above passage is that different people share common experiences of bodies and lands (which is the realm of existence in which they are born, the world) as the result of the common basis in the transformations of their eighth consciousnesses. The second point is that people's sense organs are private. If this is juxtaposed with the idea of remote and close *ālambanapratyaya*, it becomes clear that in the two aspects of our cognitive structure, namely the perceiving and the perceived aspects, the perceiving aspect is the sense organ and it is private, but the perceived aspect has both a personal dimension vis-à-vis the close *ālambanapratyaya* and a collective dimension vis-à-vis the remote *ālambanapratyaya*.

However, there appears to be a conflict in Xuan Zang's discussion of the relationship between the remote and the close *ālambanapratyaya*. In one passage, Xuan Zang (544) argues that consciousness may or may not have a remote *ālambanapratyaya* but it necessarily has a close *ālambanapratyaya*, whereas in another passage (ibid.) he contends that the remote *ālambanapratyaya* is the cause of the close *ālambanapratyaya*, which means that consciousness cannot have the close one without the remote. Xuan Zang appears to be struggling between an intentional analysis of consciousness and a causal explanation. Intentional analysis, as Edmund Husserl—the father of phenomenology in the twentieth century —defines it, is to see consciousness as essentially that which is *of* an object; on the other hand causal explanation takes consciousness as that which is *by* an object, which means that it is causally connected with things-events in the natural world. When Xuan Zang argues that consciousness may or may not have a remote *ālambanapratyaya*, he is clearly aware of the intentional structure of consciousness within which the remote *ālambanapratyaya*, or real object in Husserl's terminology, is not a necessary component. However, when he contends that the remote *ālambanapratyaya* is that which "produces" the close *ālambanapratyaya*, he appears to resort to the causal analysis in explaining the relationship between the remote and the close *ālambanapratyaya*. The causal analysis contradicts the intentional analysis in this particular case because in the former passage the remote object is a necessary condition for the close object, whereas in the latter passage the remote object is not a necessary condition for the close object. Nevertheless Xuan Zang clearly privileges the intentional analysis over the causal explanation by virtue of the fact that he devotes much of his *CWSL* to the former while paying little attention to the latter. Such a position can be justified in that the causal explanation presupposes the intentional analysis because only the intentional analysis can locate the cause in the causal explanation. Put differently, to locate the remote object *as* the cause of the correlating close object, one must investigate that very close object through the intentional analysis, whereas the causal explanation, without the intentional analysis, falls into an infinite regress. But we are still left with this question: What is the relationship between the remote object and the close object? I will return to this when I discuss the self-externalization of consciousness later in this chapter.

The last condition that Xuan Zang talks about is *adhipatipratyaya*, condition *qua* contributory factor, defined as "a real *dharma* (conditioned or unconditioned, as opposed to imaginary *dharmas*), possessing potent energy and capable of promoting (first nine *hetus*) or counteracting (tenth *hetu*) the evolution of another *dharma*" (Wei Tat, 547).[25] Needless to say, the real *dharmas* here refer to the eight consciousnesses, and this means that the eight consciousnesses are *adhipatipratyaya* to one another (Xuan Zang, 570). This conditioning factor addresses the subjective—hence the private—aspect of conditioning, which involves the support of sense organs as the perceiving aspect in the structure of our cognition. This is the simultaneous support of consciousness. Specifically, the five senses have four supports: five sense organs as the object support, *manovijñāna* as the discriminating support, *manas* as the pure-impure support, and *ālayavijñāna* as the root support (266–268). *Manovijñāna*, which normally functions with the five senses in their discriminatory cognitive function of the external world, may be functioning alone while the activities of the five senses have stopped (e.g., in a dream). It has as its support *manas* and *ālayavijñāna*. *Manas* has as its support *ālayavijñāna* while also taking *ālayavijñāna* as its object (280). *Ālayavijñāna* has *manas* as its support. More interestingly, Xuan Zang claims that all three previous conditions are *adhipatipratyaya* (546). This means that all the causes and conditions are essentially activities of the eight consciousnesses. He needs this postulate to complete his idealist system by bringing all the conditions back to different manifestations of consciousness itself. This is what Xuan Zang means when he states that it is the present consciousness that is manifested as the semblance of cause and effect, past and future.

To sum up:

> In the transformations of the eight consciousnesses as a group, there must be *adhipatipratyaya* amongst them but not *hetupratyaya* or *samanantarapratyaya*. There may or may not be *ālambanapratyaya*. (570)

Hetupratyaya involves the relationship between the eight consciousnesses and *bīja*s, an intra-moment relationship, whereas *samanantarapratyaya* deals with the relationship between the eight consciousnesses as a group at one moment and the succeeding moment, an inter-moment relationship. *Ālambanapratyaya* and *adhipatipratyaya*, in explaining our sense of externality, address the internal relationship among the eight consciousnesses at each moment, an intra-moment relationship; the former is the perceived/objective aspect and the latter the perceiving/subjective aspect as well as the perceived/objective aspect, as expressed in the following remark: "The same *nimittabhāga* is both *ālambanapratyaya* and *adhipatipratyaya* of the *darśanabhāga* whereas the *darśanabhāga* is only *adhipatipratyaya* of the *nimittabhāga*" (572).

Through this detailed analysis of the relationship among the consciousnesses, Xuan Zang has firmly established the realm of consciousness as both necessary and sufficient in explaining our experiences, personal as well as collective. The formulation of *ālayavijñāna* as the ground of our experience not only incorporates the three kinds of continuity previously listed but also expands that scheme. As we have seen, Xuan Zang has actually accepted the Sarvāstivādins' position on the simultaneity of cause and effect, except that Sarvāstivādins fall into the trap of substantialism in its extreme form by maintaining that *dharma*s in the past, present, and future all exist simultaneously. Xuan Zang, on the other hand, interprets the simultaneity between cause and effect as the cause grounding the effect, although the ground, *ālayavijñāna*, is itself always in the process of transformation. Moreover, since *bīja*s are potential, not actual, their causal succession takes place undetected. Due to the homogeneity between the successive *bīja*s, their succession can be misidentified as some entity persisting through the change. Mediated by *bīja*s, there is a congruity between successive dharmic moments, but not direct causality, as we have seen earlier. This view is shared by Sautrāntikas. By recognizing a structure of past, present, and future within each moment that manifests itself in the semblance of the past and the future (Xuan Zang, 174), Xuan Zang incorporates the third approach to continuity I discussed earlier that effectively does away with the instantaneous nature of a moment.

These three scenarios of continuity encapsulate the first two kinds of conditioning discussed in the *CWSL*, namely *hetupratyaya*, condition *qua* cause, and *samanantarapratyaya*, condition *qua* antecedent. The latter two kinds, namely *ālambanapratyaya*, condition *qua* object, and *adhipatipratyaya*, condition *qua* agent, examine the causal conditioning from both the objective and the subjective sides; they enable Xuan Zang to explain our experience of externality and subject/object duality without appealing to the actual existence of any external objects independent of consciousness.

The Self-Externalization of Consciousness. Now that Xuan Zang has established that the relationship between different kinds of consciousness is governed by the causal law, the next step is to explain how an internal process vis-à-vis the consciousness activities can give rise to the sense of externality, so as to complete his case that the actual existence of an external world is irrelevant.[26] Two issues are at stake in this effort. First, Xuan Zang needs to make the case that externality is the result of the self-externalizing activities of consciousness. Second, he has to explain how an essentially private self-externalizing activity of an individual can account for the collectivity of our experience of the external world.[27]

On the first issue, we find the following remark in the CWSL:

> At the moment the perceived is apprehended, it is not grasped as external; only later manovijñāna, in its discriminatory function, creates the illusion of the external. Therefore, the domain of the perceived is the result of the transformation of nimittabhāga of consciousness itself. In this sense, the perceived exists. However, when it is grasped by manovijñāna as externally real objects, it does not exist. Moreover, in the domain of objects, the objects are not objects even though they appear so; they are not external even though they appear so. They are like dream objects, which should not be grasped as real and external objects. (520)

According to Xuan Zang, the sense of externality does not arise at the moment when immediate perception takes place. In other words, at the moment of immediate perception, there is no differentiation between the internal and the external. There is perception *only*. The sense of externality only arises as a result of the discriminatory function of manovijñāna, the sixth consciousness, which transforms a percept into the image aspect of manovijñāna, namely nimittabhāga. Xuan Zang uses a dream to illustrate his point that consciousness itself is capable of creating the sense of externality. In a dream state, even though the five senses have stopped their functions, the continued activities of manovijñāna still create the sense of externality (266). This is a clear indication that it is manovijñāna that creates the sense of externality, and that the sense of externality does not have to be premised upon the actual existence of external objects independent of consciousness.

However, what is it that manovijñāna externalizes that makes us experience the externality of the world? This has to do with the objectification of consciousness. We have seen earlier in this chapter that two conditions are responsible for the objective dimension in our cognitive structure, according to Xuan Zang's Yogācāra scheme, namely the ālambanapratyaya, condition qua object, and the adhipatipratyaya, condition qua agent. According to Xuan Zang, the ālambana of manovijñāna includes ālayavijñāna, manas, and the five senses (570), and these objects of manovijñāna are also themselves consciousnesses, namely adhipatipratyaya. What is relevant to our purpose here is ālayavijñāna. In this regard, we find Xuan Zang stating that "when *ālayavijñāna* itself is born through the power of causes and conditions, it is manifested internally as *bīja*s and a body with sense organs and externally as the world" (136). Here Xuan Zang points out that *ālayavijñāna* manifests itself into two realms, internal and external. The internal refers to the *bīja*s and the body with sense organs, and the external to the world. When this is juxtaposed with the claim that it is *manovijñāna* that differentiates the external from the internal, it is clear to us that the dual manifestation of *ālayavijñāna* is the result of externalizing activities of *manovijñāna*.

What is even more interesting, however, is that, according to the *CWSL*, there are common or universal *bīja*s in *ālayavijñāna* that provide the objective basis for externality: "The word 'place' (*sthāna*) in the stanza refers to the fact that the ripening consciousness (*vipākavijñāna*) manifests as objects in the external world through the ripening of its universal *bīja*s" (144). This means that there are two kinds of seeds, private and universal. Private seeds give rise to one's own body with its sense faculties, namely the seven consciousnesses, whereas universal seeds generate non-private *dharma*s, which appear to be the external major elements and derived matter. As Junshō Tanaka rightly points out, the universal *bīja*

> is postulated as the foundation for the possibility of collective experience. Collective experience means that which is manifested as an existing entity in the consciousnesses of the majority [of sentient beings] and is therefore commonly experienced. (277)

Tanaka further differentiates four subcategories of entities in terms of their private and universal seeds: the common in the common, the non-common in the common, the non-common in the non-common, and the common in the non-common (278). Accordingly, the common in the common refers to entities like mountains and rivers, the non-common in the common private properties like houses and land, the non-common in the non-common one's own body, and the common in the non-common other people's bodies (ibid.).

Moreover,

> even though the consciousnesses of sentient beings are manifested differently, what are manifested are similar, with no difference in terms of locality. This is just like many lamps lit together, such that the lights appear as one single light. (Xuan Zang, 144)

In this passage, which immediately follows the previous one in the *CWSL* arguing for the universal *bīja*s as the ground for collective experience of the world, Xuan Zang seems to backpedal from the position of that preceding passage by saying that the common world is the result of the manifestation of private consciousnesses. The idea of the universal *bīja*s does not even appear to be necessary. The message Xuan Zang is trying to convey here, if we look at the two passages together, is that the commonness of the world as we experience it is not a real one but an apparent one. Such a common world is constituted by the manifestation of essentially individual and private conscious processes, whose *apparent* commonness is attributed to the working of the universal *bīja*s. In other words, the universal *bīja*s do not account for a real common world but only an apparent one. This is tantamount to claiming that the universal *bīja*s themselves do not share the same degree of reality as the private *bīja*s in Xuan Zang's Yogācāra system.

If we bring in the close and the remote *ālambanapratyaya* discussed earlier, it becomes obvious that the remote object of consciousness refers to the *dharma*s generated by the universal *bīja* and the close object by the private *bīja*. Because the remote/universal object is only apparent, not real, its universality is then premised upon its seeming externality resulting from the externalizing activity of *manovijñāna*. In other words, the universality of *bīja* is directly linked to the externalizing activity of *manovijñāna*. This means that the universal *bīja* correlates with the externalizing activities of *manovijñāna* in that there is a universal structure in what is externalized by *manovijñāna*. The *sense* of the remoteness of an object is the result of such an externalization of *manovijñāna*. To be more exact, the sense of the remote object is constituted by the externalizing activity of *manovijñāna*, which has a universal structure. As to whether such a remote object actually exists or not, it is not a question that can be explained within Xuan Zang's qualified idealist system. Neither is he interested in such a question. This explains Xuan Zang's claim that while the close object is a necessary condition for consciousness, the remote object is not. Therefore, the issue concerning the relationship between the remote and the close objects is resolved by attributing the origin of their *senses* to the operation of *manovijñāna* while shelving the metaphysical question of whether a remote object actually exists or not.

Consequently, for Xuan Zang, there are three different senses of the "world": 1) the apparent common receptacle world that is the result of the operations of all eight consciousnesses of an individual that belong to the community of individuals in the everyday waking state; 2) the private world that results from the operations of *manovijñāna, manas,* and *ālayavijñāna* of an individual in dreams; and 3) the world of the enlightened. He uses the second to explain the first while leaving the third out of the explanatory scheme regarding the externality and commonness of the objects of our everyday experience. What distinguishes the first from the second is the cooperation of the five senses.

At this juncture, let us focus our attention on the first sense of the "world" because this is where the issue concerning the experience of a common world is at stake. Xuan Zang enumerates three kinds of non-private *dharma*s, namely, the receptacle world, another person's mind, and another person's body. The receptacle world is what appears to be a common world, the sense of which is constituted by a community of individual consciousness. As for another person's mind, Xuan Zang treats it no differently from any external physical object, as is evident in the following remark:

> One's consciousness can comprehend another mind as a seemingly external object like a mirror where what appears to be an external object appears. However, such a comprehension is not direct. What can be comprehended directly is the transformation of the mind itself, not another mind. (522)

In other words, another person's mind is the unfolding of one's own mental activities; it can be understood within the discriminatory cognitive structure of the grasper and the grasped in one's own conscious process.

With regard to another person's body, Xuan Zang contends that on the one hand sense faculties and their supporting physical body are the result of the maturing of private *bīja*s (148). On the other hand,

> because of the power of the ripening of the universal *bīja*s, this *vipā-kavijñāna* transforms itself in such a way that it resembles other persons' sense organs in the locus of their bodies. Otherwise, one would not be able to enjoy the sense organs of other persons. (ibid.)

Put simply, even though one's sense faculties or body are developed out of one's own particular series of seeds, the operations of the five sense faculties give rise to the sense of collectivity of the human body.

To sum up, in Xuan Zang's Yogācāra system, the private and the collective, the individual and the universal, are identical entities, with different senses attributed to them by the operation of *manovijñāna* and the cooperation of the five sense faculties. Thereby, Xuan Zang has made his case that the *apparent* commonness or collectivity of the world is the result of the externalization of a community of individuals, each of which is constituted by eight consciousnesses.

Ālayavijñāna and the Self

Finally, we are faced with the question we set out to answer: Has Xuan Zang achieved his objective in explaining continuity within the Buddhist orthodoxy through his presentation of *ālayavijñāna*? To answer this question, we first have to know what kinds of continuity Yogācāra Buddhists like Xuan Zang are concerned about. This can be detected in the list of logical arguments Xuan Zang gives in support of the existence of *ālayavijñāna* in the CWSL.[28] He states (202–244) that *ālayavijñāna* is

1) the *vipākacitta* that holds *bīja*s;
2) the uninterrupted retributive mind;
3) the mind in the course of reincarnation;
4) that which appropriates the body;
5) the support for life and heat;
6) the mind at conception and death;
7) exists by reason of *nāmarūpa*;
8) the substance of consciousness-food on which the other three foods (food in mouthfuls, food by contact, and food through aspiration) depend;
9) the mind in *nirodha-samāpatti*;
10) the foundation for pure and impure *dharma*s.

Obviously Xuan Zang is preoccupied with the continuity of subjectivity, within one lifetime and between lives. In the final analysis, his theoretical effort to explain the continuity of subjectivity is aimed at accounting for the self as a continuum; this is evidenced by the three meanings of *ālayavijñāna* given in the CWSL, one of which asserts that *ātman* is the result of attachment to the eighth consciousness (104), as we have seen previously. His explanation of an external object as a continuum is the extension of the continuity of subjectivity; for him the continuity of subjectivity and the continuity of objectivity are two aspects of the same cognitive process. The former holds primacy over the latter, while the actual existence of external objects independent of consciousness is rendered irrelevant. Let us now take a closer look at how Xuan Zang explains our sense of self as a continuum within the Yogācāra theoretical edifice he has presented. Because he regards *ātman* as the result of attachment and misidentification of the continuum of *ālayavijñāna* as an identity, my efforts will focus on examining how such a misidentification takes place.

According to the *CWSL*, attachment to *ātman* is of two kinds: that which is innate and that which results from mental discrimination (20). The innate kind is always present in the individual, and it operates spontaneously without depending on external false teachings or mental discriminations (ibid.). It is itself divided into two kinds:

> The first is constant and continuous, and it pertains to the seventh consciousness, which arises together with the eighth consciousness and grasps the mental image of the latter as the real self.
>
> The second is sometimes interrupted and it pertains to the sixth consciousness and the five aggregates that are the result of their transformations; the mental image that arises with them individually or as a group is grasped as the real self. (ibid.)

Xuan Zang differentiates two senses of self here: one is constant and the other is sometimes interrupted. Such a differentiation is made with an eye on our different senses of the self in the waking state, the dream state,[29] and the deep meditative state, which, it may be recalled, is the primary concern in the initial postulation of *ālayavijñāna*. If our sense of self is limited to the waking and even the dream state, wherein the content of consciousness is recollectable, it would run the risk of being lost during the deep meditative state. This is the reason behind the differentiation made between these two senses of self. In the first case, the sense of self that is constant pertains to the seventh consciousness, *manas*, which adheres to *ālayavijñāna* as the self because both *manas* and *ālayavijñāna* are constant and never interrupted until enlightenment is reached. In the second case, the sense of self that can be interrupted pertains to the sixth consciousness, which operates with the five senses as in the waking state or without them as in the dream state. The second sense of self is interrupted during certain deep meditative states.

In the case of the first sense of self, we have learned that *ālaya-*

vijñāna has three aspects: the perceiving (*darśanabhāga*), the perceived (*nimittabhāga*), and the self-corroboratory (*svasaṃvittibhāga*), which are manifested as the external world on the one hand and the internal *bīja*s and sense organs possessed by the body on the other. Which aspect is the one to which *manas* attaches itself and which is misidentified as the self? In this connection, Xuan Zang says:

> *Manas* appropriates only the *darśanabhāga* of the *ālayavijñāna*, not its other *bhāga*s, because *darśanabhāga* has, since before the beginning of time, been a continuous and homogeneous series, as if it were a constant and an identical entity. Because this *bhāga* is the constant support of various *dharma*s, *manas* attaches to it as the inner self. (282)

So it is the perceiving aspect, *darśanabhāga,* of the eighth consciousness that *manas* takes as its object and misidentifies as the self, but *darśanabhāga* is a homogeneous continuum even though it appears as eternal and one. This is how continuity is misconstrued as identity.

The "self" in the second sense of the word is due to the activities of the sixth consciousness, *manovijñāna,* with or without the cooperation of the five senses. However,

> *manovijñāna,* like the visual consciousness, et cetera, must have its own support manifesting its own name. Such a support does not arise from condition *qua* immediate antecedent (*samanantarapratyaya*), but from condition *qua* agent (*adhipatipratyaya*) instead. (Xuan Zang, 328)

As Wei Tat rightly points out, such a support of *manovijñāna* is *manas,* the seventh consciousness (329). Put simply, the sixth consciousness should have its own sense organ, just as the eye is the sense organ for visual consciousness. Here *manas* is viewed as the sense organ for *manovijñāna.* However, as we have previously seen, *manas* is also said to be one of the *ālambana*s of *manovijñāna* (Xuan Zang, 570). This means that *manas* is both the support *qua* sense organ and the support *qua* object of *manovijñāna.* This is in line with Xuan Zang's general position, which treats subject and object as two aspects of the same experiential process. Because one of the functions of *manovijñāna* is its externalizing activities, if all these are juxtaposed side by side, the overall picture we get of the generation of the self involves the following processes: the perceiving aspect, *darśanabhāga,* of *ālayavijñāna* is an ever-evolving continuum to which *manas* attaches and misidentifies as an identity; this identity is then externalized by the activities of *manovijñāna* as *ātman* standing outside the cognitive structure of subject and object.

There is another sense of self that Xuan Zang talks about, in contradistinction to the above two innate senses of self. It is caused by mental discrimination and derived from the force of external factors including false teachings and discriminations. This sense of self pertains exclusively to *manovijñāna*. Attachment to *ātman* is also of two kinds:

> The first, preached by certain heterodox schools, refers to the aggregates that arise out of the mental images in *manovijñāna*. Through discrimination and intellection, *manovijñāna* attaches to those aggregates as a real self.
>
> The second refers to the characteristics of the self, preached by certain heterodox schools, that arise out of the mental images in *manovijñāna*. Through discrimination and intellection, *manovijñāna* attaches to those characteristics as a real self. (22)

In the first case the self is conceived as the object of self-belief. This is the view held by Vātsīputrīyas. Xuan Zang refutes that it is the five *skandhas*, not *ātman*, that is the object of self-belief. Because the five *skandhas* are themselves impermanent, the permanence of *ātman* is hence rejected. In the second case the self is the product of various *ātman*-concepts of a false teaching that refers to the Vedic teaching of *ātman*. Because these typical Buddhist refutations of other views of self in defense of their own position are common knowledge to students of Buddhism, I will not go into them in detail here.

It is worthwhile to take note of Xuan Zang's own violation of suspending judgment on the existential status of any extra-conscious entities when he declares that *ātman* does not exist, since its existential status is suspended within his philosophy. All he can actually do is reject the existential question of *ātman* altogether on the grounds that it can neither be affirmed nor denied within the confines of consciousness.

Conclusion

In this chapter I have tried to present the concept of *ālayavijñāna*, as well as the rationale behind Yogācāra's effort in formulating the concept, as expounded by Xuan Zang in the *CWSL*. Xuan Zang is very conscious of the limitations imposed by Buddhist orthodoxy on his theoretical endeavor. In my opinion, he is largely successful in explaining subjectivity as a continuum and the continuity of experience by analyzing consciousness alone without appealing to anything outside and by ably rendering externality irrelevant in his system. His effort underscores a vigorous attempt to fortify the Buddhist doctrine against any form of reification and substantialization. In explaining the self as a subliminal continuum he effectively endorses the view that our sense of self is closely related to some subliminal mental activities of which we are largely unaware in our daily life; this view is echoed by modern psychoanalysts like Freud, Jung, and others.

In the following chapters, I will compare Xuan Zang's Yogācāra approach with that of modern psychologists, including Freud and Jung, in order to test the viability of approaching the Yogācāra notion of *ālayavijñāna* through the notion of the unconscious developed by Freud and Jung in modern psychology. In so doing, I also hope to expose the underlying issues that are addressed in the way these theories are formulated in search of larger implications for the traditions they represent to promote possible future integrations.

3

THE
UNCONSCIOUS

FREUD AND JUNG

IN THE LAST CHAPTER, I examined in detail the concept of *ālaya-vijñāna* within the context of Yogācāra Buddhism as presented in the *CWSL*. I attempted to defend the viability of Yogācāra's qualified idealist system and the indispensable role of *ālayavijñāna* in that system. As we have seen, *ālayavijñāna* is formulated to account for the continuity of our experience without resorting to any form of reification.

Given the subliminal nature of *ālayavijñāna,* the concept appears to have a natural affinity with the notion of the unconscious as it has been developed in modern Western psychology, first by Freud and later Jung.[1] In fact, some Buddhist scholars (e.g., Thomas Kochu-muttom, 135) simply use the term "unconscious" when they try to explain *ālayavijñāna.* There is an apparent advantage in doing so, namely rendering a complicated Buddhist concept comprehensible to a modern audience. However, there are also serious problems that come with this practice. "Unconscious" as it is employed in modern psychology has been developed in a totally different cultural, historical, and philosophical milieu from *ālayavijñāna.* In this chapter I will deal with the theoretical frameworks of Freud and Jung as they are related to their conceptualizations of the unconscious respectively, so that a comparison can be carried out between *ālayavijñāna* and the unconscious when they are brought into a dialogical context in the chapters that follow.

Freud's Theory of the Unconscious

Freud's theory of the unconscious undergoes a series of major revisions, hence it is difficult to present a single picture in this regard.

However, without being distracted by the historical vicissitudes of his theory, for the purpose of this presentation we will be concerned with his theories of the unconscious in the two major systems that he established to explain human subjectivity; these are known as the topographical system and the structural system. The topographical system is laid out in Freud's monumental work *The Interpretation of Dreams,* first published in late 1899, wherein the mind is stratified into the unconscious, preconscious, and conscious. The structural system represents a major shift in Freud's theoretical endeavor in the 1920s; it is best summarized in his last major theoretical work, *The Ego and the Id,* published in 1923, wherein the mind is structured into id, ego, and superego. Let us examine how the two systems are laid out by focusing primarily on these two works and drawing on relevant insights from his other writings.

The Interpretation of Dreams is the foundational text of the movement of psychoanalysis launched by Freud. The significance of the work lies in its revolutionary way of interpreting patients' dreams, which led to Freud's "discovery" of the existence of a dynamic subliminal mental process;[2] in Freud's own words, "*The interpretation of dreams is the royal road to a knowledge of the unconscious activities of the mind*" (1965, 647, original italics). The central theme of this work is that a dream is a fulfillment of an unrecognized wish:

> Dreams are psychical acts of as much significance as any others; their motive force is in every instance a wish seeking fulfillment; the fact of their not being recognizable as wishes and their many peculiarities and absurdities are due to the influence of the psychical censorship which they have been subjected during the process of their formation; apart from the necessity of evading this censorship, other factors which have contributed to their formation are a necessity for the condensation of their psychical material, a regard for the possibility of its being represented in sensory images and—though not invariably—a demand that the structure of the dream shall have a rational and intelligible exterior. (572–573)

Here Freud is making three points crucial to the interpretation of dreams, namely, what a dream is, why its intended wish is not recognizable, and how it is formed. A dream is a fulfillment of a wish that is normally unrecognized by the dreamer herself. Its being unrecognizable is due to the psychic structure that is responsible for its formation, namely the censoring mechanism in the mind that prevents the wish from freely expressing itself. Therefore, the formation of a dream requires evasion of censorship in order for the wish to express itself, the condensation of an enormous amount of psychical material into a short dream time, the representability of the material in images, and the intelligibility of its structure.

What interests us most at this juncture is the second point: the censoring mechanism of our mental life. It paints the picture of a stratified human mind, thus making a subliminal mentality possible. To explain the formation of dreams as the fulfillment of an unrecognized wish, Freud needs to account for two things: why there is at a dream's basis a wish and why it is unrecognized. To address the second issue, Freud proposes the following:

> We may suppose that dreams are given their shape in individual human beings by the operation of two psychical forces (or we may describe them as currents or systems); and that one of these forces constructs the wish which is expressed by the dream, while the other exercises a censorship upon this dream-wish and, by the use of that censorship, forcibly brings about a distortion in the expression of the wish. It remains to enquire as to the nature of the power enjoyed by this second agency which enables it to exercise its censorship. (1965, 177)

Freud postulates two forces or systems within the human psyche, wish and censorship. Wish is the primary motivating force behind a dream, but because it is subject to critique by a censoring agent, the wish has to disguise itself to get around that critical agent. Consequently, there is always a distortion of the wish expressed in an adult's dream.[3] However, why does a dream have to express a wish in the first place? According to Freud, "the reason why dreams are invariably wish-fulfillments is that they are products of the system Ucs. [unconscious], whose activity knows no other aim than the fulfillment of wishes and which has at its command no other forces than wishful impulses" (607).

Obviously, in order to understand the point he is making here, I must first introduce what is known as the topographical system, which Freud sets up in *Interpretation*. In its famous Chapter Seven, Freud schematizes three systems in the human mind. This is the well-known formula of unconscious, preconscious, and consciousness:

> We will describe the last of the systems at the motor end as 'the preconscious,' to indicate that the excitatory processes occurring in it

can enter consciousness without further impediment provided that certain other conditions are fulfilled:[4] for instance, that they reach a certain degree of intensity, that the function which can only be described as 'attention' is distributed in a particular way, and so on. This is at the same time the system which holds the key to voluntary movement. We will describe the system that lies behind it as 'the unconscious,' because it has no access to consciousness *except via the preconscious,* in passing through which its excitatory process is obliged to submit to modifications. (1965, 579–580, original italics)

There are two ends in the psychical apparatus that Freud proposes earlier in the chapter, the perceptual end and the motor end. Consciousness stands at the perceptual end of the apparatus, receiving stimuli from the external world, hence it is referred to as *Pcpt.-Cs.* It is the link between the external world and the internal world. In the above passage, however, Freud's focus is on the mechanism involved in the formation of a dream, what were formerly known as the critical and the criticized agents. Here they are reformulated into the preconscious system and the unconscious system. When used in the sense of a system, the preconscious is simplified as *Pcs.* and the unconscious as *Ucs.* Both of them are defined by their relations to the system of consciousness, *Pcpt.-Cs.*[5] *Pcs.* stands closer to consciousness than *Ucs.*, and its content can become conscious without much difficulty provided the *Pcs.* contents have the necessary intensity or attention; *Ucs.* has no access to consciousness except through *Pcs.* As Freud puts it, *Pcs.* stands like a screen between *Ucs.* and *Cs.*, and it holds the key to voluntary movement (579).

In his 1915 paper "The Unconscious," Freud tries to portray the unconscious itself instead of through its relationship with consciousness. The unconscious is characterized by the following features: "*exemption from mutual contradiction, primary process* (mobility of cathexes),[6] *timelessness,* and *replacement of external by psychical reality*" (1957, 187, original italics). Let us briefly examine these characteristics of the *Ucs.*

On the first point of *Ucs.* being exempt from mutual contradiction, Freud says:

The nucleus of the *Ucs.* consists of instinctual representatives which seek to discharge their cathexis; that is to say, it consists of wishful impulses. These instinctual impulses are co-ordinate with one another, exist side by side without being influenced by one another, and are exempt from mutual contradiction. When two wishful impulses whose aims must appear to us incompatible become simultaneously active, the two impulses do not diminish each other or cancel each other out, but combine to form an intermediate aim, a compromise.

There are in this system no negation, no doubt, no degrees of certainty: all this is only introduced by the work of the censorship between the *Ucs.* and the *Pcs.* Negation is a substitute, at a higher level, for repression. In the *Ucs.* there are only contents, cathected with greater or lesser strength. (1957, 186)

In other words, mutual contradiction is not even possible in the *Ucs.*, because different impulses can exist side by side without canceling each other out. The introduction of any contradiction into the psyche is the work of a censoring mechanism that screens out the undesirable psychic contents. This means the *Ucs.* is an inclusive but chaotic system, as opposed to the exclusive system of consciousness wherein contradictions become possible when an order is imposed.

On the second point, Freud argues:

The cathectic intensities [in the *Ucs.*] are much more mobile. By the process of *displacement* one idea may surrender to another its whole quota of cathexis; by the process of *condensation* it may appropriate the whole cathexis of several other ideas. I have proposed to regard these two processes as distinguishing marks of the so-called *primary psychical process.* (ibid., original italics)

Put simply, the unconscious follows the primary psychical process, which consists of two phases: that of displacement and of condensation. The phase of displacement is one in which the dream elements with high psychical value are stripped of their intensity while new values are created for elements with low psychical value, hence generating the difference between the dream-content (what is manifested in a dream) and the dream-thought (what remains latent in a dream) (Freud 1965, 342–343). Displacement is a chief method by which distortion in dreams is achieved (343) and an understanding of the distortion of a dream is critical in its effective interpretation. The process of condensation is evident when we take into consideration that "[d]reams are brief, meagre and laconic in comparison with the range and wealth of the dream-thoughts" (313). That is, the sheer gap between short dreams and their complex messages necessitates some sort of condensation in the formation of dreams.

The theory of condensation accounts for the fact that "the dream is not a faithful translation or a point-for-point projection of the dream-thoughts, but a highly incomplete and fragmentary version of them" (315).

On the point of the timelessness of the *Ucs.*, Freud states:

> The processes of the system *Ucs.* are timeless; i.e. they are not ordered temporally, are not altered by the passage of time; they have no reference to time at all. Reference to time is bound up, once again, with the work of the system *Cs.* (1957, 187)

Temporality is the work of consciousness and it has no role to play in the unconscious. This is related to the first characteristic of the unconscious, namely that it is exempt from mutual contradiction; the law of non-contradiction can only be applied to an entity that is ordered by temporality because the same mental duration cannot be occupied simultaneously by contradictory ideas.

Lastly, on the point of the replacement of external by psychical reality, Freud says:

> The *Ucs.* processes pay just as little regard to *reality*. They are subject to the pleasure principle; their fate depends only on how strong they are and on whether they fulfill the demands of the pleasure-unpleasure regulation. (ibid., original italics)

That is to say, the *Ucs.* is not interested in pleasing the external world, but rather in pleasing itself. It does not follow what Freud calls the reality principle, as consciousness does, but rather the pleasure principle.

It quickly becomes obvious that Freud uses the term "unconscious" in two different senses, descriptive and dynamic (1965, 653). Both *Ucs.* and *Pcs.* are unconscious in the descriptive sense, which merely attributes a particular *quality* to a mental state that one is not immediately and presently aware of. However, only *Ucs.* is unconscious in the dynamic sense, which attributes a particular *function* to a mental state, although Freud does not use these terms when the topographical system was initially formulated in *The Interpretation of Dreams*.[7] At this stage, the dynamic sense of the unconscious is equivalent to the repressed. There is still a third sense of the unconscious, the systematic sense, as James Strachey points out in his introduction to *The Ego and the Id*: "This implied a topographical or structural division of the mind based on something more than function, a division into portions to which it was possible to attribute a number of differentiating characteristics and methods of operating" (Freud 1960, xxx). In other words, in its systematic sense, the unconscious is understood as a process itself, distinguished from consciousness and preconscious. The *Ucs.* is also unconscious in the systematic sense. Therefore, to go back to our question of why a dream has to do with a wish, it is because a dream is a product of the *Ucs.*, whose single activity is to seek fulfillment of wishes. A dream and a wish are related to each other, almost by definition: "*The state of sleep makes the formation of dreams possible because it reduces the power of the endopsychic censorship*" (1965, 565, original italics).

However, in the course of his continuing clinical observation and theoretical deliberation, Freud became increasingly dissatisfied with the topographical system as it had been set up in *Interpretation*. The early 1920s witnessed a major theoretical shift by Freud, represented by his three works, *Beyond the Pleasure Principle* in 1920, *Group Psychology and the Analysis of the Ego* in 1921, and *The Ego and the Id* in 1923. They established what is called his structural system (Gay 1988, 394). Because the last of the trio provides the best summary of his new system, my analysis will concentrate on this work. I will also draw on Freud's *New Introductory Lectures on Psycho-Analysis*, which came soon after *The Ego and the Id*, in my discussion of the new system.

According to Freud himself, his unhappiness with the topographical system was twofold: the ambiguity of the word "unconscious" and two new clinical discoveries—unconscious ego resistance and an unconscious need for punishment (Macmillan 1997, 440).[8] As we have seen previously, the term "unconscious" is used in three different senses in Freud's writings prior to the 1920s: descriptive, dynamic, and systematic. The first refers to whatever is not immediately present to consciousness and is thus latent; the second to the repressed content that was previously in consciousness; and the third to the *Ucs.* in Freud's topographical system. One can easily see the confusion engendered by this terminology.

The second difficulty has to do with two of Freud's new clinical discoveries. Unconscious ego resistance was discovered in the clinical situation when a patient failed in the attempt to remove "the resistances which the ego displays against concerning itself with the repressed" (Freud 1960, 8). This inability is due to other resistance *from* the ego (not *against* the ego as in the first case), of which the patient is totally unaware:

> We have come upon something in the ego itself which is also unconscious, which behaves exactly like the repressed—that is, which produces powerful effects without itself being conscious and which requires special work before it can be made conscious. (8–9)

The recognition of an unconscious portion *in* the ego upsets the established "antithesis between the coherent ego and the repressed" (9), calling for a revision of the initial formulation.

The unconscious need for punishment is suggested when patients exhibit "negative therapeutic reaction," that is, they "react inversely to the progress of treatment" (49). This is a special kind of resistance, more powerful than "narcissistic inaccessibility, a negative attitude towards the physician and clinging to the gain from illness" (50). Freud elaborates:

> In the end we come to see that we are dealing with what may be called a 'moral' factor, a sense of guilt, which is finding its satisfaction in the illness and refuses to give up the punishment of suffering. . . . But as far as the patient is concerned this sense of guilt is dumb; it does not tell him he is guilty; he does not feel guilty, he feels ill. (ibid.)

This is another sign of the function of the unconscious portion of the ego. Accordingly, the terminological difficulty with the unconscious and ego, together with the two discoveries, motivates Freud to give up his topographical system:

> It had thus become apparent that, alike as regards 'the unconscious' and as regards 'the ego,' the criterion of consciousness was no longer helpful in building up a structural picture of the mind. Freud accordingly abandoned the use of consciousness in this capacity: 'being conscious' was henceforward to be regarded simply as a quality which might or might not be attached to a mental state. The old 'descriptive' sense of the term was in fact all that remained. (1960, xxxii)[9]

At this point, Freud attempts to differentiate mental regions from mental quality. His earlier difficulty arose, at least partially, out of the confusion between the two. Consequently, he makes the categories of the topographical system—preconscious, and especially conscious and unconscious—qualities of what is mental and proceeds to set up a new structural system more clearly defined in terms of mental regions; this is the well-known formula of id, ego, and super-ego to which I will now turn.[10]

Ego is a mental entity that "starts out . . . from the system *Pcpt.* [perception], which is its nucleus, and begins by embracing the *Pcs.*, which is adjacent to the mnemic residues" (16); "the other part of the mind, into which this entity extends and which behaves as though it were *Ucs.*," (17) is called id. Put differently, ego and id are two continuous compartments of a mental entity, predicated by different qualities, the former by conscious and unconscious qualities and the latter simply by what is unconscious.

According to Freud, the ego has two characteristics—its genesis from the influence of the external world and its embodiedness:

> It is easy to see that the ego is that part of the id which has been modified by the direct influence of the external world through the medium of the *Pcpt.-Cs.;* in a sense it is an extension of the surface-differentiation. Moreover, the ego seeks to bring the influence of the external world to bear upon the id and its tendencies, and endeavours to substitute the reality principle for the pleasure principle which reigns unrestrictedly in the id. For the ego, perception plays the part which in the id falls to instinct. (1960, 18–19)

The claim that the ego is part of the id is not only to reiterate the continuity between id and ego, but also to claim that the ego grows out of the id or that the id is the ground of the ego. This marks a fundamental shift in Freud's conceptualization of the unconscious. Previously, the unconscious was deemed an epiphenomenon of consciousness because the genesis of the former is the result of the repressive function of the latter. However, to view the ego as an entity that grows out of the id means that the unconscious (the id) is more than what was previously conscious and that the unconscious is not just the result of repression, forgetting, and neglecting, which are ego-centered activities.

The influence of the external world via perception is decisive in the genesis of the ego. In fact, what perception is to the ego is what instinct is to the id. Consequently, the ego serves as a mediator between the external world and the id. The ego follows the reality principle whereas the id follows the pleasure principle (Freud 1960, 19). The reality principle refers to the way by which ego brings about order and structure in consciousness. By contrast, the id, ruled by instincts, follows the pleasure principle. Ego is an organized and coherent substructure within the mind, resulting from contact with the external world via perception:

> Another factor, besides the influence of the system *Pcpt.*, seems to have played a part in bringing about the formation of the ego and its differentiation from the id. A person's own body, and above all its surface, is a place from which both external and internal perceptions may spring. . . . The ego is first and foremost a bodily ego; it is not merely a surface entity, but is itself the projection of a surface. (19–20)

The ego's bodily nature is related to its first characteristic in that it is an extension of the surface-differentiation and such surface-differentiation proceeds from the body; the ego is first and foremost an embodied ego. Only the ego with a body can make a clear demarcation between what belongs to an individual and what does not.

The concepts of id and superego are explained at length in Freud's *New Introductory Lectures on Psycho-Analysis,* and my discussion of them will draw on this work and *The Ego and the Id.* The id is "the dark, inaccessible part of our personality, . . . and can be described only as a contrast to the ego" (Freud 1964, 91). In contradistinction to the ego, the id is chaotic, instinctual, and pleasure-seeking. Logic does not apply to its functioning and contrary impulses can exist side by side without contradicting each other as they do in the ego. There is no passage of time. Temporality as an a priori form governing ego activities has no role with regard to the id. It does not abide by any moral law, and exercises no value judgments.[11] In a word, the id is what the ego is not. The id can be viewed as a reformulation of the *Ucs.* in the topographical system.

The superego is an agency in the mind that observes, judges, and punishes the ego (74). It is derived from a transformation of the child's earliest object-cathexes—referring to the investment of libido made by a child in an object or its internal representation (e.g., a parent in the case of the Oedipus complex)—into an identification with that object, namely the parental authority:

> The differentiation of the superego from the ego is no matter of chance; it represents the most important characteristic of the development both of the individual and of the species; indeed, by giving permanent expression to the influence of the parents it perpetuates the existence of the factors to which it owes its origin. (Freud, 1960, 31)

In other words, the superego is the internalization of parental authority acquired later in life. The tension between the superego and the ego gives rise to the conscience (Freud 1964, 76).

What is the relationship among the three domains of the mind? Phylogenetically, the differentiation of the ego from the id is prior to the separation of the superego from the ego (99). This means that the id is the most primitive of the three, and when it comes into contact with the external world the ego is born as a buffer zone between the instinctual id and the external world. As we have seen, this is a significant revision of Freud's earlier view, which seems more or less to equate the unconscious with the repressed because in that view consciousness, without which there is no repression to begin with, has to be phylogenetically prior to the unconscious. The role of the superego is to help the ego grapple with the conflict between the id and the external world by internalizing inhibiting parental authority into a moral agent within the individual mind. Therefore, it is clear that the ego simultaneously serves three "masters" as it were: the external world, the superego, and the id (Freud 1960, 58; 1964, 97). This means that the ego is receptive to all of the three forces from both within and without the mind.

"What distinguishes the ego from the id quite especially is a tendency to synthesis in its contents, to a combination and unification in its mental processes which are totally lacking in the id" (1964, 95). The ego's synthetic function is what brings about order in consciousness. The most fundamental orders are temporality and spatiality, both of which are forms of perception, which is the origin of consciousness *(Pcpt.-Cs.)* in Freud's topographical system. This synthetic function of the ego is indicative of its following the reality principle. Freud here may have the Kantian scheme in mind. He does not invalidate the Kantian system but rather delegates its validity to the function of the ego, which is only a (tiny) portion of the human mind. Because space and time are the forms of perceptual consciousness of the ego, the ego is rendered closer to the external world than to the internal world, which only follows the pleasure principle. This is evident in the following remark made by Freud:

> By setting up this ego ideal, the ego has mastered the Oedipus complex and at the same time placed itself in subjection to the id. Whereas the ego is essentially the representative of the external world, of real-

ity, the super-ego stands in contrast to it as the representative of the internal world, of the id. (1960, 32)

The superego represents the id whereas the ego represents the external world. On the one hand, the superego helps the ego master the Oedipus complex through identification with the parental authority; on the other hand it is the means by which the ego is subjected to the power of the id. The contents of the id can penetrate into the ego through two paths, directly or by way of the superego (58). "The ego is not sharply separated from the id; its lower portion merges into it" (17). There is no valve, as it were, between the ego and the id. Moreover,

> [t]he super-ego merges into the id; indeed as heir to the Oedipus complex it has intimate relations with the id; it is more remote than the ego from the perceptual system. The id has intercourse with the external world only through the ego. (Freud 1964, 98)

This means that the id can have access to the ego through the superego. Through the superego the ego is able to master the id.

Freud's theory of the unconscious has been challenged on many fronts, one of which was especially noteworthy because it came from within the psychoanalytic movement that Freud founded. This was the challenge posed by Carl Jung, who was once a close associate of Freud and in fact, his heir designate. In many ways, Jung's theory of the unconscious is both a challenge to and a development of Freud's.

Jung's Theory of the Unconscious

In this section I will focus on Jung's development and critique of Freud's theory of the unconscious.[12] My discussion will be based upon Jung's mature theory, and I will not go into the details of its development.[13] According to Jolande Jacobi, Jung's psychological theory consists of two parts: "(1) the structure of the psyche and (2) the laws of the psychic processes and forces" (1973, 1). Because the structure of the psyche is relevant to my discussion, I will focus on this aspect of Jung's psychology.

Due to the influence of Freud, Jung structures the psyche into the realm of consciousness and the unconscious:[14]

> By consciousness I understand the relation of psychic contents to the *ego*, in so far as this relation is perceived as such by the ego. Rela-

tions to the ego that are not perceived as such are *unconscious*. (1971, 421)

In other words, psychic contents are considered conscious if they are perceived by the ego, and they are unconscious if not perceived by the ego. What then is the ego?

> For all its appearance of unity, it [the ego] is obviously a highly composite factor. It is made up of images recorded from the sense-functions that transmit stimuli both from within and from without, and furthermore of an immense accumulation of images of past processes. All these multifarious components need a powerful cohesive force to hold them together, and this we have already recognized as a property of consciousness. Consciousness therefore seems to be the necessary precondition for the ego. Yet without the ego, consciousness is unthinkable. This apparent contradiction may perhaps be resolved by regarding the ego, too, as a reflection not of one but of very many processes and their interplay—in fact, of all those processes and contents that make up ego-consciousness. Their diversity does indeed form a unity, because their relation to consciousness acts as a sort of gravitational force drawing the various parts together, towards what might be called a virtual centre. For this reason I do not speak simply of *the ego*, but of an *ego-complex*, on the proven assumption that the ego, having a fluctuating composition, is changeable and therefore cannot be simply *the ego*. (1969a, 323–324)[15]

This preceding passage is concerned with two crucial points regarding the ego: its existence as a composite and its relationship with consciousness. First, there is a clear tension between the apparent unity and the actual composite nature of the ego for Jung. He concurs with Freud on the idea that ego consists of images transmitted from both within and without the mind as well as from its own past experience. Consequently, the ego cannot be a singular self-contained entity, but rather has a fluctuating composition. In other words, the ego is a changing entity.

Due to this composite nature, there is a need to hold the different components together and place them into a coherent structure. However, for Jung, this is the function of the ego as well as of consciousness. Therefore, the ideas of the ego and consciousness seem to presuppose each other, hence creating the dilemma of how to differentiate the two, if this is possible at all. If they cannot be differentiated, what is the point of postulating two concepts with completely identical definitions? This is the second issue addressed in the above passage. Jung is fully aware of the predicament here, and he suggests a solution by rendering the ego as the interplay of all the processes that are underway in consciousness. This point is made clearer in Jung's rather succinct definition in *Psychological Types*: "By ego I understand a complex of ideas which constitutes the centre of my field of consciousness and appears to possess a high degree of continuity and identity" (1971, 425).[16] Put differently, ego is the center of the field of consciousness that is well structured and organized, generating the sense of continuity and identity in an individual: "There can be no consciousness when there is no one to say: '*I* am conscious'" (Jung 1969a, 283).

There is one more important point in the above passage, namely the ego is an ego-complex.[17] This is crucial in differentiating the concept of ego from the concept of consciousness in Jung's theory. Because the complex in Jung's scheme has its origin in the unconscious, let us examine this concept by first looking into Jung's theory of the unconscious.

As we have seen previously, Jung understands the unconscious as a psychic process whose relationship with the ego is not perceived by the latter as such (1971, 421). The unconscious for Jung has two dimensions, personal and collective:

> The personal unconscious consists firstly of all those contents that became unconscious either because they lost their intensity and were forgotten or because consciousness was withdrawn from them (repression), and secondly of contents, some of them sense-impressions, which never had sufficient intensity to reach consciousness but have somehow entered the psyche. The collective unconscious, however, as the ancestral heritage of possibilities of representation, is not individual but common to all men, and perhaps even to all animals, and is the true basis of the individual psyche. (1969b, 153–154)[18]

To put it briefly, the personal unconscious includes forgotten or repressed conscious materials and residues of sense-impressions.[19] The collective unconscious is not related to the experience of the individual but is rather the totality of inherited possibilities of representation and the basis of the individual psyche.

Eventually, Jung concludes that the personal unconscious consists of feeling-toned complexes (1969a, 42) and the collective unconscious instincts and archetypes (1969b, 133–134). A complex is defined by Jung as the phenomenon of the "feeling-toned groups of representations" in the unconscious (Jacobi 1959, 6), which are of "an intrapsychic nature and originate in a realm which is beyond the objective control of the conscious mind and which manifests itself only when the threshold of attention is lowered" (7).[20] In other words, a complex is a psychic phenomenon originated in the personal unconscious and manifested in the consciousness when the attention level is lowered. The keys to understanding the concept of a complex are its uncontrollability by the conscious mind and its origin in the unconscious:

> According to Jung's definition every complex consists primarily of a "nuclear element," a vehicle of meaning, which is beyond the realm of the conscious will, unconscious and uncontrollable; and secondarily, of a number of associations connected with the nuclear element, stemming in part from innate personal disposition and in part from individual experiences conditioned by the environment. (8–9)

A complex has a nuclear center and a number of associations with it. The core of a complex has a high degree of autonomy and independence from the ego whereas its associated elements are more receptive to influence from the outside world via the ego. To be aware of a complex, as in the case of its manifestation in consciousness, does not alter its effects, and the only way to dissolve it is to discharge its energy through emotional assimilation.[21]

As we have seen, in Jung's view the ego is a complex, the ego-complex. It is one among many complexes in the psyche: "[I]nasmuch as the ego is only the centre of my field of consciousness, it is not identical with the totality of my psyche, being merely one complex among other complexes" (Jung 1971, 425). Because a complex has its origin in the personal unconscious, this means that the ego *qua* complex is rooted in the personal unconscious. That is, the ego originates in the personal unconscious. However, because a complex intrudes into the realm of consciousness when the level of consciousness is lowered, can the same be said of the ego-complex? If so, that would be tantamount to saying that the ego as a complex is an intrusion into the consciousness; this position cannot be held in Jung's psychology because the ego is the very condition of consciousness. The origin of this apparent contradiction can be traced to Jung himself; he randomly tosses around ideas as he goes along without giving consistent definitions of his concepts.[22] If we are to solve the above dilemma, we have to claim that the ego must be a special kind of complex. One possibility is to interpret the ego as an organizing principle of consciousness, and as such the center of consciousness, providing a coherent structure of continuity and identity to consciousness. This organizing principle is itself unconscious even though that which it holds together is conscious. This means that the ego is itself only a structure; the psychic contents become conscious when structured by the ego, but the ego itself remains concealed. Hence both the unconscious nature of the ego as a complex and the conscious nature of the ego as the precondition of consciousness can be accommodated. Consequently, the psyche is turned into a master complex system, consisting of various complexes, of which the ego is one. The ego-complex is apparently the most powerful among its peers, and its structuring activity gives birth to the field of consciousness of which it is the center.

In this connection, we find Jacobi claiming that "complex actually constitutes the structure of the psyche" (1959, 25). That is, because the ego is one of the complexes and the personal unconscious is constituted by complexes, complexes become the structure of an individual psyche.[23] Because it is only a structure, a complex can take on a content that is either personal or collective. This means that the individual psychic structure constituted by complexes is private, whereas its content can be either personal or collective, as Jacobi points out:

> If a "nodal point" [the nuclear element of a complex] is enriched only by mythical or universal human material, we may speak of a complex originating in the realm of the collective unconscious; but if individually acquired material is *superimposed* on it, i.e., if it appears in the cloak of a personally conditioned conflict, then we may speak of a complex originating in the domain of the personal unconscious. (25, original italics)

This is how Jung connects the personal unconscious with the collective unconscious. There is indeed a kinship between the concepts of the complex and the archetype that are constitutive of the personal unconscious and the collective unconscious, respectively, as Jacobi observes (30). Therefore it is appropriate for us now to turn to the concept of the collective unconscious, which is one of Jung's most seminal and controversial theories.

In Jung's clinical observations, he discerned that there is a dimension in the psyche that is not acquired through personal experience (1969b, 42). It is universally distributed and inherited in the psyche and is most vividly manifested in the mythologies and religions of the world. This non-personal dimension of the psyche is what Jung calls the collective unconscious. The collective unconscious consists of two aspects, instinct and archetype. Let us begin with Jung's concept of instinct:

> [I]nstincts are impersonal, universally distributed, hereditary factors of a dynamic or motivating character. . . . Moreover, the instincts are not vague and indefinite by nature, but are specifically formed motive forces which, long before there is any consciousness, and in spite of any degree of consciousness later on, pursue their inherent goals. (43) [24]

Here instincts are characterized by their universality, hereditariness, and dynamism. More interestingly, Jung suggests here that instinctual forces are teleological, orienting themselves toward some inherent goals. However, a question naturally arises: What goals are the instinctual forces pursuing and what is the mechanism in such a pursuit? It is with these questions in mind that Jung makes the following remarks:

> I regard the characteristic *compulsiveness* of instinct as an ectopsychic factor. None the less, it is psychologically important because it leads to the formation of structures or patterns which may be regarded as determinants of human behaviour. Under these circumstances the immediate determining factor is not the ectopsychic instinct but the structure resulting from the interaction of instinct and the psychic situation of the moment. The determining factor would thus be a *modified* instinct. . . . Instinct as an ectopsychic factor would play the role of a stimulus merely, while instinct as a psychic phenomenon would be an assimilation of this stimulus to a *pre-existent psychic pattern* [italics added]. A name is needed for this process. I should term it *psychization*. Thus, what we call instinct offhand would be a datum already psychized, but of ectopsychic origin. (1969a, 115, original italics unless noted) [25]

It is clear that Jung's concept of instinct has a distinct somatic character to it, and it is through what he calls a "psychization" process that the original compulsiveness of instinct is modified. Hence, Jung differentiates two kinds of instinct: the original one, which is ectopsychic or somatic in origin, and the modified one resulting from psychization. The original instinct is somatic but the modified one becomes structured and patterned through the psychization process. According to Jung, the modified—hence structured—instinct is determinative of behavior. Consequently, Jung uses the term "instinct" in its psychized sense while acknowledging its ectopsychic or somatic origin. Or in Jung's words: "In the last analysis, instincts are ectopsychic determinants" (1969a, 118). He lists five main groups of instincts: hunger, sexuality, activity, reflection, and creativity. The order in which Jung lists them suggests that the instincts are hierarchical from the natural to the cultural:

> The psychized instinct forfeits its uniqueness to a certain extent, at times actually losing its most essential characteristic—compulsiveness. It is no longer an ectopsychic, unequivocal fact, but has become instead a modification conditioned by its encounter with a psychic datum. As a determining factor, instinct is variable and therefore lends itself to different applications. Whatever the nature of the psyche may be, it is endowed with an extraordinary capacity for variation and transformation. (115–116)

Instinctual forces pursue their inherent goals through the psychization process, which transforms somatic forces to psychic ones. The possibility of the transformation of instincts lies in their empowerment by the libido, or psychic energy. Libido is a concept Jung takes over from Freud, but he significantly expands it. The Freudian libido is sexual energy whereas the Jungian libido is psychic energy. To reduce psychic energy to sexual energy is characteristic of Freud's reductionist approach. Jung needs a neutral form of energy in the psyche to make the transformation of instinctual forces possible. The goals of such a transformation are what Jung refers to as "the pre-existent psychic patterns" in the passage cited above, and they are what he later calls "archetypes."

Jung's concept of archetype, as essential as it is in his psychological framework, is so difficult to define and so full of ambiguities and contradictions that the best way to approach it is by "talking around" it, as Jacobi suggests (1959, 31). Hence, we find Jung saying:

> Archetypes are, by definition, factors and motifs that arrange the psychic elements into certain images, characterized as archetypal, but

in such a way that *they can be recognized only from the effect they produce*. They exist preconsciously, and presumably they form the structural dominants of the psyche in general. . . . As a priori conditioning factors they represent a special psychological instance of the biological 'pattern of behavior,' which gives all things their specific qualities. (Quoted in Jacobi 1959, 31, original italics)

There are several points that interest us here. First, archetypes are essentially a priori forms in the unconscious. They "are not disseminated only by tradition, language, and migration, but . . . they can realise spontaneously, at any time, at any place, and without any outside influence" (Jung 1969b, 79). They are pre-existent forms not developed individually, but inherited.

The second point is related to the first one. Because Jung emphatically insists that archetypes are only formal and are empty of contents, archetypes per se can never be known as such, and they can only be recognized through the effects they produce. The effects that archetypes produce are what Jung calls archetypal images. Therefore, he draws a distinction between an archetype per se and an archetypal image. By making such a distinction, Jung hopes to achieve two goals: retaining the hereditary nature of archetypes and accounting for the inevitable differences in our experience of the same archetypes from individual to individual and from group to group. That is, only archetypes are inherited; archetypal images, which are what we actually experience in encountering archetypes, vary among individuals as well as groups.[26]

As for the origin of archetypes, Jung's position is not consistent. On the one hand, he states that such a question is essentially unanswerable because it is ontological: "Whether this psychic structure and its elements, the archetypes, ever 'originated' at all is a metaphysical question and therefore unanswerable" (1969b, 101). On the other hand, however, he refutes his own position with the following remark:

There are as many archetypes as there are typical situations in life. Endless repetition has engraved these experiences into our psychic constitution, not in the form of images filled with content, but at first only as *forms without content*, representing merely the possibility of a certain type of perception and action. (48, original italics)

Jung is rather explicit that the origin of archetypes is the repetitive experience of some typical situations in life that engrave the forms of those experiences into our psychic constitution. Here we see another instance of his fluctuating stance between idealist and empiricist positions, although this can be resolved by resorting to the difference between the archetype, which is formal and inherited, and the archetypal representation, which is empirical and acculturated.[27]

According to Jung, instincts and archetypes determine each other: *"Instincts are typical modes of action"* (1969a, 135, original italics); *"Archetypes are typical modes of apprehension"* (137, original italics); "[T]he archetypes are simply the forms which the instincts assume" (157). However, the archetype gradually takes over the role previously assigned to the instinct. Jung eventually comes to the view that it is the archetypes that are constitutive of the collective unconscious (1969a, 42; 1969b, 4), making archetypes the forms "representing merely the possibility of a certain type of perception and *action*" (1969b, 48, italics added). In other words, the concept of instinct is subsumed under the concept of archetype: "the archetype consists of both—form and energy" (102).

To sum up, Jung structures the psyche into three realms: consciousness, personal unconscious, and collective unconscious. Consciousness is the realm organized by the ego, which itself originates from the personal unconscious as a complex. This means that the ego is the link between consciousness and the unconscious. The personal unconscious is constituted by complexes, which are private forms in the psyche that can take on a content that is either private or collective in its origin. The collective unconscious is constituted by inherited archetypes/instincts, but we can only experience archetypal images, the materialized archetypes as it were, in encountering the collective unconscious. Hence archetypal images become the link between the personal and the collective.

After this brief examination of Freud's and Jung's theories of the unconscious, I will reintroduce Xuan Zang into the discussion. By bringing the theories of all three into a new dialogical context I hope to clarify their differences and examine why they exist and how they are accomplished among the three formulations of the subliminal consciousness. These are the issues I will deal with in the next two chapters.

4

THREE PARADIGMS
OF THE
SUBLIMINAL
MIND

XUAN ZANG, FREUD,

AND JUNG

IN THE LAST TWO CHAPTERS, I conducted close examinations of Xuan Zang's Yogācāra Buddhist formulation of *ālayavijñāna* and Freud's and Jung's theories of the unconscious to familiarize us with the indigenous contexts of these three theories of the subliminal consciousness. In this chapter and the next, I will bring the three together by introducing them to a new context of dialogue. Within this new dialogical context, I will investigate the questions of *what* the specific thematic differences among them are, *why* they are so different, and *how* they come to be so different. The first question examines what is thematized in the three theories in order to see their differences, the second looks into the objectives of these theories, and the third examines the ways of theorization they adopt to achieve their goals, implicitly or explicitly. The basic assumption of my comparative study of these three formulations of the subliminal consciousness is that theoretical endeavors are significantly shaped by the objectives they set out to accomplish as well as by the ways of reasoning that are operative in formulating their theories; in most cases these ways of reasoning remain unschematized within their own contexts and will be more readily exposed in the new dialogical context.

In discussing what the thematic differences among the three are, my comparative approach within the newly set up dialogical context will enable us to gain better insights into some of the operative presuppositions of the three thematizations of the subliminal consciousness; these presuppositions are difficult to expose when the theories are left to themselves. I will do so by examining the theoretical paradigms within which the three concepts emerge respectively. I will argue that the paradigms that are operative in the three theories are their understandings of what a human being is and/or should be, namely personhood. Personhood has two dimensions, individual and collective, and consequently this study will concentrate on how individuality (qualities that belong to an individual person) and collectivity (qualities that belong to a group or to the humanity as a whole) are dealt with in the three theories of the subliminal consciousness and possible reasons for the differences among the three in this regard. At the core of the study are two questions: What kinds of individuality and collectivity are schematized in the three formulations of the subliminal consciousness, and what is the relationship between individuality and collectivity in the three theories? These questions crystallize what kinds of human beings are schematized in their respective schemes. That is, the formulations of the three theories are based on three different pictures of what a human being is taken to be. We will see that the three different pictures of what a human being is and/or should be are closely related to the audiences and their concerns the three theories are addressing. An understanding of the link between the two, namely what a human being is taken to be, implied by the three theories, and the audiences they are addressing, will shed important light on why Xuan Zang, Freud, and Jung have such different visions about what a human being is and/or should be.

Individuality

Let us begin with the question concerning individuality in the three theories of the subliminal consciousness. First, what kinds of individuality are schematized in the three theories? For Xuan Zang, it is the sense of self;[1] for Freud it is ego (here we will concern ourselves only with his structural system because the earlier topographical system is subsumed under the structural system). Jung's case is a bit more complicated because he formulates three concepts that are related to the idea of individuality: ego, *persona*, and Self.

As we saw in Chapter Two, Xuan Zang thematizes four aspects of the self in the *CWSL*: one pertains to *manas* (seventh consciousness) and three pertain to *manovijñāna* (sixth consciousness). The most fundamental aspect of self, and the one most relevant to this comparative study, is the first one; it is the result of *manas'* attachment to *ālayavijñāna* leading to the misidentification of the continuum as substance. That is, in Xuan Zang's view, the self is not a selfsame identity existing outside of the mental processes of a person but is rather a subliminal continuum that is mistaken as substance or substratum.[2] We have learned that *ālayavijñāna* has three aspects: the perceiving (*darśanabhāga*), the perceived (*nimittabhāga*), and the self-corroboratory (*svasaṃvittibhāga*), which are manifested as the external receptacle-world on the one hand and the internal sense organs possessed by the body on the other. It is the perceiving aspect, *darśanabhāga,* of the eighth consciousness that *manas* takes as its object and misidentifies as the self, but *darśanabhāga* is a homogeneous continuum even though it appears as eternal and one.

As we saw, due to the constraint of orthodox Buddhist doctrines against any kind of substantialization, *ālayavijñāna* is not formulated as a substratum of some sort. Instead, the *CWSL* conceptualizes it as a flux, or a continuum of subliminal mental activities that follows the rule of dependent origination. In delusion, sentient beings misconstrue *ālayavijñāna* as a substance, namely a substantive self, whereas it is only a continuum of activities. In this way the orthodox Buddhist doctrine of no-self, *anātman,* is upheld. That is, through the postulation of *ālayavijñāna,* Yogācāra Buddhists can explain away the substance of the self and substitute it with the continuity of *ālayavijñāna.* The positing of *ālayavijñāna* is a Yogācāra attempt to explain continuity without substance. Indeed, it can be argued that prior to the postulation of *ālayavijñāna,* the Buddhists did not really have a convincing explanation of the apparent sense of a self we possess. We can clearly see the significance of *ālayavijñāna* in the Yogācāra system given the "signature" doctrine of *anātman* in Buddhism.

To analyze the self *qua* substance, *ātman,* in the misidentified continuum of the storehouse consciousness indicates that Xuan Zang shares with Freud (1960, 18) and Jung (1969b, 280) the notion that individuality is closely related to the subliminal mental activities. However, this is the extent of their similarity. Significant differences remain. As we saw in the last chapter, according to Freud the unconscious process is chaotic, requiring that order be imposed from without, by the external world, represented by the ego. That is, individuality, or the ego for Freud, despite its origin in the unconscious, is the result of the contact between the internal and the external: "[T]he ego is that part of the id which has been modified by the direct influence of the external world through the medium of the *Pcpt.-Cs.*; in a sense it is an extension of the surface-differentiation" (1960,

18–19). In other words, the influence of the external world is decisive in the genesis of the ego, according to Freud. Hence it is the modification of the unconscious process by the external world that is determinative in the birth of the ego. This is what Freud means by the principle of reality followed by the ego.

For Xuan Zang, however, subliminal conscious activity is an orderly process—namely orderly succession or continuity—regulated by various kinds of causality as we saw in Chapter Two. Accordingly, in Xuan Zang's formulation, individuality/self vis-à-vis the continuum of *ālayavijñāna* follows the principle of continuity whereas for Freud individuality *qua* ego follows the principle of reality. Furthermore, for Xuan Zang individuality vis-à-vis the self is itself the subliminal consciousness, *ālayavijñāna,* but misidentified by *manas* as substance; for Freud, however, individuality vis-à-vis the ego is fundamentally different from the subliminal consciousness, the id. For the former, the self *qua* substance is the result of misidentification, but for the latter the ego is the result of modification of the unconscious id due to the decisive influence of the external world. In other words, for Xuan Zang, personal identity, if there is one, is *ālayavijñāna,* the subliminal consciousness (*manas* is not the self but it mistakes *ālayavijñāna* as the self), whereas for Freud, personal identity is not the unconscious *per se* but its modification by the external world.

Jung's conceptualization of individuality is more complicated than those of Xuan Zang and Freud. This is because Jung has three notions that pertain to individuality: ego, *persona,* and Self. As we have seen previously, Jung conceptualizes the ego as a complex which, while of an unconscious origin, is the organizing principle of the field of consciousness of which it is the center. Ego is one complex among many that are constitutive of the psyche, which is a conscious-unconscious whole. It imposes an order upon the psyche through exclusion and suppression of non-agreeable contents, which become dissociated from the ego; the order imposed by the ego generates a sense of coherent identity.

However, there is another concept of individuality that Jung formulates in his psychology, *persona. Persona* is the mask worn by actors to indicate the role they play:

> It is, as its name implies, only a mask of the collective psyche, a mask
> that *feigns individuality,* making others and oneself believe that one

is individual, whereas one is simply acting a role through which the collective psyche speaks. . . . [T]he *persona* was only a mask of the collective psyche. Fundamentally the *persona* is nothing real: it is a compromise between individual and society as to what a man should appear to be. . . . [I]n relation to the essential individuality of the person concerned it is only a secondary reality, a compromise formation, in making which others often have a greater share than he. The *persona* is a semblance, a two-dimensional reality, to give it a nick-name. (Jung 1966, 155–156, original italics)

Here Jung makes two important observations. First, a *persona* is collective in its nature but appears individual. Second, a *persona* is a compromise between individual and society. This means that a *persona* is a social mask that people wear in their interactions with one another. It is collective because it is essentially social, but it is also individualistic because it is worn by an individual and is taken to be his/her own. Hence it is a two-dimensional secondary reality that is a derivative of the social, being imposed upon the individual.

Jung's *persona* is close to Freud's notion of the ego because the influence of the external world is decisive in the genesis of both. In fact, Jung acknowledges that the concepts of *persona* and ego-consciousness are identical (158). There is, however, a difference in the way Jung uses these two terms. That is, when an individual's self is considered in and of itself, ego is used; when an individual's self is considered in its interactions with society, *persona* is used. It is hence appropriate to distinguish two senses of the individual self in Jung's usage: internal and external. The internal self is a complex that is at the center of an individual consciousness. The external self is the social mask that an individual takes on in interaction with other people. Obviously, Freud's notion of ego resembles the external self.

To Jung, neither the internal self nor the external self is the real individuality, even though both are important to a certain extent in maintaining a healthy psyche. The real individuality is that which lies at the center of the entire psyche, not just the realm of consciousness. This is what Jung calls the Self. It is "our life's goal, for it is the completest expression of that fateful combination we call individuality" (Jung 1966, 240). As with many of Jung's concepts, there is no coherent definition of the Self. Warren Colman differentiates four aspects of the Jungian Self: the totality of the psyche, an archetype, a personification of the unconscious, and a process (4).[3]

However, the first meaning of the Self overlaps with Jung's definition of the psyche itself: "[T]he psyche is a conscious-unconscious whole" (1969a, 200).[4] The third meaning, which equates the Self with the unconscious (1966, 158), can be subsumed under the second meaning—namely Self as an archetype—because the archetype is the form of the collective unconscious. The fourth meaning is covered by Jung's notion of individuation. Therefore, I will focus on the second meaning of "Self" as an archetype.

The Self is the archetype of wholeness (Jung 1969, 223), and as such it is the most important archetype (266). Wholeness means the union of conscious and unconscious in the psyche. Psyche is a conscious-unconscious whole. Consciousness and the unconscious, taken by themselves alone, are only parts of the psyche. The psyche that is dominated by the ego, which is the usual case, is one-sided. As we have seen, the ego is the center of consciousness, not of the whole psyche. Its domination over the psyche is the result of its imposition upon the rest of the psyche through suppression and exclusion; the result is that a large part of the psyche is left in the dark, repressed. In order for the psyche to become healthy, to restore its balance from ego domination, it needs to orient itself toward the Self as its new center. This is because the Self is the archetype of wholeness that integrates the previously disjointed psyche and organizes it into a harmonious totality.[5] The psychic order brought about by the Self differs from the ego in that the latter is achieved through exclusion and suppression while the former comes about through inclusion and integration. As a result, the Self transforms the ego-dominated, one-sided psyche to a more balanced and healthy psyche:

> As the apotheosis of individuality, the self has the attributes of uniqueness and of occurring once only in time. But since the psychological self is a transcendent concept, expressing the totality of conscious and unconscious content, it can only be described in antinomial terms. . . . [T]he self: as the essence of individuality it is unitemporal and unique; as an archetypal symbol it is a God-image and therefore universal and eternal. (Jung 1969c, 62–63)

The Self is unique to an individual, but as a God-image in the psyche it is also universal. It is both immanent and transcendent at the same time in relation to the psyche. As an immanence, it is what makes an individual a unique being in time; as a transcendence, it points to the collective dimension of spirituality beyond time.

However, there appears to be a contradiction in Jung's formulation of the Self. On the one hand, the Self is the true individuality; it is what makes an individual truly individual. On the other hand, as an archetype the Self is essentially collective. Thus the Self is both individualistic and collective. In fact, it is both individualistic and collective par excellence.[6] This suggests that in Jung's view true individuality correlates with true collectivity. Individuality without collectivity is egoistic, individuality identified with collectivity leads to ego-inflation. True individuality is the result of the transformation of the ego through vitalization by the archetypal power of the Self without being swamped by it. Such a transformation is what Jung calls "individuation":

> There is a destination, a possible goal [in psychic development]. That is the way of individuation. Individuation means becoming an "individual," and, in so far as "individuality" embraces our innermost, last, and incomparable uniqueness, it also implies becoming one's own self. We could therefore translate individuation as "coming to selfhood" or "self-realization." (Jung 1966, 173)

Individuation is becoming an indivisibly whole human being beyond the divided state wherein conscious and unconscious are in an uneasy relationship. In other words, individuation is the process of realizing the Self by integrating what is normally ignored in the psyche, be it the anima[7] in a man or the animus[8] in a woman—the shadow that the ego casts in the psyche through neglect and suppression. Put simply, it is a process to cultivate a balance amongst psychic functions, superior and inferior,[9] depending upon the psychic constitution of an individual, by integrating consciousness with the unconscious. By contrast, the order brought about by the ego is simply imposed upon the rest of the psyche, hence a large part of the psyche is marginalized. As a result, the psyche is one-sided and unhealthy. Individuation reorganizes the psyche by dislocating the ego from the center of the psyche through what Jung calls the transcendent function:

> Although it [the ego] is able to preserve its structure, the ego is ousted from its central and dominating position and thus finds itself in the role of a passive observer who lacks the power to assert his will under all circumstances, not so much because it has been weakened in any way, as because certain considerations give it pause. That is, the ego

cannot help discovering that the afflux of unconscious contents has vitalized the personality, enriched it and created a figure that somehow dwarfs the ego in scope and intensity. (Jung 1969a, 224)[10]

The Self, approached in the course of the individuation process, ousts the ego from the center of the psyche it used to occupy on the one hand and rejuvenates and revitalizes the psyche on the other. Therefore, the transformation that the individuation process brings about in the psyche is both structural and energic. It is obvious that the postulation of the Self accounts for the goal of individuation as a process of spiritual transformation.

However, Jung makes a distinction between wholeness/completeness and perfection (1969c, 68–69). The individuation process is geared towards wholeness, not perfection. Wholeness is a psychological concept, whereas perfection is a metaphysical concept. This is how Jung fends off any accusation of psychologizing the divine, which is perfection. Nevertheless, it should be clear that for Jung collectivity is the source of spirituality. As such, it seems to be a far cry from Freud's notion of collectivity, even though the difference between Jung and Freud on this issue is actually much more subtle.

Collectivity: The Source of Human Spirituality

Before dealing with Freud's conceptualization of collectivity in his theory of the unconscious, we need to clarify one common mischaracterization of Freud's theory:

> A study of the theory of repression as developed by Freud should make it abundantly clear that Jung's repeated statement reducing Freud's repressed-unconscious to nothing other than "a subliminal appendix to the conscious mind" did not do justice to the theoretical concepts of Freud. Jung's remark that the unconscious as described by Freud represented "nothing but the gathering place of forgotten and repressed contents" likewise was not quite fair to Freud's basic concept. (Frey-Rohn, 120)

It is misleading to equate Freud's unconscious with Jung's personal unconscious. Freud's concept of superego, which is unconscious, is essentially collective. The conceptualization of the superego in Freud's structural system is a radical shift from his earlier topographical system in that the superego represents a heightened awareness on Freud's part of the role of the collective in an individual's psychic life.[11] Let us take a closer look at Freud's conceptualization of the collective dimension of the unconscious.

What kind of collectivity is schematized in the formulation of the superego? In this connection, we are told that the formation of the superego is the result of internalization of parental authority into the psyche. When the external restraint is internalized, "the superego takes the place of the parental agency and observes, directs and threatens the ego in exactly the same way as earlier the parents did with the child" (Freud 1964, 77). Moreover, we are also told that

> a child's super-ego is in fact constructed on the model not of its parents but of its parents' super-ego; the contents which fill it are the same and it becomes the *vehicle of tradition* and of all the time-resisting judgements of value which have propagated themselves in this manner from generation to generation. (84, italics added)

Here Freud is explicit about what kind of collectivity the superego represents; it is the vehicle of tradition. "Tradition" in this context mainly refers to the moral values of a society and culture that are the achievement of human civilization.

As Freud sees it, there is an inherent conflict between the individual and the collective. The individual, driven by pleasure-seeking instinct, always finds himself at odds with the social values that put a check on his pursuit of instinctual gratification. As Freud puts it bluntly, "every individual is virtually an enemy of civilization" (1961b, 6) due to the instinctual renunciation that civilization demands of the individual. As a child, such a demand is issued by the parental authority, especially in the face of the powerful Oedipus complex. The internalization of the parental authority into the psyche as the superego is the product of civilization. That is, civilization "obtains mastery over the individual's dangerous desire for aggression by weakening and disarming it and by setting up an agency within him to watch over it, like a garrison in a conquered city" (Freud 1961a, 84).

In addition to its role as the vehicle of tradition, the superego also contains the germ of all (Judaeo-Christian) religions:

> Religion, morality, and a social sense—the chief elements in the higher side of man—were originally one and the same thing. . . . [T]hey were acquired phylogenetically out of the father-complex: religion and moral restraint through the process of mastering the Oedipus com-

plex itself, and social feeling through the necessity for overcoming the rivalry that then remained between the members of the younger generation. (Freud 1960, 33–34)

Freud is making a crucial observation here: The higher forms of human spirituality, namely religion and morality, originate from the father-complex in the mastery of the Oedipus complex. This means that spirituality is the achievement of the collective unconscious of our psyche epitomized in the formation of the superego.

The view that spirituality is essentially collective in nature is shared by Jung in his formulation of the archetype. However, there is a crucial difference between the two positions with regard to human spirituality. For Freud,

[e]ven if conscience is something 'within us,' yet it is not so from the first. In this it is a real contrast to sexual life, which is in fact there from the beginning of life and not only a later addition. (1964, 77)

In other words, human spirituality, represented by the superego, is a later acquisition in life, the result of internalization of an external authority; this is true even if it is granted that spirituality is within the person. This means, according to Freud, that spirituality is forced upon an individual from the outside. Jung's critique of Freud claims that he views the spiritual principle "only as an appendage, a by-product of the instincts" (1969a, 55) and hence as little more than the source of restraint and suppression that works against an individual. Human beings fail to recognize the true nature of religious ideas, the highest form of human spirituality, which like all of the other achievements of civilization arise "from the necessity of defending oneself against the crushingly superior force of nature" (Freud 1961b, 26–27). Hence Freud claims that religious ideas

are illusions, fulfillments of the oldest, strongest and most urgent wishes of mankind. The secret of their strength lies in the strength of those wishes. As we already know, the terrifying impression of helplessness in childhood aroused the need for protection—for protection through love—which was provided by the father; and the recognition that this helplessness lasts throughout life made it necessary to cling to the existence of a father, but this time a more powerful one. (38)

Freud immediately clarifies what he means by illusion. He makes a distinction between illusions and delusions:

> What is characteristic of illusions is that they are derived from human wishes. In this respect they come near to psychiatric delusions. But they differ from them, too, apart from the more complicated structure of delusions. In the case of delusions, we emphasize as essential their being in contradiction with reality. Illusions need not necessarily be false—that is to say, unrealizable or in contradiction to reality. (39)

Put simply, the key difference between a delusion and an illusion is that the former is contradictory to reality whereas the latter is not necessarily so.[12] Therefore, to claim that religious ideas are illusions is not the same as saying that they are wrong or in contradiction with reality. Nevertheless Freud still maintains the view that religious ideas are illusory fulfillments of human wishes. They have their origins in the infantile longing for fatherly protection.

In a word, Freud's view of human spirituality, epitomized in his formulation of the collective unconscious—the superego—can be summarized in three aspects: It is derived from the sexual instinct, is acquired through the internalization of a protective and prohibitive external authority, and is essentially illusory in that it represents the collective wish-fulfillments of humanity. This is in sharp contrast with Jung.

As we have seen previously, for Jung as well as for Freud, collectivity is the source of spirituality. However, Jung differs from Freud in holding the view that spirituality is the goal toward which all our psychic development is *naturally* oriented, and as such it comes from the interior of an individual, not from the exterior. This is the very rationale for Jung's postulation of archetype: "Psychologically . . . the archetype as an image of instinct is a spiritual goal toward which the whole nature of man strives" (1969a, 212).[13] That is, the postulation of archetypes is to account for the teleological orientation of the psyche and therefore the spiritual goal to be accomplished in the individuation process. In order to avoid a view similar to Freud's that spirituality is derivative of, hence secondary to, the sexual instinct, Jung makes the bold move of claiming that archetypes are inherited, not derived from something else. Both men are mindful of the significance of Jung's claim. When talking about the collective unconscious, Freud writes:

I fully agree with Jung in recognizing the existence of this phylogenetic heritage; but I regard it as a methodological error to seize on
a phylogenetic explanation before the ontogenetic possibilities have
been exhausted. I cannot see any reason for obstinately disputing the
importance of infantile prehistory while at the same time freely
acknowledging the importance of ancestral prehistory. (Quoted in
Jacobi 1959, 20, n28)

Freud is trying to dispute Jung's view on methodological grounds,
but such a critique simply misses Jung's intention in postulating the
archetype as an inheritance, namely it is formulated by Jung as that
toward which all human spiritual transformation is directed naturally: "It is not sufficient to point out the often obviously archetypal
nature of unconscious products, for these can just as well be derived
from acquisitions through language and education" (Jung 1969b,
44). Consequently, two totally different pictures of humanity emerge:
For Freud a human being is primarily a sexual being whereas for
Jung a human being is both instinctual and spiritual. This is at the
very core of the differences between Freud and Jung. In viewing
human beings as inherently spiritual, Jung is closer to Xuan Zang,
to whom I now turn.

I have already discussed in Chapter Two the three kinds of collectivity that Xuan Zang thematizes in *CWSL:* the physical world,
other people's bodies, and their minds. However, where does the
spiritual dimension fit in Xuan Zang's theory of *ālayavijñāna*?[14] After
all Yogācārins are concerned, more than anything else, with the possibility of Buddhist enlightenment, *nirvāṇa*. In light of our discussion of spirituality in Freud and Jung, one question naturally arises:
Is Buddhist enlightenment addressed by Xuan Zang's theory of individuality or by his theory of collectivity? Let us make a closer examination of Xuan Zang's treatment of spiritual transformation in
Buddhism.

The spiritual transformation in Yogācāra Buddhism is called
"*āśraya-parāvṛtti.*" "*Āśraya*" means "ground" or "basis," and "*parāvṛtti*" means "revolving" or "transformation." Hence the word as
a whole means "the basis on which one relies, revolves, and turns
into a different basis (or non-basis); the ground itself on which one
stands, overturns, revealing a new world, illuminated by a new light"
(Nagao, 115). This basis that needs to be transformed is *ālayavijñāna*,
as Xuan Zang points out: "The *āśraya* that holds the *bīja*s refers to

the root consciousness, *mūlavijñāna*. This *āśraya* can hold the *bīja*s of impure and pure *dharma*s, and as such it is the basis for both impure and pure *dharma*s" (754). *Parāvṛtti* "connotes a 'rolling towards,' a becoming intent upon, a reaching for, a happening or occurrence that will lead to a tendency, that will take on a projectorial trait" (Lusthaus 1989, 306). This means that *āśraya-parāvṛtti* is the transformation of the storehouse consciousness in reaching a goal, namely *nirvāṇa* in the Buddhist context. In other words: "The *āśraya-parāvṛtti* is the turning-up of one's basis; namely, it is the conversion of the *ālayavijñāna* which stores all seeds" (Osaki, 1063).

However, this transformation of consciousness does not necessarily suggest that in Xuan Zang's scheme, the psychic activity is only teleological, as it is conceptualized by Jung. For Jung, psychic activity is inherently teleological in orienting one toward the wholeness represented by the archetype of the Self, whereas for Xuan Zang there are two kinds of psychic activities: *parāvṛtti* and *pariṇāma*. *Parāvṛtti* is a teleological activity of the psyche, but *pariṇāma* refers to the intrapsychic dynamics involving the eight consciousnesses in the Yogācāra scheme as we discussed in the previous chapter, and it "implies an aporia, a movement unsure of its direction" (Lusthaus 1989, 306). Put simply, ordinary psychic activity is in disarray, whereas psychic activity in the course of *parāvṛtti* is geared toward enlightenment.

Then what makes it possible for the *pariṇāma* activity of the psyche to be reoriented toward the *parāvṛtti* activity in order for the spiritual transformation to take place? According to Xuan Zang, two conditions are required in this regard: the pure *bīja*s and the perfuming of them by the pure *dharma*s, which allows for the pure *bīja*s to increase:

> The pure *dharma*s arise in dependence upon the pure *bīja*s. These pure *dharma*s perfume in turn and thus produce new pure *bīja*s. (120)

The pure *bīja*s are the seeds of *nirvāṇa* and the pure *dharma*s mean the true *dharma* preached by the Buddha himself. As a supramundane reality, *nirvāṇa* cannot be contained in this world. Being unconditioned, it cannot be supported by the eighth consciousness. But in order for it to be reachable by deluded sentient beings, Xuan Zang has to bring it into this mundane world. Hence, we find him claiming that the storehouse consciousness contains the seeds of enlightenment, but not enlightenment itself (190). The pure seeds alone do not constitute a sufficient condition to achieve *nirvāṇa* because they still require the pure *dharmas*' perfuming for their growth and fruition.

In order to establish the theoretical possibility of achieving enlightenment by way of increasing the pure seeds through perfuming, Xuan Zang has to postulate the inborn pure seeds carried in the storehouse consciousness.[15] If *bīja*s of pure *dharma*s (here only the pure *bīja*s are the concern) were not inborn, there would be no pure *bīja*s because the pure can not be born out of the impure by the perfuming;[16] thus, it would be impossible to achieve *nirvāṇa*.

The other indispensable aspect that makes *āśraya-parāvṛtti* possible is the perfuming of the pure *bīja*s by pure *dharma*s. The rationale is based upon the stipulation of the characteristic of *bīja*s by which *bīja*s depend on a group of conditions in order to actualize their capacity to produce an actual *dharma* (Xuan Zang, 126–128). In other words, without proper conditions, the pure *bīja*s cannot by themselves engender their fruit of *nirvāṇa*. In the *CWSL,* it is the pure *srutavasana,* the hearing of the Buddha's teaching, that perfumes the pure *bīja*s and causes them to grow: "When the meditater hears the true *dharma*, the inborn pure *bīja*s are perfumed to grow and transform gradually till a supramundane mind is born" (122). The true *dharma* here refers to "the efflux of the pure *dharmadhātu*" (Wei Tat, 115) that is experienced by the meditator in her meditation.[17]

Two different kinds of teaching are presented in *CWSL:* impure and pure (122). Rujun Wu interprets the former as good advice and/or instruction of any ordinary teachers or even of the vast majority of unenlightened Buddhist monks and nuns due to the fact that their knowledge is acquired through reading books. The latter refers to the direct preaching of the Buddha, the enlightened one (55–57). The former, being defiled in nature, is not able to perfume the pure *bīja*s of the practitioner while the latter, being pure, has such a capacity.[18] It suggests that there is a transference of the Buddha's power to the listener when she hears the direct preaching of the Buddha. Accordingly, listening to the true *dharma*, which is the Buddha's direct teaching, is far more than mere listening; according to Buddhism, it can drastically facilitate the spiritual transformation of the listener by increasing her pure *bīja*s.[19]

Given the necessary and sufficient conditions, namely inborn pure *bīja*s and the increase of those pure *bīja*s through the perfuming of the true *dharma* preached by the Buddha himself, the possibility of *āśraya-parāvṛtti* has thus been established. Achieving *āśraya-parāvṛtti* is a gradual progression, and *CWSL* schematizes five stages. I will leave the actual process of *āśraya-parāvṛtti* to Chapter Five, where I compare different modes of access to the subliminal mind.

What is striking about Xuan Zang's theory of spirituality is that it is not located in the collective dimension of the mind, as it is for Freud and Jung. Rather, it is schematized as that which transcends the mental realm, even though the possibility of achieving spiritual transformation vis-à-vis pure seeds is retained in the collective dimension of *ālayavijñāna*. This means that for Xuan Zang there is a path toward enlightenment contained in the collective dimension of *ālayavijñāna,* even though enlightenment transcends the deluded mental activities, personal and collective.

Xuan Zang's positing of the inborn pure seeds, the necessary condition of *āśraya-parāvṛtti,* renders him closer to Jung. For both Xuan Zang and Jung there is an inborn tendency of a human being toward spirituality. However, for Xuan Zang that tendency alone does not lead to (Buddhist) spiritual transformation. This means that spiritual transformation for Xuan Zang is by no means an automatic and natural process of life because it requires both rigorous cultivation on the part of the practitioner and crucial assistance from an enlightened being.[20] For Jung, on the other hand, the individuation process toward psychic wholeness is always going on even when it is unbeknownst to the person herself, although some people become more individuated than others in part because of their intentional effort or attention. This difference between Xuan Zang and Jung is due to the fact that *nirvāṇa* is schematized by Xuan Zang as that which transcends the deluded mind, personal or collective, even though the possibility of achieving spiritual transformation is retained in the collective dimension of *ālayavijñāna;*[21] for Jung, on the other hand, the archetype of the Self is in the collective unconscious and the maturation of the psyche is necessarily geared toward the Self. For Xuan Zang spiritual transformation is a mere possibility due to the existence of the inborn pure seeds, which renders spiritual transformation possible on the one hand but requires the collaboration of a practitioner's own effort and the assistance of an enlightened being on the other; for Jung it is an inherent possibility due to the teleological orientation of our mental life toward wholeness and individuation; and for Freud, it is a forced necessity because it is necessary for human beings' very survival in society even though it is against the wishes of the pleasure-seeking id.[22]

Let us sum up our discussion so far on individuality and collectivity schematized in the three theories. On the issue of individuality, we have seen that in Xuan Zang's system, it is primarily the ego resulting from the attachment of *manas* to the ever-changing but homogeneous *ālayavijñāna*. In Freud's case, it is the ego, the genesis of which is the modification of the id by the external world. In Jung's theory, it has three aspects, first as ego-complex (internal), which occupies the center of the psyche by marginalizing other elements; second as *persona* (external), which is the external representation of the ego; and third as the Self, which represents the wholeness of the psyche. On the issue of collectivity, we have seen that in Xuan Zang's system it includes the receptacle physical world, other people's bodies, and other people's minds, and that spirituality is not included in the collective dimension of the deluded subliminal consciousness, although its seeds are; in Freud's case, it is the superego that represents tradition and moral values internalized in the course of the socialization of a human being; in Jung's theory, it includes the archetype and the instinct, the former being spiritual and the latter material.

Although I have carried out a comparative study of Xuan Zang's, Freud's, and Jung's theories of the subliminal consciousness with a focus on how individuality, collectivity, and their relationship are schematized in these three theories, the question remains: Why are there such differences in these formulations of the subliminal consciousness? Although there are many possible answers to this question, I will argue that one of the major reasons for the differences lies in the fact that the objectives the three theories set out to achieve are different. The difference in their objectives has greatly contributed to the difference in the contents of the three theoretical formulations of the subliminal consciousness. Let us now turn to these objectives. In examining them, I will reveal their underlying assumptions about what a human being is and/or should be.

Personhood: Three Premises, Three Paradigms

What are the objectives that Xuan Zang, Freud, and Jung set out to achieve in their formulations of the subliminal consciousness? Let us look at this issue from the perspectives of individuality and collectivity that were outlined above.

On the issue of individuality, Xuan Zang, as an orthodox Buddhist, has to defend the Buddhist notion of *anātman* against the Brahmanical notion of *ātman*. In other words, Xuan Zang's analysis of the self, on the one hand, rejects the metaphysical notion of *ātman* as an obstacle to reaching enlightenment through meditative practices prescribed by Yogācārins, while on the other hand it explains the reason for our having a *sense* of self. Consequently, continuity becomes crucial in Xuan Zang's conceptualization of *ālayavijñāna*; continuity is misidentifiable as substance and therefore it can be used to both dispute a substantive interpretation of the self and explain a misunderstanding as the result of misidentification. Hence continuity becomes the principle of the subliminal consciousness in Xuan Zang's theory. Accordingly, *manas*, whose attachment to *ālayavijñāna* gives rise to the metaphysical sense of self, is characterized by four afflictions (*kleśa*): self-delusion, self-belief, self-conceit and, self-love (Xuan Zang, 288), all of which point to the delusory nature of a metaphysical self. But there is no sense of chaos in Xuan Zang's formulation of *ālayavijñāna*, and there is no reason to posit chaos for him either. Rather, the subliminal consciousness in Xuan Zang's theory is an orderly process. *Manas* does not impose any order upon *ālayavijñāna*, but only attaches to it instead. As a result, there is no sense of conflict between *manas* and *ālayavijñāna* in the genesis of the self in Xuan Zang's theory, although it is prominent in Freud's formulation of ego, id, and superego.

The naturally ordered process of *ālayavijñāna* is in sharp contrast to the two subliminal mental processes in Freud's structural system, the chaotic and pleasure-seeking id that defies order and the severe and suppressive superego that imposes order. Freud's analysis of the ego means to find ways to fortify the poor ego against the assault of the unconscious world—be it the superego or the id—in addition to the external world; in doing so he seeks to help his patients who suffer from neurosis restore and maintain sanity.[23] Put differently, in Freud's case, the unconscious is the culprit in human insanity, and the strengthening of the ego is essential to restore the psychic order in psychoanalytic practices. The issue of its being empirical or metaphysical does not arise at all in the context of psychoanalysis. For Xuan Zang, however, the attachment to a metaphysical self, *ātman*, is the hurdle that needs to be overcome through rigorous meditative practices in order to reach enlightenment.[24] The sense of an intense struggle of the ego we see in Freud's theory is completely missing in Xuan Zang's formulation. There is, instead, only attachment.

Jung's analysis of the ego falls somewhere between Xuan Zang's and Freud's. This can be attributed, at least partially, to the fact that Jung is concerned with psychotic patients whose ability to deal with the world is severely damaged.[25] This explains the fact that Jung does not embrace the ego-centered perspective of Freud. For Freud, the neurotic patient's ego is impaired but not yet destroyed, hence his goal is to restore that ego for the patient. For Jung, the psychotic patient's ego is so severely damaged that its treatment calls for more dramatic measures than simply to restore the lost ego; he tries rather to subjugate the ego to a larger organizing power within the psyche, the Self. As a result, for Jung, not only is the ego not the totality of the psyche (a view shared by Freud), it should not even be at the center of the psyche. Nor does Jung advocate a rejection of the ego, a position held by Xuan Zang. Instead, Jung contends that the ego should be transformed through what he calls the transcendent function in the individuation process. That is, Jung hopes to substitute for the ego what he calls the Self, the whole of personhood, in developing a healthy and balanced psyche.

On the issue of collectivity, we have found that different kinds of collectivity are schematized in the three theories. Xuan Zang thematizes the external world, other people's bodies, and other people's minds; Freud thematizes the superego as the vehicle of tradition, including morality and religion; and Jung thematizes the collective unconscious constituted by instincts and archetypes.

The differences in the kinds of collectivity among the three are striking. In Xuan Zang's theory, the social, historical, and cultural aspects of the collectivity are nowhere to be found, whereas they loom large in Freud's theory. There are various possible explanations for such a difference between the two, one of which could be the very development of our theoretical effort in thematizing history, society, and culture in the history of philosophy.[26] However, I would like to suggest that such a conspicuous missing element in Xuan Zang's theory of the subliminal consciousness can also be explained in terms of the objective of his theory, namely to account for the possibility of enlightenment. A practitioner's meditative practice is regarded as essential and the meditative experience is largely individualistic, so that history, society, and culture are not directly involved. In fact, to achieve enlightenment is to transcend the very conditionality of history, society, and culture, even though it can also be argued that the very possibility of such a meditative practice lies in a specific historical, social, and cultural environment. Nevertheless this environment remains unthematized in Xuan Zang.

For Freud, collectivity—as the vehicle of tradition—and individuality exist in a rather hostile relationship. This is because Freud, in locating the problem of the forced renunciation of an individual's sexual instincts in the collective, is trying to help his psychologically disturbed patients cope with the stifling challenges posed by the collective. Because for Freud collectivity is the source of both spirituality and suppression, spirituality becomes one imposed from without, and the result primarily of sexual frustration. This explains Freud's observation that the superego "seems to have made a one-sided choice and to have picked out only the parents' strictness and severity, their prohibiting and punitive function, whereas their loving care seems not to have been taken over and maintained" (Freud 1964, 78). Because the collective is deemed as antagonistic to an individual, the spirituality which is located within the collective can only be strict and severe in the eyes of the individual. However, that does not have to be the case, as Jung's conception of collectivity shows.

In the case of Jung, spirituality vis-à-vis the archetype of the Self is deemed as the inherent goal toward which the psyche is naturally oriented in the individuation process.[27] As such, it is not imposed upon an individual from without, as in the case of Freud. For Jung, a human being is both an instinctual and a spiritual creature,[28] but in the course of her *natural*—though not necessarily smooth or easy—growth, she evolves from a more instinctual being in her earlier life to a more spiritual being in her later life.[29]

However, Jung has one major problem in his conceptualization of the collective unconscious: It lies with his concept of archetype. Jung formulates the concept of archetype in order to achieve two goals: the possibility of spiritual transformation and an explanation of commonality in our experience. These two objectives are not entirely compatible because the former requires inheritance and the latter acculturation. The former one is unique to Jung; the latter one overlaps with Freud's notion of the collective unconscious, the superego. Jung's theory explains the formal aspects of collectivity well, but it has serious problems in accounting for the acculturation aspect of collectivity. In order to reconcile the conflict between these two objectives in the postulation of the archetype, Jung introduces the notion of archetypal representation. However, this does not seem to solve the problem at all because many of the archetypal representations are confined to race, gender, nation, and family and belong to the realm of acculturation; as such they do not seem to have any correlating formal archetypes-per-se, which are the preconditions of the archetypal representations to begin with.[30] The introduction of the archetypal representation seems to be a kind of *ad hoc* solution instead of a well-thought-out one.

It is conceivable that Jung in his theoretical endeavor proceeded from spirituality to collectivity and Freud from collectivity to spirituality. This leads to the confusion in their theories because neither explicitly stipulates where spirituality and collectivity coincide and where they depart. Xuan Zang's idea to differentiate spirituality from collectivity on the one hand and to place the seeds of spirituality in collectivity on the other hand offers one possible way to avoid the confusion we see in Freud's and Jung's theories of the subliminal consciousness.[31]

There are two common denominators among the three theories of the subliminal consciousness: consciousness, in the narrow sense of the word, is not the totality of the mind; and the genesis of the ego is in the subliminal realm. However, their differences are unmistakable. Clearly three kinds of persons are schematized in the three theories. In Xuan Zang's theorization we see a lone meditator engrossed in rigorous practice to achieve enlightenment; in Freud a desperate fighter trying to survive in an antagonistic society; and in Jung a seeker attempting to fight off the tendency to withdraw into herself by embarking on a spiritual journey. Underlying such differences are three different premises about what a human being is and/or should be. That is, for Xuan Zang, a human being is a deluded being and the way out of such a delusion is through meditative practices prescribed by Yogācāra teachings. For Freud, a human being is essentially a sexual being who is trying to be spiritual in order to survive in society. For Jung, a human being is both a sexual and a spiritual being and an ideal personhood is that which embraces the Self through the individuation process.

To conclude, it should become clear to us that Xuan Zang's *ālaya-vijñāna* is neither Freud's unconscious nor Jung's unconscious with respect to their thematic contents, operative presuppositions, and objectives. Xuan Zang, Freud, and Jung are working within three different paradigms, to use Thomas Kuhn's term. As such, their theories of the subliminal consciousness follow different rules and address different concerns of different audiences. Xuan Zang addresses the problematic of the possibility of awakening primarily to Buddhist practitioners; Freud addresses the issue of depression initially to his neurotic patients; and Jung addresses the more serious case of schizophrenia originally to his psychotic patients. Even though Freud's and Jung's theories would come to address a much wider audience, the points of departure for them were very different and that had a significant impact on the subsequent development of their theories.

Now that we have come to an understanding that the three theories belong to different theoretical paradigms, the next step is to examine how they are formulated. I will conduct an inquiry into the modes of reasoning by which the subliminal consciousness is conceptualized in the three paradigms respectively, hence contributing to their differences. We will see that, in addition to the thematic focus, targeted audience, and tacit assumptions, the mode of reasoning also plays a significant role in shaping a theory in its articulated form. This will be my topic for the next chapter.

5

ACCESSIBILITY
OF THE
SUBLIMINAL MIND

TRANSCENDENCE VERSUS

IMMANENCE

IN THE LAST CHAPTER, I carried out a comparative study of Xuan Zang's formulation of storehouse consciousness, Freud's unconscious, and Jung's unconscious by focusing on their thematic differences and operative presuppositions, as well as the different objectives they set out to accomplish. I concluded that these theories belong to radically different theoretical paradigms, designed to address completely different audiences and their concerns. I will now address how their particular modes of reasoning contribute to the accomplishment of their objectives.

As we discussed in Chapter Four, the objective of Xuan Zang's Yogācāra theory is to help Buddhist practitioners reach awakening; the original purpose of Freud's theory is to assist his neurotic patients in curing their mental diseases; and the initial motive of Jung's theory is to aid his psychotic patients in overcoming their debilitating mental disorder. According to the Yogācāra theory, in order to reach enlightenment, Buddhist practitioners must be able to perceive *ālayavijñāna* directly. In other words, a practitioner has to have direct access to *ālayavijñāna* to achieve enlightenment. By contrast, patients receiving psychoanalytic treatment rely on their analysts for access to their unconscious activities through an elaborate interpretative scheme provided by psychoanalytic theories. As a result, access to the unconscious is indirect. This indirect access to the unconscious of a patient provided by the interpretation of a trained psychoanalyst has been taken for granted. This chapter problematizes the very indirectness of access by introducing Xuan Zang's formulation, which provides direct access to the subliminal mind. Direct access is crucial in Xuan Zang's system; for Yogācārins it holds the key to a practitioner's *own* effort to reach enlightenment. Indirect access, however, is critical in both Freud's and Jung's systems because it leaves room for the mediating and assisting role played by an analyst/doctor in both theories, which is essential in the eventual cure of mental disorders.

The primary objective of this chapter is not just to reveal these different modes of access to the subliminal activities provided in three formulations of the subliminal mind. More importantly, I will use these different modes of access as a clue to expose underlying ways of reasoning these theories employ and embody. My assumption here is that different ways of reasoning have a major impact on the content of a theory, and this becomes all the more compelling when I juxtapose several theories that deal with a similar subject but are radically different from one another. More specifically, by probing into the philosophical significance of the subliminal mind along the bias of its access, I will argue that these three different formulations correspond to different models of "transcendence" and "immanence." By looking into these two principles, I hope to provide some insight regarding how their methods of theorization contribute to achieving their objectives. In other words, I am claiming that how the three theories are supposed to be used is closely related to the two principles operative in them.

Let us be clear what transcendence and immanence mean in this context. Here "transcendence" is defined broadly as "that (A) to which reference can be made only by denying that the referent lies within the boundaries of the world of phenomena (B) but to which (A) the explanation of the world of phenomena (B) has to resort, not vice versa."[1] Plato's conceptualization of form in relationship to matter is a prototype of transcendence. To apply this definition to our discussion of the various formulations of the subliminal mind, when the subliminal mind is claimed to be a transcendence, it should be understood as saying that the subliminal mind lies outside the boundary of consciousness, which is the world of phenomena in the mental region, and that our conscious life is explained by resorting to the subliminal mental activities. Immanence is the opposite of transcendence, defined as that to which reference can be made by allowing the referent to lie within the boundaries of the world of phenomena wherein a two-way, or reciprocal, dependency exists between them. Therefore, when the subliminal mind is said to be an immanence, this should be understood as meaning that the subliminal mind lies within the boundary of consciousness and that they explain each other.

The main objective of my study here is to reveal the *modus operandi* of the three theories respectively—the underlying principles operative in the theorizations à la transcendence and immanence— by problematizing access to the subliminal mental activities. My argument is that a major portion of Jung's formulation of the subliminal mind resorts to the principle of transcendence, Freud's to both immanence and transcendence, and Xuan Zang's to immanence. Transcendence, represented by Jung's formulation of the collective unconscious, has been the dominant mode of reasoning in the mainstream Western intellectual tradition. Freud's formulation, which blurs the boundary between transcendence and immanence, is a challenge to this, and immanence characterizes the mode of reasoning in the mainstream Buddhist tradition. I will reveal that the involvement of the transcendence principle in Freud's and Jung's theories, to different extents, renders any direct access to the unconscious impossible, whereas Xuan Zang's immanence-based formulation of the subliminal mind makes direct access possible within his framework. I will begin with Freud.

Transcendence/Immanence and the Mode of Access in Freud's Conceptualization of the Unconscious

We learned in Chapter Three that there is a major revision in Freud's conceptualization of the mind from his earlier topographical system to his later structural system. The topographical system is laid out in his monumental work, *The Interpretation of Dreams,* wherein the mind is stratified into the unconscious, preconscious, and conscious. The structural system is best summarized in his *The Ego and the Id,* published in 1923. In this system the mind is structured into id, ego, and superego. Let us first examine the topographical system.

The topographical system is designed to explain a key insight in Freud's psychoanalytic framework, that is, a dream is the fulfillment of an unrecognized wish. An important element in this system is the preconscious, which is postulated as a filter, as it were, that lies between consciousness and the unconscious. Therefore, by definition, the unconscious cannot become consciousness: The unconscious "has no access to consciousness *except via the preconscious,* in passing through which its excitatory process is obliged to submit to modifications" (Freud 1965, 580, original italics). The unconscious that "enters" consciousness is already modified by the preconscious. By resorting to such a framework, Freud is able to explain that a dream is the fulfillment of a wish due to the activities of the unconscious and that the unrecognizability of such a wish is due to the censoring function of the preconscious. The wish becomes recognizable only through the methods of interpretation prescribed by Freud's psychoanalysis. The ideal scenario is to have a psychoanalyst who is trained in Freud's theory interpret the dream. The unrecognizability of the wish expressed in a dream points to the fact that there is no direct access to the unconscious, and psychoanalysis via a trained analyst provides the only access, albeit an indirect one.

The lack of direct access to the realm of the unconscious will be carried into Freud's later structural formulation, which divides the human mind into the id, ego, and superego. Here the ego is envisioned as part of the id. This means that the ego grows out of the id or that the id is the ground of the ego. As I pointed out in Chapter Three, this marks a fundamental shift in Freud's conceptualization of the unconscious. That is, in the structural system, the id is more fundamental than the ego in that the latter grows out of the former; in the topographical system, however, consciousness is more primary than the unconscious in that the latter is the result of the repressive function of the former. This shift in the primacy of consciousness to the unconscious in Freud's thought can also be seen in the fact that consciousness in the structural system has to presuppose the unconscious, instead of the other way around as is the case in the topographical system. The significance of such a shift becomes even clearer when it is seen from the perspective of the change in the modes of reasoning the shift represents. Therefore let us take a look at how the modes of reasoning à la transcendence and immanence operative in Freud's formulations of the subliminal mind have impacted the way the relationship between consciousness and the unconscious is conceptualized in his two systems.

Freud is ambiguous with respect to the role transcendence and immanence play in his theories. First of all, the principle of immanence is clearly involved in Freud's formulation of the unconscious, whether in his earlier topographical system or the later structural system. That is, in both systems there is a mutual dependency between consciousness and the unconscious. They define each other: The unconscious stores the forgotten or repressed contents of consciousness, while consciousness is heavily influenced by unconscious activities, most of which are out of the control of consciousness. Thus the relationship between the two is reciprocal, instead of a one-way dependency that would be indicative of transcendence.

What makes Freud's conceptualization of the unconscious challenging, however, is that it also involves the transcendence principle. This is manifested in the lack of direct access, *in principle,* to the unconscious as such in Freud's formulation, which renders the unconscious outside the realm of consciousness. According to Freud, there is no direct access to the unconscious: *"The interpretation of dreams is the royal road to a knowledge of the unconscious activities of the mind"* (1965, 647, original italics). In other words, access to the unconscious is gained only through interpretation. This is tantamount to claiming that access to the unconscious is achieved through reasoning only. If access to the unconscious is achieved only through interpretation and analysis, it renders the unconscious a product of rational postulation or hypothesis, not unlike the Platonic form in *this* regard. Thus conceived, the unconscious is clearly a transcendence with respect to consciousness: It is outside of the realm of consciousness but explains our conscious life. However, the crucial difference between Plato's form/matter relationship and Freud's unconscious/consciousness relationship is that in Plato's case the relationship between form and matter is that of one-way dependency with the latter depending on the former, a normative scenario of transcendence; on the other hand, Freud's unconscious is not a simple transcendence with respect to consciousness, but also an immanence in the sense that the relationship between the unconscious and consciousness is a reciprocal dependency.

There is, however, a subtle but significant difference between Freud's earlier topographical system and his later structural system with respect to the roles played by transcendence and immanence principles in them. Even though both systems deny direct access to the unconscious, the relationship between consciousness and the unconscious changes—and the significance of this change—is better appreciated when seen in light of the principles of transcendence and immanence. That is, Freud is leaning more toward the transcendence principle in his structural (as opposed to his topographical) formulation of the unconscious.

The mutual dependency of consciousness and the unconscious in Freud's topographical system is more pronounced than that of the ego and id in his later system. (I will deal with the superego later.)

To be more specific, in the topographical system, the unconscious stores the repressed or forgotten content of what used to be in consciousness, but it also influences the activities of consciousness. The content of the unconscious as the repressed or forgotten conscious materials was known prior to its sinking into the unconscious; this is indicative of the dependency of the unconscious on consciousness in the former's acquisition of its content; consciousness has no direct access to such content once it sinks into the unconscious, due to the censoring function of the preconscious. However, in the structural system, the ego grows out of the id. Even as they influence each other, some part of the id remains unknown because it always contains something that was never present in the ego. In other words, a certain part of the id becomes somewhat independent of the ego. It is therefore clear that the id is a stronger transcendence with respect to the ego in Freud's structural system when compared with the transcendence of the unconscious with respect to consciousness in his topographical system.

To recap what we have discussed so far, the lack of direct access to the unconscious points to its transcendent nature in both the topographical and the structural systems; on the other hand, the reciprocal relationship between the two in both systems is also indicative of the operation of the immanence principle. This means that transcendence and immanence in both of Freud's systems are rather peculiar. The unconscious is not strictly immanent with respect to consciousness due to the lack of direct access to the former by the latter in principle; neither is the unconscious strictly transcendent with respect to consciousness due to the mutual dependence of the two. In fact the line between transcendence and immanence is blurred in Freud's theories.

Let us call the relationship between consciousness and the unconscious in Freud's topographical system a case of "asymmetrical immanence": on the one hand, the basic relationship between the unconscious and consciousness in the topographical system is that of immanence, in the sense that the unconscious stores the forgotten or repressed contents of consciousness while consciousness is heavily influenced by subliminal mental activities, most of which are out of the control of consciousness; on the other hand, the unconscious cannot be accessed directly by consciousness, rendering the former a transcendence with respect to the latter.

Let us call the relationship between the id and ego in Freud's structural system "asymmetrical transcendence"; here Freud is clearly appealing more to transcendence in his formulation of the unconscious, or id. However, the relationship is asymmetrical due to the fact that the ego still retains its impact on the id even though such an impact is significantly diminished when compared with the impact consciousness exerts on the unconscious in Freud's topographical system. In a word, "asymmetrical" is used to indicate the presence of the other principle within the dominant principle. That is, asymmetrical immanence indicates the presence of transcendence in the predominantly immanence-oriented conceptualization, whereas asymmetrical transcendence denotes the presence of immanence in the predominantly transcendence-oriented conceptualization.

The operative principle behind Freud's conceptualization of the collective unconscious, the superego, in his structural system is also consistent with what lies behind the conceptualization of the id, namely asymmetrical transcendence. As we learned in Chapter Three, the formation of the superego results from the internalization of parental authority. When the external restraint is internalized, "the super-ego takes the place of the parental agency and observes, directs and threatens the ego in exactly the same way as earlier the parents did with the child" (Freud 1964, 77). Furthermore,

> a child's super-ego is in fact constructed on the model not of its parents but of its parents' super-ego; the contents which fill it are the same and it becomes the vehicle of tradition and of all the time-resisting judgments of value which have propagated themselves in this manner from generation to generation. (84)

Thus the superego represents the vehicle of tradition, and tradition in this case specifically refers to the moral and religious values of a society and culture that are the achievement of human civilization.

The relationship between the superego vis-à-vis tradition and the ego vis-à-vis an individual is that of asymmetrical transcendence because the former shapes and defines the latter while the latter exerts very little impact on the former—save for those individuals who are able to reshape the received tradition. Given the very possibility of a tradition being reshaped by certain powerful individuals and to a much lesser extent by average people, the transcendence of tradition is not absolute but asymmetrical in the sense defined above.

This asymmetrical transcendence in Freud's conceptualization of the collective unconscious vis-à-vis the superego is in sharp contrast with Jung's formulation of the collective unconscious. As we will see presently, Freud's earlier asymmetrical immanence and later asymmetrical transcendence evolve into a full-blown transcendence in certain prominent aspects of Jung's psychology, especially in his formulation of the collective unconscious vis-à-vis archetype. It will be apparent to us that transcendence, to the exclusion of immanence, dictates Jung's conceptualization of archetype. The contrast between Freud and Jung is sharpest here and most relevant to our discussion; I will now turn to the concept of archetype according to Jung's formulation.

Transcendence in Jung's Conceptualization of Archetype

As we learned in our brief examination in Chapter Three, Jung's psychology is known for its schematization of the personal unconscious and the collective unconscious. Although there is a significant overlap between Jung and Freud in their formulations of the unconscious due to their common interest and their personal and professional ties, it is with the conceptualization of archetype, among other ideas, that Jung took a wide turn away from Freud and made his mark on the study of the unconscious.

Jung's formulation of the personal unconscious is a clear case of asymmetrical transcendence. As we learned in Chapter Three, according to Jung, the personal unconscious consists of feeling-toned complexes (1969a, 42). The core of a complex has a high degree of autonomy and independence from the ego consciousness, whereas its associated elements are more receptive to influence from the ego consciousness. This means that transcendence dominates Jung's conceptualization of the personal unconscious while immanence retains some lingering influence, a typical case of asymmetrical transcendence, as we saw previously.

If Jung's formulation of the personal unconscious resorts to asymmetrical transcendence, we will see that his theory of the collective unconscious is a case of full-blown transcendence. Because it is to the collective unconscious, especially to the concept of archetype, that Jung devoted much of his creative energy and it is what Jung is particularly known for, I will look into this part of his theory in some detail. My focus will be on the way Jung constructs his system, examining the role played by the principle of transcendence in his conceptualization of the archetype. By focusing on the concept of archetype in Jung's psychology, I am drawing attention to the part of his psychology that is drastically different from Freud's. In highlighting their differences, I will show that Jung's formulation of the collective unconscious follows decidedly the principle of transcendence. That is, in Jung's formulation of archetype, transcendence plays an exclusive role—unlike its more ambiguous involvement in Freud's theorization.

As we saw in Chapter Three, in Jung's mature theory, the collective unconscious consists of instincts and archetypes (Jung 1969b, 133–134). However, the concept of instinct is eventually subsumed under the concept of archetype in constituting the collective unconscious. Hence the concept of archetype is essential to Jung's postulation of the collective unconscious. According to Jung, archetypes are a priori forms in the unconscious: They are "factors and motifs that arrange the psychic elements into certain images, characterized as archetypal, but in such a way that *they can be recognized only from the effect they produce.* They exist preconsciously, and presumably they form the structural dominants of the psyche in general" (quoted in Jacobi 1959, 31, original italics). They "are not disseminated only by tradition, language, and migration, but . . . they can release spontaneously, at any time, at any place, and without any outside influence" (Jung 1969b, 79). Archetypes are forms that preexist individuals and are inherited by individuals. Jung is rather unabashedly univocal about the involvement of the transcendence principle in his conceptualization of the archetype.

In order to stress the a priori nature of the archetype, Jung compares it to the Platonic form (1969b, 75) and the Kantian categories (1969a, 136).[2] This is indicative of his oscillation between a metaphysical position (Platonic) and a transcendental position (Kantian) on the archetype.[3] He also insists that "the concept of the collective unconscious is neither a speculative nor a philosophical but an empirical matter" (1969b, 44).[4]

However, Jung's notion of archetype is closer to Platonic forms than to the Kantian categories in an important sense. The ultimate Platonic forms of the true, the good, and the beautiful are teleological, representing the perfection toward which all natural beings strive; by contrast, the Kantian categories of causality, et cetera, are descriptive forms that constitute the limits of rationality. Jung postulates the notion of archetype, as the form of the collective unconscious, in order to explain spiritual development, what he calls "individuation." The teleological orientation of archetypes echoes that of the Platonic forms.

Jung emphatically insists that archetypes are only formal and are empty of contents, hence archetypes per se can never be known as such; they can only be recognized through what Jung calls "archetypal images/representations," which are pictorial representations of archetypes. Therefore, he draws a distinction between an archetype per se and an archetypal representation. By making such a distinction, Jung hopes to achieve two goals: retain the hereditary nature of archetypes and account for the inevitable differences in our experience of the same archetypes from individual to individual and from group to group. That is, only archetypes are inherited, but archetypal representations, which are what we actually experience in encountering archetypes, vary among individuals as well as groups.[5] The positing of archetypal representations is apparently an attempt to bridge the gap between the empirical and the metaphysical in his system.

Jung's postulation of archetype represents a transcendent "turn," as it were, in his psychology, and as a result, the concept of archetype, key to his theory, becomes a decidedly metaphysical notion despite his disclaimer that an archetype is neither speculative nor philosophical but empirical. The archetype is formal; it transcends the realm of personal experiences. Hence an archetype per se is not accessible, by definition. Nevertheless, it is both that which governs our mental life and that toward which our mental life is oriented.[6] The relationship between archetypes and our mental life is that of one-way dependency, with the latter dependent upon the former but not vice versa. The transcendent nature of the archetype cannot be more pronounced.

To sum up, our study of Freud and Jung has demonstrated the changing roles transcendence and immanence play in their respective systems. Between the early Freud, the later Freud, and the mature Jung we can clearly see an increasing reliance on transcendence in their theoretical efforts, from asymmetrical immanence to asymmetrical transcendence in Freud and from asymmetrical transcendence in Jung's theorization of the personal unconscious to the exclusive operation of the transcendence principle in his formulation of archetype. This increasing reliance on transcendence in the conceptualization of the unconscious renders the unconscious less and less accessible by consciousness. Interestingly, however, the reliance on transcendence is not shared by Xuan Zang's conceptualization of the subliminal consciousness, to which I now turn.

Immanence in Xuan Zang's Conceptualization of *Ālayavijñāna*

If the way of reasoning governs the mode of access in the formulation of the subliminal consciousness, the involvement of the transcendence principle in Freud and Jung makes direct access impossible within their systems. Instead, only indirect access, that is, through interpretation and analysis, is provided. In this section, I will argue that Xuan Zang conceptualizes *ālayavijñāna* (storehouse consciousness) by appealing to the principle of immanence alone, and I will look into how the operation of the immanence principle renders possible direct access to the subliminal consciousness in Xuan Zang's system.

As we saw in Chapter Two, the conceptualization of *ālayavijñāna* is an attempt by Yogācāra Buddhists to account for the sense of the self and the continuity of our experience. There is a clear reciprocity between *ālayavijñāna* and the other forms of consciousness in Yogācāra theory. We have learned that, according to the *CWSL*, the eight consciousnesses in the Yogācāra scheme can be viewed in terms of a threefold process: the retribution process, the self-cogitation process, and the cognition of objects other than the self (Xuan Zang, 96). The retribution process refers to the subliminal activities of the storehouse consciousness; the self-cogitation process takes the storehouse consciousness as its inner self and cogitates on the ground of such a "self"; and the process of cognition of "external" objects refers to the activities of the first six consciousnesses—the five sensory consciousnesses and the sense-centered consciousness that coordinates the activities of the five.

As Xuan Zang points out, the three processes are simultaneous and intricately intertwined with one another:

> We cannot say that in terms of their natures the eight consciousnesses are definitely the same. This is because their activities, their dependent conditions, and their associated qualities are different. Also when one ceases, the others might not. And they are different in terms of the perfuming [the seven consciousnesses] and the perfumed [the eighth consciousness]. Nor are they definitely different. As a *sūtra* explains,

the eight consciousnesses are like water and waves that cannot be
differentiated from each other, because, if they were definitely different, they could not be as cause and effect to one another. (498)

This is a crucial observation with respect to the relationship among
the eight consciousnesses: they cannot be separated from one
another, or as Brian Brown puts it, the relationship between the storehouse consciousness and the other seven consciousnesses is that of
"the differentiated identity" (209). Such an inseparability, or differentiated identity, between them is a clear indication that no form of
consciousness is outside of, therefore transcendent to, the others;
the nature of their relationship is that of immanence, and as such
they require each other to explain themselves.

We have seen that the relationship among the eight consciousnesses in the Yogācāra system is governed by four kinds of conditions: *hetupratyaya* (condition *qua* cause), *samanantarapratyaya*
(condition *qua* antecedent), *ālambanapratyaya* (condition *qua* perceived object), and *adhipatipratyaya* (condition *qua* contributory factor). Without having to repeat the details of our discussion in Chapter
Two regarding the intricate relationship among the eight consciousnesses, it should be clear that the relationship between the storehouse consciousness and the other seven consciousnesses is reciprocal.
This is an unequivocal case of immanence in operation.

However, in light of our discussion of Freud and Jung, we must
ask the more important and interesting question: Can there be direct
access to the storehouse consciousness as Xuan Zang conceptualizes
it? The answer to that is yes. As he clearly states in the *CWSL*,

> The Bodhisattvas, who have embarked upon the path of insight and
> have achieved true vision, are called "superior Bodhisattvas." They
> can reach *ālayavijñāna* and understand it. (192–194)

An accomplished Yogācāra practitioner, a Bodhisattva, who has
achieved an unimpeded penetration into reality in her meditation
practice, is able to access the storehouse consciousness herself
directly. Let us take a closer look at how the immanence principle
makes possible direct access to the subliminal consciousness in Xuan
Zang's Yogācāra system.

Direct access to the subliminal consciousness becomes a problem
only when the subliminal consciousness is regarded as that which
is outside the domain of consciousness (in the more restricted sense

of the term) due to the involvement of the transcendence principle. This means that, to some extent, the problematic of access is created by the way the unconscious is defined by Freud and Jung, perpetuated by their modes of reasoning involving transcendence. If the subliminal consciousness is not so defined, direct access to it is no longer a problem because the subliminal consciousness, thus conceived, is no longer considered a separate mental region to begin with.

The immanence-based formulation of the mind does not divide our mental activities into separate regions or realms, with a blocking mechanism lying between them, thus rendering the subliminal consciousness transcendent to, or outside of, the region of consciousness. Rather, the immanence-based conception of the mind regards our mental life as an integrated domain with varying degrees of awareness of various aspects of its activities. The question for Xuan Zang is how to increase the level of awareness and realization of various activities in our mind. Put simply, access to the subliminal consciousness for Xuan Zang means an experiential access vis-à-vis the increasing level of awareness and realization of the mental activities undetected within the everyday mode of experience. Such access is direct, unlike the indirect access through interpretation and analysis provided in Freud and Jung.

As Brian Brown aptly puts it, in the Yogācāra conception "[h]uman consciousness is by nature the processive advance to an ever more perfect *self*-consciousness in which it finally awakens to the plenitude of its identity with the *Ālayavijñāna*" (225–226, original italics).[7] Except for the somewhat Hegelian undertone in his take on *ālaya-vijñāna*, Brown's interpretation of the Yogācāra enlightenment process as the increasing awareness of *ālayavijñāna* and the ultimate realization of the consciousness-only nature of reality brought about by such an awareness offers some valuable insights into the immanent character of Xuan Zang's formulation of the storehouse consciousness. According to the *CWSL*, this increasing awareness and realization of the storehouse consciousness, namely the direct experiential access to the storehouse consciousness, is accomplished through Yogācāra Buddhist meditation practice.

As I pointed out at the outset of our discussion of Yogācāra Buddhist philosophy, this school, as its name suggests, is particularly known, even within the Buddhist meditation tradition, for its overwhelming preoccupation with the possibility of awakening and lib-

eration through vigorous meditation practices. In fact, the very origination of the concept of *ālayavijñāna,* as we learned in Chapter One,
is closely related to the theoretical necessity of accounting for certain aspects of Buddhist meditation. Therefore, it is only natural for
Xuan Zang to appeal to the experience of meditation to provide direct
access to the storehouse consciousness.[8] Because the discussion of
Yogācāra meditation in the *CWSL* involves many technical and doctrinal considerations that have little relevance to my purpose here,
I will briefly summarize the meditation process without going into
great detail.

According to the *CWSL,* in order to transform ignorance to
enlightenment, a Yogācāra practitioner needs to go through five stages
in her meditation practice: moral provision, intensified effort, penetrating understanding, sustained cultivation, and ultimate realization (664). In the stage of moral provision, the practitioner acquires
and accumulates right knowledge pertaining to the characteristic
nature of consciousness, cultivating a deep faith and understanding
of such knowledge (666). In the stage of intensified effort, the practitioner is able to overcome the belief in subject/object duality, thus
developing the right view of non-dual reality (ibid.). In the stage of
penetrating understanding, the practitioner can penetrate and com-
prehend such a non-dual reality in her meditation experience (ibid.).
In the stage of sustained cultivation, she continues to cultivate what
she has accomplished in the previous stage, while gradually cleans-
ing the remaining two mental barriers, *kleśāvaraṇa* (the barrier of
vexing passions) and *jñeyāvaraṇa* (the barrier hindering supreme
knowledge and enlightenment) (ibid.). In the last stage, ultimate realization, she completely overcomes the two barriers and reaches complete enlightenment; she is now able to strive for the enlightenment
of all sentient beings (ibid.).

In a nutshell, the first stage is the preparatory stage for a practitioner to acquire the necessary knowledge and cultivate the moral
requirements for the practice; in the second stage she starts to put
her knowledge to use by embodying the knowledge; in the third stage,
she experiences the non-dual reality in her meditation, verifying the
knowledge she has acquired; in the fourth stage, the meditative experience deepens with sustained effort on her part to overcome the
residue of the two barriers; and the last stage is the complete overcoming of the two barriers and final enlightenment. The third stage
marks the critical point in the practitioner's meditation because it

is at this stage she comes to an experiential awakening to reality, and the last two stages serve to deepen this experience. It is also in the third stage that she realizes *ālayavijñāna*.

The Yogācāra meditation practice is essentially a process of gradually overcoming two mental barriers that obstruct the non-dual reality, comprehending the world as consciousness-only (*vijñaptimātratā*), and thus transforming ignorance into enlightenment. Of the two mental barriers, *kleśāvaraṇa* is given rise to by the belief in the reality of an independent, autonomous ego (*ātmagrāha*). *Jñeyāvaraṇa* stems from adherence to the notion of discrete, self-subsistent entities or things (*dharmagrāha*); it is "any moment of empirical consciousness that fails to perceive the mutual interdependence of all phenomena in their ultimate dependence as the forms of absolute consciousness (*Ālayavijñāna*)" (Brown, 213). As Xuan Zang points out, "*Karma*, the two *grāha*s, *saṃsāric* existences, none of these is separated from consciousness because they are in their nature mind and its concomitant activities, *cittas-caittas*" (582). It is clear that these two mental barriers, generated by the attachment of an independent self and subsistent entities, are the very cause of the wheel of suffering, *saṃsāra*, and an obstruction to enlightenment.

It is important to point out, however, that the two barriers mentioned here are not structural in nature. Rather they refer to the defiled activities of the mind that can be purified or transformed in the course of meditation practice. In fact, the term "*varaṇa*," translated as "barrier," means concealing, obscuring, hiding, and veiling; this points to the process nature of the barrier, or the activities of mental defilement in this connection. More specifically, such defilements refer to the dualistic activities of consciousness that assert an independent and autonomous self on the one hand and discrete and self-subsistent entities on the other. Dualism gives rise to attachment, which is the primary cause of suffering according to the orthodox Buddhist teaching because attachment operates under the illusion that there is a real self that is attached to real entities.

Therefore, in the Yogācāra teaching, meditation practice is a form of purification that is geared toward overcoming the pernicious dualism underlying all of pre-enlightenment experience. In this consideration, the two barriers, which are the causes of subject/object dualism, are dispositional, not structural, and as such are subject to being purified and transformed. If the barriers were structural, like the Freudian preconscious, which can never be overcome *in princi-*

ple, the storehouse consciousness would be rendered a transcendent entity or process. There is no concept of a structural barrier that blocks the entrance to the storehouse consciousness. It is just a lack of awareness of the subtlety of the mental process that characterizes the storehouse consciousness. Meditation is essentially a practice that is designed to help the practitioner overcome the dispositional defilements that characterize our everyday consciousness and transform everyday consciousness into an enlightened mind by removing the two barriers, the root of which is subject/object dualism. Put simply, meditation clears the mind in a way that renders possible access to the non-dual reality that is "veiled" by the dispersing activities of the everyday mind.

Furthermore, we should be reminded that, in Xuan Zang's account, the storehouse consciousness ceases to exist *as ālayavijñāna* once the practitioner reaches enlightenment. As we discussed in Chapter Four, for Xuan Zang enlightenment is not contained within the storehouse consciousness while the seeds of enlightenment are contained in the collective dimension of the storehouse consciousness. In light of our discussion here, the Yogācāra enlightenment must not be understood as something that exists separate from everyday mental life. Rather it should be interpreted as a *new way* to experience the world, that is, non-dualistically, when the two mental barriers are removed through vigorous meditation practice. In other words, enlightenment is the very transformation of the way we experience the world, from the dual mode to the non-dual mode. Enlightenment is that very transformation; it does not point to a separate mental region.

To sum up, this chapter concludes my comparative study of the three formulations of the subliminal mind by Freud, Jung, and Xuan Zang. Here I have focused on the how of the three theories, namely how their differences came to be embodied, by examining their different modes of reasoning à la the roles transcendence and immanence play in them. I have used the various access to the subliminal mind each theory allows in its system as a clue to reveal the role played by transcendence and immanence in the three theories.

In a way, it is necessary for Freud and Jung to deny direct access to the unconscious, thus saving the critical space for their own theories to be appealed to in interpreting the unconscious. More importantly, indirect access leaves room for analysts trained in their systems to interpret the messages the unconscious conveys to their patients. As Gay Watson observes, "All contemporary psychother-apies concur in the importance of the presence of the therapist and see the relationship with the client as central to the healing process" (250). By contrast, for Xuan Zang, direct access is crucial in a Buddhist practitioner's effort to realize the source of ignorance and delusion, which characterize our everyday mental life, to transform such a ground of ignorance and delusion, and hence to reach the Buddhist awakening. However, this does not preclude a teacher from pointing a disciple in the right direction. Nevertheless, it is the practitioner's own immediate experience that counts in reaching awakening, not someone else's interpretation. As we saw in Chapter Four, there is a difference between listening to an ordinary teacher's instruction and experiencing the Buddha's preaching directly in the course of deep meditation—the former being the impure teaching, the latter the pure. In light of our discussion in this chapter, we can see that the former refers to interpretations and instructions regarding Buddhist doctrines and practices whereas the latter refers to the direct experience of awakening.

The purpose of this chapter, as well as the rest of the book, is not to demonstrate which theory is better in dealing with specific issues. Rather, I have hoped to show how differences in the purported usages of the three paradigms are aided by the different modes of reasoning they appeal to. If the traditional study of the subliminal mind tends to focus on how our experience informs our reasoning, it is my hope that this chapter has helped to expose to what extent our experience is shaped by our reasoning.

CONCLUSION

AN EMERGING NEW WORLD
AS A NEW CONTEXT

THIS BOOK IS AN EXERCISE in comparative thought on the notion of the subliminal mind as it moves through a series of contexts. I have shunned the question of the actual nature of the subliminal mind. Instead, my focus has been how discussions on the actual nature of the subliminal mind have been formulated and defended within different cultural, historical, and philosophical contexts. Indeed, we have seen that the question concerning the actual nature of the subliminal mind cannot be totally detached from such contextual settings, without which the question itself does not even make sense. In other words, there is no meta-context, as it were, that is free from specific cultural, historical, philosophical, and religious influences.

This study has taken us from the context of seventh-century Yogācāra Buddhism to that of twentieth-century modern psychology and eventually to the unfolding contemporary context of increasing cross-cultural dialogical engagement. I began by examining how the notion of the subliminal mind has been thematized within the different cultural and historical settings of Yogācāra Buddhism, Freud's psychoanalysis, and Jung's analytic psychology. I then put the three together in a new setting of dialogical engagement to investigate their presuppositions and reveal the different paradigms of personhood, as well as the different modes of reasoning operative within the theoretical frameworks. My attempt to engage the three theories of the subliminal mind has focused on three aspects of the theories: content (the what), objective (the why), and mode of reasoning (the how). My overarching assumption is that the what, why, and how are integral components of the articulated theory itself, contributing to its merits as well as its limitations. I closely examined what the theories' differences are, why they are so different, and how their different modes of reasoning help them to accomplish their different objectives.

As we have learned, the Yogācāra conceptualization of *ālaya-vijñāna* à la Xuan Zang's work achieves two purposes: to overcome a certain tension among established Buddhist doctrines and to make Buddhist enlightenment an attainable goal. In the case of the first purpose, we have seen that there is a tension in the attempt to conceptualize continuity, given the Buddhist rejection of substance/identity. Such a tension is played out in the Buddhist struggle to reconcile Buddha's key teachings, such as no-self versus *karma*, impermanence versus dependent origination, et cetera. To resolve these doctrinal tensions, Xuan Zang maneuvers within the boundary of the orthodox Buddhist position of non-substantialization and non-reification, as clearly laid out in such central Buddhist principles as *śūnyatā*. His strategy is to explain away any idea of substance or identity by resorting to the idea of continuity. In doing so, Xuan Zang renders a manifested *dharma* a moment of consciousness that is grounded in a continuous series of subliminal flux. The idealist tendency in the development of Buddhist philosophical deliberations, culminating in the Yogācāra system, makes the dharmic moment a moment of consciousness, hence prioritizing human subjectivity as the basis of our experience. In the case of the second purpose, *ālayavijñāna* is thematized as the ground that supports the vigorous effort by a Buddhist practitioner during deep meditative states wherein all discernible activities of consciousness are brought to a halt. In other words, it is the ground of our existence.

Due to its subliminal nature, *ālayavijñāna* has often been compared to the notion of the unconscious as developed in the West by Freud and Jung. Indeed, as I pointed out in the introduction, the Western interpretation of *ālayavijñāna* is the culmination of the search for a Buddhist notion of the unconscious. To be sure the concept of the unconscious has colored the effort of modern Western scholarship to approach and appreciate *ālayavijñāna*. However, my comparative study of Xuan Zang, Freud, and Jung has shown that the Yogācāra notion of *ālayavijñāna* and the unconscious in modern psychology operate within vastly different paradigms.

First of all, in terms of thematic content, the three formulations of the subliminal consciousness drastically differ from one another.

For Xuan Zang, *ālayavijñāna* follows, above all, the principle of continuity; it is a continuum governed by the rule of dependent origination. For Freud in his earlier topographical system, the unconscious is the land of desires and chaos, and any order comes from the external world; in his later structural system the id takes over the function previously assigned to the unconscious in the topographical system, and the order in the structure of the ego is brought about by the external world via a powerful internalized agent, the superego. For Jung the unconscious has a personal and a collective dimension, with the former accounting for chaotic desires and the latter primarily for the possibility of spiritual transformation.

We have learned that three theories schematize three kinds of persons. Indeed, these images of personhood have set the paradigmatic parameters within which Xuan Zang, Freud, and Jung construct their respective theoretical frameworks. Xuan Zang's theory schematizes a lone meditator striving toward awakening in the Yogācāra Buddhist sense of the term; Freud's theory schematizes a frantic fighter who, sandwiched between various inner and outer forces, is trying to survive in a hostile social environment; and Jung's theory schematizes a person embarking on a spiritual journey so as to fend off the tendency to withdraw into herself. In other words, underlying such thematic differences are three vastly different visions about what a human being is and/or should be. From Xuan Zang's Buddhist perspective, a human being is primarily an ignorant and deluded being whose only "way out" is through meditative practices prescribed by Yogācāra teachings. In Freud's case, a human being is essentially a sexual being whose spiritual effort is the operation of her survival instinct in a prohibitive society. For Jung, a human being is a combination of sexual and spiritual drives; an ideal person is one who embraces the Self through the individuation process.

Second, the differences in the thematic contents of the three formulations are closely related to the objectives Xuan Zang, Freud, and Jung purport to achieve in their theories. That is, they are addressing very different audiences with their different concerns. More specifically, Xuan Zang needs to explain, primarily to Buddhist practitioners, the root of delusion—the tenacious attachment to a self—which constitutes the ultimate barrier in their journey toward Buddhist awakening. Freud treats mostly neurotic patients who are caught between the inner and the outer worlds; his psychoanalysis gives him a powerful paradigm to explain the origin of depression, which is the main symptom of his neurotic patients. Jung helps his psychotic patients rebuild a larger sense of Self to overcome a severely impaired ability to deal with the world.

Lastly, I have argued that the vast differences in the contents and objectives among the three theories of the subliminal consciousness are perpetuated by the different modes of reasoning they resort to in their conceptualizations. We have looked into the different kinds of access to the subliminal mind the three theories provide: Xuan Zang offers direct access whereas Freud and Jung only allow indirect access. The issue of access is crucial because it is closely related to the ways Xuan Zang, Freud, and Jung intend their theories to be used. That is, the denial of direct access in Freud's and Jung's theories saves room for psychoanalysts in treating their patients; by contrast, direct access to the storehouse consciousness is considered a necessary condition for reaching Buddhist enlightenment according to Xuan Zang's Yogācāra theory. In discussing the different modes of access provided by the three theories, I have uncovered the different roles played by the principles of transcendence and immanence within them. Xuan Zang's conceptualization of the storehouse consciousness is characterized as an immanence-oriented formulation; Freud's formulation of the unconscious in his topographical system is characterized as asymmetrical immanence, while that of the id and superego in his structural system is seen as asymmetrical transcendence; Jung's theorization of the personal unconscious is characterized as asymmetrical transcendence and his theorization of the collective unconscious vis-à-vis archetype as transcendence. My argument is that there is a clear increase in the reliance on transcendence in the conceptualizations of the subliminal consciousness from Freud to Jung, resulting in a subliminal mind that is more and more distant from and less and less accessible to consciousness.

It is fair to maintain that all three theories have achieved an impressive level of success and influence, some more so than others, to the extent that each of them is able to provide an amazingly compelling and cogent framework to accomplish the objectives it sets for itself. However, it is undeniable that Freud's and Jung's conceptualizations of the unconscious enjoy a broad acceptance in the modern world. (Critiques of them are part and parcel of their wide currency.) As a result of the popularity of Freudian, Jungian, and other modern psychologies, the images of personhood schematized in them have become the norm of what a human person is taken to be in the modern world.

By bringing Xuan Zang's Yogācāra Buddhist conception of *ālayavijñāna* into the modern world and setting up a new dialogical context with Freud and Jung, I question many of the tacitly accepted norms regarding personhood. The vast difference between the theories should make it clear to us that all three are, to an extent, constructs, conditioned by their social, cultural, and historical contexts. That is, the theories of the subliminal mind, on the one hand, are conditioned by their contexts, while, on the other hand, they help to shape that very condition to a greater or lesser extent.

The wide gap between the articulated theories from different cultures demonstrates the shockingly different sensitivities these traditions have demonstrated toward different aspects of mental phenomena. Jack Engler records two instances of such sharply different problems Buddhism and modern psychology are sensitive to:

> When Burma's most renowned scholar and meditation master, Ven. Mahasi Sayadaw, visited America in 1980, he held a meeting with Western vipassana teachers about teaching. I remember Jack Kornfield asking in his intrepid way, "What do you do when students bring psychological problems to you?" There was a hurried consultation with the other sayadaws (teachers) and some evident confusion. He turned back to Jack and asked, "What psychological problems?" At the end of his U.S. visit, the sayadaw remarked on how many Western students seemed to be suffering from a range of problems he wasn't familiar with in Asia. A "new type of suffering," he said— "psychological suffering"! As is now well known, the Dalai Lama, too, on his first visits to the West, expressed shock at the degree of low self-esteem and self-hatred he encountered in Western practitioners. (2003, 45)

The gap between Buddhist and modern psychological sensibilities is indeed astonishing. This is consistent with Engler's observation regarding the different theoretical foci between Buddhism and modern psychology:

> Systematic Buddhist psychology (Abhidhamma) lists fifty-two mental factors defining discrete states of consciousness and their karmic value, including a range of afflictive emotions—greed, envy, hatred, doubt, worry, and so on. But there is no mention of sadness, except as a kind of unpleasant feeling that can tinge other mental states. There is no mention of depression, no mention of mental illness as

we understand it or of psychiatric disorders. No mention of personality, family, or relationship issues as such. (ibid.)

Clearly, in some of these areas traditional Buddhism can learn a great deal from modern psychology, not so much because modern psychology is more advanced, even though it might very well be the case. More importantly if Buddhism is to modernize and address a more Western-educated audience, it has to face these psychological issues with their underlying assumptions of what a human person is and should be as described in modern psychology and widely but tacitly accepted in the modern world. Buddhism needs to find ways to deal with these psychological issues and eventually help to transform some of the norms regarding human beings. As Harvey Aronson astutely points out, "Once we acknowledge our differences, it becomes possible for us to consider if there is something we wish to alter in our orientation. The more differences we can discern, the more opportunities we have to reflect on who we are and what we may wish to become" (xvi).

The Buddhist theory of the subliminal mind can show us a different way of theorizing human beings that takes ignorance seriously as the source of suffering. That is, Buddhism has a lot to contribute in bringing about healthy and enlightened living in the modern world once its way of looking at human beings is taken more seriously. For example, the Buddhist insight on how to live with suffering, instead of trying to escape from it, can be very helpful:

> In the Mahayana Buddhist tradition, for example, it is emphasized that samsara (i.e., conditioned, unenlightened existence, or the wheel of life and death) is no different from nirvana (i.e., the state of enlightenment in which all self-centered craving ceases to exist). In other words, there is no paradise or ideal state to be attained. There is only this world and this present moment, and enlightenment consists of the experiential realization of this. (Safran 2003b, 27–28)

Indeed, anybody who is familiar with Freud's theories can clearly see the resonance between the Buddhist and Freud's concern of how to live with suffering. As Gordon Pruett points out, "[I]t is supremely clear that both [the Buddha and Freud] hold that human existence is suffering in origin and nature" (9). However, the sources of our suffering are very different according to Buddhism and modern psychology à la Freud. In Jeremy Safran's words, "Always the icono-

clast, realist, and destroyer of illusions, Freud insisted on remind-
ing us that in the end, for all of our noble aspirations and preten-
sions, we are ultimately animals motivated by sexual and aggressive
instincts" (2003b, 27). This echoes the view of human nature
enshrined in modern science since Charles Darwin's theory of evolution. As Frank Sulloway points out, "Freud stands squarely within
an intellectual lineage where he is, at once, a principal scientific heir
of Charles Darwin and other evolutionary thinkers in the nineteenth
century and a major forerunner of the ethologists and sociobiolo-
gists of the twentieth century" (5). In contrast, many strands of Buddhism embrace a very different norm of human nature. For example,
as Richard Davidson and Anne Harrington observe:

> [T]he dominant note of the biobehavioral sciences in the West has
> been tragic-machismo: We find our origins in ancestors we call "killer
> apes," ponder our potential for violence, explore the genetic and bio-
> chemical bases of our capacity for selfishness, depression, and anx-
> iety. In contrast, Tibetan Buddhism has long celebrated the human
> potential for compassion, is dedicated to studying the scope, expres-
> sion, and training of compassionate feeling and action, and sees com-
> passion as a key to enduring happiness and, even more fundamentally,
> spiritual transformation. (v)

It should become apparent to us that by bringing different elements into this widening dialogical discourse, we are enriching the
pool of our human experiences as well as our conceptualization of
such experiences in sensitizing ourselves to some previously ignored
or simply unknown aspects of human experiences and potentials.
This helps traditions involved in the dialogue to expand their hori-
zons and inspires fresh effort to take these traditions to exciting new
territories. John Welwood, in developing what he calls "a psychology of awakening," puts it bluntly: "[A]*wakening needs psychology just as much as psychology needs awakening*" (xvi, original
italics) because "Western psychology has mostly neglected the spiritual domain, to its detriment, while the contemplative paths have
lacked an adequate understanding of psychological dynamics, which
inevitably play a major part in the process of spiritual development"
(ibid.). Psychological analysis without the search for spiritual growth
can lead to narcissistic self-obsession, while searching for spiritual
growth without proper psychological analysis can blind the spiritual effort of the psychological *dynamics*—not just structure—that

are involved. For example, Buddhism can learn a good deal from modern psychology on the analysis of psychological dynamics in the genesis of ignorance and attachment, both of which are regarded by Buddhism as the causes of suffering. On the other hand, modern psychology can take more seriously the Buddhist diagnosis of human ignorance as the cause of suffering so that the goal of psychological analysis can be reoriented toward some form of spiritual pursuit to free us from such ignorance instead of being overly obsessed with the mental dynamics as an end in itself. To be sure, there are many reasons that ignorance—in the broadly spiritual sense of the term—is not taken seriously in modern psychology, which regards itself as a largely scientific endeavor. To orient psychology too much toward spiritual ends might provoke the fear, quite often legitimately, of compromising the scientific integrity of psychology. But such a concern should not and need not cripple psychologists' efforts to cautiously accommodate spirituality in their work. As for what specific direction the mutual transformation between modern psychology and Buddhism will take, it is well beyond the moderate design of this book to speculate.

Before I conclude, I would like to reflect on the very context in which these three theories of the subliminal consciousness could be brought together. The contemporary world is an increasingly interconnected one. This interconnectedness of the emerging new world provides the ultimate new context that has been brewing the popularity of comparative approaches to ideas across cultural and historical boundaries. Cross-cultural dialogue and engagement point to a new reality, a new world, and a new context that traditional scholarship can no longer afford to ignore. Such an approach to ideas can be both enriching and risky, as I pointed out in the Introduction. Edward Said puts his finger on a very troubling foundation in the Orientalist endeavor in his acute observation of the pervasiveness of power and domination in this cross-cultural discourse. However, Said's totalizing characterization of Orientalism has been critiqued in recent scholarship. For example, Bernard Faure points out:

> Said is not sufficiently sensitive to the reasons that prevented earlier scholars, who were not always simply agents of Western imperialism, from escaping the trap of Oriental categories. He therefore fails to question the sociohistorical and epistemological changes that have

allowed him (and us, dwarves sitting on the shoulders of Orientalist giants) to perceive this trap. By denying all earlier attempts, within the framework of Orientalism, to question Orientalist values, Said forgets to acknowledge his own indebtedness to this tradition and the epistemological privilege that made his own vision possible. In other words, Said paradoxically shows us how easy it is to fall into methodological scapegoatism: in condemning individuals for failures that are ultimately owing to epistemological constraints, we tend to forget, just as the Orientalists did, that our vision is not entirely our own, that it is grounded in specific time and now. (6–7)

It is important that we recognize the very condition that underlies Said's critique of Orientalism. An effective way to deal with the problem Said has sensitized us to is not to discontinue the cross-cultural dialogical discourse altogether, but rather to treat it as part and parcel of the ongoing discourse. In other words, Said's critique of Orientalism is itself part of the Orientalist discourse. It is a clear indicator that Orientalism is not a homogeneous discourse, but rather that it has its own internal dynamics, which in the long run are able to correct its own problems so long as it is an open discourse. The very possibility of Said's critique is the accomplishment of the Orientalist discourse he critiques.

If I apply the above observation to my case, it should be abundantly clear that the fact that Xuan Zang, Freud, and Jung can be meaningfully brought together under the same rubric at all within a single work points to a world that is vastly different from the one the three used to live in. As stated in the Introduction, an important reason why the work of Xuan Zang, a seventh-century Chinese Yogācārin, is chosen to engage in a dialogue with modern psychology over that of contemporary Buddhist figures has to do with the interesting way the West has approached Buddhism. Yogācāra Buddhism, despite its lack of monastic affiliations in contemporary Asia, has attracted a significant amount of attention in contemporary Western scholarship on Buddhism. Historically, Yogācāra Buddhism represents a high point in the philosophical and psychological development of Mahāyāna Buddhism, and as such, it is very appealing to many Western scholars. Their detailed studies of this school have provided many significant insights into Buddhism in general, thus impacting the way Buddhism is received in the West as well as its engagement with other disciplines, including psychology.

Therefore, the study of Yogācāra Buddhism is not simply of historical and scholarly significance, but also of contemporary relevance in the mutual understanding of Buddhism and the West—in this case their radically different assumptions and understandings of human beings. Such a fruitful dialogue between the East and the West points to some of the constructive aspects of the Orientalist discourse. As J. J. Clarke comments:

> The perceived otherness of the Orient is not exclusively one of mutual antipathy, nor just a means of affirming Europe's triumphant superiority, but also provides a conceptual framework that allows much fertile cross-referencing, the discovery of similarities, analogies, and models; in other words, the underpinning of a productive hermeneutical relationship. It is not simply that the East has frequently been elevated to exalted heights of perfection and sublimity in European eyes—the 'romanticisation' hypothesis would serve to explain as much—but rather that this elevated status has been a source of creative tension between East and West, and has been exploited as a position from which to reappraise and reform the institutions and thought systems indigenous to the West. (1997, 27)

In other words, the Orientalist discourse, despite its limitations and problems, addresses an increasingly interdependent and interconnected world that obscures traditional boundaries, be they historical, cultural, religious, social, or philosophical. It is ultimately this emerging new world that sets the context for intellectual discourses, breaks down old barriers, and fosters an increasingly globalized world community.

NOTES

Introduction

1. Herbert Guenther proposes rendering *ālayavijñāna* as "foundational cognitiveness" (82).

2. The title of William Waldron's book, *The Buddhist Unconscious: The Ālayavijñāna in the Context of Indian Buddhist Thought,* suggests such a tendency, even though it deals with Western psychology only in passing.

3. It is interesting to note that this comparative section was dropped from Waldron's book, which is based on his dissertation.

4. To be fair to Waldron, the rest of his dissertation deals with exactly that context. However, it seems to matter little in the comparative section of his dissertation. In other words, the contexts of both Western psychology and Yogācāra Buddhism do not appear to be an integral part of the comparative study at all. Waldron justifies such a practice thusly: "[A]s with most comparative studies of different systems of thought, what we lose in context we gain in perspective" (1990, 405). I will argue here that contexts should be an integral part of the comparative study.

5. The term "Orientocentrism" is taken from Rubin 1996.

Chapter 1: The Origin of the Concept of *Ālayavijñāna*

1. For example, Lambert Schmithausen's *Ālayavijñāna: On the Origin and the Early Development of a Central Concept of Yogācāra Philosophy* is the most comprehensive study of the origin of *ālayavijñāna;* William Waldron's doctoral dissertation, "The Ālayavijñāna in the Context of Indian Buddhist Thought: The Yogācāra Conception of an Unconscious," is a solid study of *ālayavijñāna* in some canonical Indian Mahāyāna Buddhist scriptures and it complements Schmithausen's work. Waldron's book *The Buddhist Unconscious: The Ālayavijñāna in the Context of Indian Buddhist Thought* is based on his dissertation.

2. Steven Collins observes, "Throughout Buddhist thought, we must recognise this reaction of opposition to Brahmanical ideas and practices: the denial of self (*ātman*) is the most fundamental example, and symbol, of this attitude" (84).

3. The dates of Vasubandhu, the author of *Abhidharmakośa,* and his affiliation have been heatedly debated by scholars. According to Louis de La Vallée Poussin's

introduction to *Abhidharmkośa* (and whose French translation was in turn translated into English by Leo M. Pruden), Vasubandhu appears to be a different figure from the person known as Asaṅga's younger brother and a Yogācāra master (13–15). The Vasubandhu of the *Abhidharmakośa* is neither a Vaibhāṣika nor a Sarvāstivādin. He also has evident sympathies for Sautrāntikas and utilizes the opinions of Yogācārins, especially Asaṅga. However, *Abhidharmakośa* is a presentation of the Vaibhāṣika (a subschool of Sarvāstivāda) system, whereas the prose commentary *Abhidharmakośabhāṣyam* incorporates Vasubandhu's personal opinions, objections, and the positions of diverse schools and masters rejected by the Vaibhāṣika School (Poussin, 3–4). According to Stefan Anacker, who is willing to accommodate the traditional history of Buddhism, there is only one Vasubandhu who was an unorthodox Vaibhāṣikan (as reflected in the conflicting positions he adopts in the *Abhidharmakośa*, which is a Vaibhāṣika work, and in the autocommentary *Abhidharmakośabhāṣyam,* wherein he adopts the Sautrāntika position) before finally becoming a Yogācārin (1998, 17–18). Akira Hirakawa concurs with Anacker in maintaining that there is only one Vasubandhu, but he puts him in the fifth century (400–480) rather than the fourth (316–396) (Hirakawa, 137). In Erich Frauwallner's view, "Vasubandhu did not himself belong to the school of Sarvāstivādin, but to that of the Sautrāntika" (186). Although the *Abhidharmakośabhāṣyam* has generally been regarded as Vasubandhu's autocommentary to his *Abhidharmakośa,* some scholars are suspicious of this view (Anacker 1999, 516).

4. Steven Collins cautions scholars on accepting such a claim by Buddhists at face value. For Collins, scholars of Buddhism should see *anattā/anātman* as an ideological stance that is a social, intellectual, and soteriological strategy:

> Among those Buddhists who are concerned with, and pay explicit allegiance to, the doctrine of *anattā,* it provides orientation to social attitudes and behaviour (particularly *vis-à-vis* Brahmanical thought and the ritual priests who purveyed it), to conceptual activity in the intellectual life of Buddhist scholastics, and to soteriological activity in the life of virtuoso meditators. Thus, anyone who accepts the Buddhist virtuoso Path accepts submission to the strategy, and applies the modes of psychological analysis to himself which Buddhist doctrine recommends. Other religious traditions have different views and different strategies, and it is open to the syncretistic thinker to construct his own explanation of the 'reality' to which they all might refer. Scholarship must remain silent, content to show the logic and function of the particular forms of words which each tradition has chosen to embody its message.
>
> What scholarship can do is two-fold: first, to try to see what it was in the values and presuppositions of contemporary Indian religious thinking which allowed the Buddha to adopt this strategy; and second, to examine how it was and can be applied to the life and experience of the Buddhist monks. (78)

5. As Steven Collins observes, the opinions regarding the interpretation of the denial of the self could be classified into two groups: "those who refuse to believe that the 'real' doctrine taught by the Buddha is what the canonical teaching of *anattā* appears to be; and those who do accept that the doctrine of *anattā* is what the Buddha taught, and that it means what it appears to say, but who then deduce from it a final evaluation that Buddhism is 'nihilistic', 'pessimistic', 'world-' and 'life-denying', and so on" (7). However, this observation was made in the late 1970s and recent scholarship on Buddhism has generally come to accept the sec-

ond opinion while rejecting the evaluation of Buddhism as nihilistic, pessimistic, or life/world-denying.

6. Apparently, this is the Theravāda Buddhist interpretation of the *Suttas Piṭaka* (Werner, 95).

7. The following is a list of early Pāli scriptures in chronological order according to Hajime Nakamura (27):

1) Pārāyana (of the Suttanipāta);

2) a. The first four *vaggas* of the *Suttanipāta* and the first *Sagāthavagga* of *Saṃyutta-nikāya;*

    b. Itivuttaka, Udāna;

    c. The first eight *vaggas* of *Nidāna-saṃyutta* of the *Saṃyuttanikāya* II and *Vedalla* as mentioned by Buddhaghosa;

3) The twenty-eight *Jātaka*s found at Bharhut and *Abbhutadhamma* as mentioned by Buddhaghosa.

8. When David Kalupahana quotes this passage, he adopts the translation of "no-self" instead of "not-self" (1992, 69). However, the text here clearly favors the latter translation over the former.

9. The early Suttas refer to the *Sutta-piṭaka* of the Pāli Canon, the oldest sections of which are in the first four *Nikāya*s and parts of the fifth. They are known as the *Dīgha Nikāya, Majjhima Nikāya, Saṃyutta Nikāya, Aṅguttara Nikāya,* and *Khuddaka Nikāya* (Harvey, 10).

10. The term "experience" is used here in the most general sense.

11. Steven Collins summarizes the way personality is discussed within Buddhist discourse:

> In the conception of personality, Buddhist doctrine continues the [Upaniṣadic] style of analysis into non-valued impersonal constituents: indeed it is precisely the point of not-self that this is *all* that there is to human individuals. Examples are the two-fold 'name-and-form' (*nāma-rūpa);* the four-fold '(things) seen, heard, thought, cognised'; the very widespread and influential five 'categories' (*khandha*), that is 'body, feelings, perceptions, mental formations, consciousness'; the six-fold 'sense-bases' (*āyatana*), that is, the five senses plus 'mind'; and on into the huge variety of classifications found in Buddhist scholasticism *(Abhidhamma).* (82)

12. In the *Abhidharmakośabhāṣyam,* where Vasubandhu is defending the doctrine of *anātman* against the Personalists who advocate that the Buddha accepts the existence of a (metaphysical) self in his teaching, we do find arguments that are somewhat Kantian in that the Buddha is represented here as rejecting the *pudgala*, or self, as a possible object of cognition, thus discrediting the opponents' contention for the existence of such a self (1321).

13. This argument echoes Steven Collins' observation that in the non-Mahāyāna traditions the teaching of *anattā/anātman* "is a form of the denial of self which . . . has been of most importance in the ethical and psychological dynamics of spiritual education, while in other traditions, especially *Mahāyāna* schools, it has been much developed as a topic of epistemology and ontology, under the general name of 'Emptiness' *(śūnyatā)"* (116).

14. As Issai Funabashi observes, it is Sarvāstivāda—of which Vaibhāṣika (the position the *Abhidharmakośabhāṣyam* embraces) is a subschool—that links up

the two categorizations of *karma,* although in the early scriptures the relationship between the two is not entirely clear (38–39).

15. Vasubandhu does not explain why he regards speech as the ultimate action.

16. As Genjun Sasaki observes,

The basic concept of *kamma* in relation to *anatta* has two references, the one a prescriptive reference by way of theoretical reasoning to non-substantiality, the other an empirical cognitive reference by way of the ethical postulates of activity. It is the former of these two references which corresponds to the non-substantiality of *anatta;* it is the latter which is in compliance with the postulate for the positiveness of *anatta* (not-self). Thus, the two references of *kamma* have come to correspond to those of the *anatta* concept. This fact indicates that both concepts of *kamma* and *anatta* are actually a genuine unity: *kamma,* in turn, usually finds itself involved in the experience of not-self, which could, as we have seen, not appear but through *kamma; kamma* is first of all tested in *anatta; kamma* is not separated from not-self *(anatta),* but it is the categorical form of not-self. Therefore, we may say that the *kamma*-concept may be postulated but nothing else. The thought of not-self can then be interpreted as effectively as the concept of *kamma.* (39)

17. Nāgārjuna forcefully demonstrates the absurd consequences of reifying the agent as separate from actions in Chapter VIII of his *Mūlamadhyamakakārikā.*

18. This problematic of continuity can also be seen in terms of the tension between the momentariness of consciousness and the doctrine of dependent origination. As Paul Schweizer astutely observes:

[I]f consciousness is indeed momentary, then the principle of dependent origination, which was initially introduced to account for the apparent relation of coherence between successive instants of external existence, is now needed to support the logically prior notion that there is a relation of systematic dependence between the internal moments of consciousness. (82)

Here Schweizer challenges the Buddhist position that consciousness is momentary by pointing out its conflict with the Buddhist doctrine of dependent origination. Recognition of the regularity of dependent origination requires a coherent observing consciousness, and this coherency of observing consciousness can be warranted by nothing but the principle of dependent origination itself. If the observing consciousness is momentary, as Buddhists maintain, the succession of conscious moments becomes haphazard, hence rendering that which it observes, namely, the external world, chaotic and irregular, with the consequence of invalidating the principle of dependent origination by which the world is ordered:

Thus the external DO [dependent origination] principle can be inferred from experience only if an analogous internal principle is presupposed to obtain with respect to momentary consciousness. But then there is no possible evidence which could confirm the principle as applied to conscious moments, and so the line of reasoning in support of the dependency principle becomes viciously circular. (Schweizer, 89)

Simply put, if consciousness is indeed momentary, it has to abide by the principle of dependent origination in order for such a consciousness to observe the external world as dependently originated. Obviously the reasoning involved becomes hopelessly circular because what is to be proved is already presupposed in the argument. Hence Schweizer concludes that "either the original principle of *pratītyasamutpāda* must be abandoned as empirically unconfirmable, or else consciousness must be held to be non-momentary" (ibid.); Schweizer chooses the latter as the more desirable alternative because the former "would undermine the basic regularities and law-like patterns by which the world is made comprehensible and predictable" (90).

The issue of circularity raised by Schweizer is indeed a difficult one. He points out that "already in the basic tenets of Buddhistic thought lay the logical seeds of the later Idealistic versions of the moments, such as the Yogācāra school, which embrace the essentially Upaniṣadic position that Consciousness (*vijñāna*) is ultimately real" (ibid.). However, the conclusion he reaches is a bit too hastily drawn. It is indeed only Yogācārins who meet Schweizer's challenge head on; furthermore, they do not quite so easily give in to the Upaniṣadic position, however tempting:

> In order to dispense with the attachment to seemingly real entities outside the mind and its concomitant activities, we put forward the teaching that nothing exists except the transformation of consciousness. However, those who regard consciousness as real existents are also attached to *dharma*s, just like the attachment to the illusory external entities. (Xuan Zang, 86)

Here Xuan Zang—a prominent figure in the Yogācāra tradition during the seventh century whose work will be the focus of Chapter Two—cannot be more unequivocal in rejecting the Upaniṣadic position on the ultimate reality of consciousness: "Outer objects, as postulates whose existence depends on inner consciousness, are conventional entities. Insofar as consciousness is the basis of the postulated and unreal external entities, it can be said to exist" (12). In other words, the reality of consciousness is recognized only in the context of disputing the externality of objects. Outside this context, it cannot be said to exist, just like external objects. The postulation of *ālayavijñāna* takes up Schweizer's challenge of circularity. The solution will become clearer in Chapter Two when we discuss *ālayavijñāna* in detail.

19. Here the word "Hīnayāna" is not used derogatorily as Mahāyānists meant it to be when they coined the term. It is used descriptively as an umbrella term to include non-Mahāyāna schools such as Sarvāstivāda, Sautrāntika, and others.

20. Alexander von Rospatt's *The Buddhist Doctrine of Momentariness* is an extensive survey of Buddhist literature on the evolution of the Buddhist doctrine of momentariness. According to Rospatt, among the early Buddhist schools, Mahāsāṅghikas did not accord any particular importance to the doctrine of momentariness of conditioned *dharma*s although some of their subsects did accept it (29–32). Most other major non-Mahāyāna Buddhist schools, including Sthaviras, Sarvāstivādins, Sautrāntikas, and Theravādins, accepted, in one way or another, this doctrine (32–33). Regarding the evolution of the definition of *kṣaṇa,* or moment, Rospatt states:

> The usage of *kṣaṇa* in the sense of momentary entity documents that the change in the conception of the term *kṣaṇa* was brought to its logical conclusion. Starting out with the basic meaning of "very short time," the *kṣaṇa* came to be understood—reflecting an atomistic conception of time—as "the shortest unit of time," the length of which came to be equated with the duration of mental entities (or transient entities in general) as the briefest conceivable events. Conversely, these entities were understood to be momentary so that the characterization of the moment became a characterization of momentary entities, a constellation which—

in the context of the definition of *kṣaṇika* (lit. endowed with a moment; i.e. momentary)—prompted the conceptualization of the moment as the evanescent nature of these entities. Given this identification of the moment with a (or in the case of Śāntrakṣita possibly even **the**) nature of the entity, it is understandable that *kṣaṇa* was also used to refer to the entity itself, which is after all held to be nothing beyond its properties. (110)

21. Phenomenologist Edmund Husserl is famous for articulating this scheme in his discussion of the structure of time consciousness, which argues that a temporal object never appears within our consciousness as an isolated momentary now, but rather always as a temporal horizon constituted by the immediate past and the immediate future. He elaborates on this scheme in his *On the Phenomenology of the Consciousness of Internal Time (1893–1917)* (1991, translated by John Barnett Brough, Dordrecht, The Netherlands: Kluwer Academic Publishers).

22. Although Sarvāstivāda also adopts the third view, as Kalupahana observes (1975, 73), the first view dominates much of its discourse. Consequently, I will focus on this aspect of the Sarvāstivāda stance.

23. As Steven Collins points out, Sarvāstivāda and Sautrāntika figure much more prominently in Mahāyāna texts as examples of "Hīnayāna" (20–21fn). This suggests that Sarvāstivāda and Sautrāntika are more important than other "Hīnayāna" schools (e.g., Theravāda) in the doctrinal debate with Mahāyāna and that the former two play a crucial role in helping to shape Mahāyāna doctrines. Hence, I will focus on Sarvāstivāda and Sautrāntika in tracing the origin of the Yogācāra concept of *ālayavijñāna*.

24. I am using the term "intentional" in the way defined by Edmund Husserl. According to Husserl, consciousness is, in its nature, always directed toward an object. That is, consciousness is always *of* something. There are two kinds of object, the intended and the intentional, the distinction between which is crucial to the intentional study of consciousness. Clearly, the object that is intended is not the same as the intentional object. The intended object may or may not exist but the intentional object necessarily exists as a correlative of the intentional act. The intentional object is an essential component to the intentional structure of consciousness, not the intended object. Clearly Sarvāstivādins do not distinguish intentional objects from intended objects. In this regard, I disagree with Paul Griffiths' observation that "[t]he essentially intentional model of consciousness used by the theorists of the Sarvāstivāda requires that every object of cognition and every referent of a proposition should exist: according to this model one cannot cognize a non-existent" (52). If Sarvāstivādins were using the intentional model of consciousness in the Husserlian sense of the term, they would not have had to insist that the cognized necessarily exists. Only a causal model of consciousness could have forced them to do so.

25. "Conditioned things are the fivefold *skandhas*, matter, etc." (Vasubandhu, 61). Unless noted otherwise, *dharma*s referred to in this chapter are all conditioned *dharma*s.

26. Unconditioned *dharma*s refer to space and the two types of extinctions: extinction due to knowledge (*pratisaṁkhyānirodha*) and extinction not due to knowledge (*apratisaṁkhyānirodha*) (Vasubandhu, 59).

27. As David Kalupahana points out, "Interestingly, Dharmatrāta [a prominent Sarvāstivādin] avoids a positive assertion that there is a permanent *(nitya)* element over and above the changing forms, probably realizing that this form of

assertion would openly contradict the Buddhist doctrine of impermanence. Yet such an evasion does not help Dharmatrāta, for the distinction he is making [between the substance (*dravya*) of a *dharma* and its changing manner or mode (*bhāva*) of appearance] will remain meaningless unless he is committed to the view that the so-called substance is permanent and eternal" (1992, 128).

28. As to the question whether things do exist in all three times or not, "that was part of the established doctrine of the school and is already presupposed by all the attempts" (Frauwallner, 188).

29. The Sarvāstivādin postulation of this *dharma* as an independent entity also accounts for the difference between an Arhat in his everyday state and an ordinary person. But Sautrāntika does not regard *prāpti* as

> a dharma constituting a separate thing in and of itself, . . . but a certain condition of the person: 1) the seeds of defilement have not been uprooted through the Path of the Saints; 2) the seeds of defilement have not been damaged by means of the worldly path; 3) the seeds of innate good have not been damaged through false views; and 4) the seeds of good 'obtained through effort' are in good condition at the moment when one wants to produce this good. When the person is in such a condition, this is what we call 'possession of defilement.' (Vasubandhu, 210–211)

In other words, for Sautrāntikas, *prāpti* is nothing more than a "dharma of designation" (212).

30. Sarvāstivādins appear to be aware of the danger of infinite regress in the postulation of *dharma*s. Their defense is summarized in *Abhidharmkośabhāṣyam* (217–218), but their effort to dispel such a suspicion does not seem at all convincing.

31. As Katsumi Mimaki points out, "Sautrāntika was established in critiquing Vaibhāṣika [a subschool of Sarvāstivāda], but it is not clear historically at what point Sautrāntika was established" (92). According to Hirakawa, however, the Sautrāntika School broke away from the Sarvāstivāda School "during the fourth century after the Buddha's death" (111).

32. Also in contrast with Sarvāstivādins, Sautrāntikas advocate that "there is no actual difference between the object, the subject, and the cognition because they are one and the same entity and because the division into three parts is merely a logical construction" (Kajiyama, 119).

33. "The Sautrāntika School emphasized the importance of *sūtras* over *śāstras* and claimed that its teachings originated with Ānanda, the monk who had chanted the *sūtras* at the First Council" (Hirakawa, 111). Padmanabh Jaini cites a specific example: "[T]he Theravādin as well as the Vaibhāṣika interpretation of the term *sānuśaya,* and the subsequent identification of the *anuśayas* with *paryavasthāna* are contrary to the *sūtra* quoted above. They show a determined effort to uphold the Abhidharma in preference to the *sūtra*. The Sautrāntika takes strong exception to the Ābhidharmika theories and puts forth his theory of *bīja*" (242).

34. Katsumi Mimaki has a good summary of the Sautrāntika's metaphysics (some form of atomism) and epistemology (existence recognized through inference) in his "Shoki Yuishiki Shoronsho ni Okeru Sautrāntika Setsu" (The Thoughts of the Sautrāntikas as Revealed in the Works of Early Vijñānavādins).

35. A more detailed analysis of the debate between Sarvāstivādins and Sautrāntikas on the problem surrounding the attainment of cessation can be found in

Paul Griffiths' succinct and clear presentation in Chapter Two of his *On Being Mindless*.

36. Although some scholars have ably demonstrated the appearance of conceptualizations of certain mental phenomena that are subliminal in nature in the general Indian philosophical and religious literature, it is fair to say that the concept of *ālayavijñāna,* especially in its fully developed form, is amongst the earliest, if not *the* earliest, methodical attempt of its kind against that backdrop.

37. The doctrine of *anātman* can be viewed as an application of the doctrine of impermanence to the human personality.

38. Thus Lambert Schmithausen claims that "such a nuance [the secondary nuance that the new kind of *vijñāna* was a part of the basis-of-personal-existence that is clung to as Self by ordinary people] was, originally, not intended but came to be evoked afterwards automatically due to the predominant use of '*ālaya*' in Buddhist texts, especially when the close connection of *ālayavijñāna* with *nirodhasamāpatti* or similar states had weakened" (25). I will return to this issue later in the book.

39. As Katsumi Mimaki points out, according to Sautrāntikas, "[W]hat we cognize is not the external object itself but the image that was projected into the knowledge of the external object. . . . The cognition of an object is the self-revealing of that cognition itself. That is, it is nothing other than the self-cognition of knowledge itself" (82). This means that Sautrāntika epistemology is not a simple causal model, but rather it has a clear recognition of the constitutive function of consciousness in a cognitive act.

40. The question of whether Yogācārins are metaphysical idealists or not is a long-standing controversy. My position is that they are metaphysical idealists in a qualified sense. I will deal with this question in Chapter Two.

41. An earlier discussion of the two streams of Yogācāra thought can be found in Yoshifumi Ueda's "Two Main Streams of Thought in Yogācāra Philosophy." A more detailed discussion of the two streams can be found in John Keenan's introduction to *The Realm of Awakening*, a book coauthored by Paul Griffiths and others.

Chapter 2: *Ālayavijñāna* in the *Cheng Weishi Lun*

1. Unless noted otherwise, the *CWSL* translations cited in this book are my own. The only complete English translation of the *CWSL* is by Wei Tat, from which I have benefited a great deal. Wei Tat's impressive translation, includes many interpretative insertions that are helpful for understanding the text, but some may find it too liberal. The paginations of my translations are from the Chinese portion of Wei Tat's work; they are provided for those readers who may want to check both the original Chinese text and Wei Tat's translation as well as his interpretation. Occasionally I have used Wei Tat's interpretative translations due to the terseness, and therefore vagueness, of Xuan Zang's text, and these are identified as such. In other words, I am treating Wei Tat's work more as an interpretation than as a strict translation.

2. Xuan Zang also wrote an autobiographical travelogue, *Da Tang Xi Yu Ji* (Record of Countries West of Tang China). As Sally Wriggins notes, "No one had made fresh observations after traveling the length and breadth of India before: Xuanzang has become a major source for historians studying the India of the seventh century—before the coming of Islam" (180).

3. Shunkyō Katsumata's *Bukkyō ni okeru Shinshikisetsu no Kenkyū* (*A Study of the Citta-Vijñāna Thought in Buddhism*) offers a detailed comparison between Dharmapāla, as represented by Xuan Zang, and Sthiramati on their interpretations of Vasubandhu's *Triṃśikā*.

4. Scholars have questioned the peculiar nature of the *CWSL*. For example, Shunkyō Katsumata (9–10) laments that a translator as great as Xuan Zang composed the text by compiling selective translations of various commentaries instead of translating all ten commentaries themselves, thus losing for posterity an invaluable source for the works of ten prominent Indian Yogācārins. (The *CWSL* remains, however, important in the study of Yogācāra thought.) He notes that such a practice is rather inconsistent with Xuan Zang's usual custom of being overly faithful to original texts in his translations. Traditionally it is believed that the particular style of the *CWSL* was adopted at the request of Xuan Zang's favorite disciple, Gui Ji. Dan Lusthaus goes even further in claiming that "from its inception, the *Ch'eng wei-shih lun* represents Ku'ei-chi's [Gui Ji] aspirations, not Hsüan-tsang's [Xuan Zang's], and it is Ku'ei-chi who has invested it with catechismic significance" (2002, 399). Here I am not concerned with these questions.

5. See the more detailed discussion about the three approaches on p. 33.

6. According to Dan Lusthaus, Xuan Zang's effort to argue for the non-difference of Madhyamaka and Yogācāra is due to the influence of Dharmapāla, under whose disciple Xuan Zang studied at Nālandā (2002, 404).

7. This is what J. N. Mohanty calls "consciousing" (34).

8. Various Hindu schools have made their own list of metaphysical categories. The most famous one is given by the Vaiśeṣika School, which lists seven categories: substance, quality, action, universal, individual, inherence, and absence/negation. *Ātman* is included under the category of substance. Buddhists in general do not accept the validity of these categories, rejecting them as nothing more than the result of pure intellectual abstraction. This is evidenced in the *CWSL*, where the Buddhist position is defended. The basic strategy in the *CWSL* in dealing with the opponents' views on the metaphysical categories is to link the categories to consciousness in arguing that they are perceivable only through sense organs. Hence they do not have a separate existence apart from consciousness. Because the arguments are not directly related to the theme of this chapter, they will be filtered out. Buddhists reduce these categories to two, self (*ātman*) and elements, or entities *(dharma)*, namely the non-physical/internal and the physical/external—or at least they hold these two as representatives of metaphysical categories, the postulation of which should lay to rest any lingering concerns regarding other metaphysical categories. This is the way *Triṃśikā* treats metaphysical categories.

9. "If such words [as *ātman* and *dharma*s] are metaphorical expressions, on what ground can they be established? They are both metaphorical postulates resulting from the transformations of consciousness" (Xuan Zang, 10).

10. This is different from subjective idealism, which emphasizes the ultimate reality of the knowing subject (and it may either admit the existence of a plurality of such subjects or deny the existence of all save one, in which case it becomes solipsism). It will become clear that to Yogācārins, neither the knowing subject nor the known object is the ultimate reality. Xuan Zang's Yogācāra idealism is also different from objective idealism, which denies that the distinction between

subject and object, between knower and known, is ultimate and maintains that all finite knowers and their thoughts are included in an Absolute Thought.

11. In order to solve this problem, Nyāya philosophers argue that misperception is not misperception of objects but rather misperception of place. In defending such a solution, they resort to rather convoluted arguments as to how that can be the case. I will not go into the details of these arguments, which are interesting but unconvincing—or to use M. Hiriyanna's words, "subtle rather than profound" (228). (Hiriyanna was not necessarily referring to this particular point when he made the comment about some of the Naiyāyika theories.)

12. This is the title of Bina Gupta's book, which is a study of *sākṣin*, a concept critical to Advaita Vedānta epistemology. The translation of the term "*sākṣin*" as "disinterested witness" is attributed to Husserl's idea of the phenomenological ego as "disinterested on-looker" (Gupta, 5).

13. The Yogācāra system dealt with in this chapter is based on Vasubandhu's *Triṃśikā* (*Thirty Verses*) and its commentaries compiled by Xuan Zang in the *CWSL*. Regardless of whether Vasubandhu himself was an idealist or not, his teaching has been interpreted along the lines of metaphysical idealism in the mainstream Indian Buddhist tradition with only a few exceptions. As for what Vasubandhu himself advocates in this respect, here are the following positions found in modern Buddhist scholarship: Lusthaus: epistemological idealism; Kochumuttom: realist pluralism; Wood: idealist pluralism; Sharma: absolute idealism; Stcherbatsky: spiritual monism; Murti: idealism par excellence; Conze and Griffiths: metaphysical idealism. Among them, Lusthaus and Kochumuttom can be grouped together because both of them reject the ontological idealist interpretation of Yogācāra; the others can be viewed as variations on interpreting Yogācāra as advocating metaphysical idealism.

14. According to Diana Paul, Paramārtha's interpretation of Yogācāra also falls along the lines of qualified metaphysical idealism although she does not use that term: "Although there are philosophical inconsistencies from one text to another, for Paramārtha, at least, Yogācāra is a system in which the world we experience evolves from acts of cognition continually in operation, and no other world is ours to *experience* (which is not the same thing as saying that no other world *exists*)" (Paul, 8). Paramārtha, as a prominent translator of Buddhist texts into Chinese during the sixth century, greatly influenced Xuan Zang's understanding of Yogācāra philosophy (Paul, 4), even though their overall approaches to Yogācāra philosophy would turn out to be very different as Xuan Zang eventually followed Dharmapāla's interpretation.

15. Bimal Matilal comes up with four possible positions regarding the nature of physical objects:

One is *regressive*: the physical object is there in the first place to give rise to the sense-datum, and thus we have a causal theory or representationalism. The other is *progressive*: the physical object is a construction out of these immediately given data, and thus we have phenomenalism, which says that we build up our world with these bits and pieces of what is given in immediate sensory experience. Moreover, we know that there is also a third position that is possible: physical objects do not exist, and it is a myth to assume that they do. This is the position of Vasubandhu in his *Vijñaptimātratā-siddhi*. . . . The third position may or may not be implied in the second, although the critics of the second assert, more often than not, that it leads to the third position. The fourth position is . . . direct realism. (232–233)

16. "Some *sūtra*s say that there are six consciousnesses and we should know that this is only an expedient way of explanation. They pronounce six conscious-nesses on the ground of six sense organs, but the actual categories of conscious-nesses are eight" (Xuan Zang, 336).

17. Xuan Zang lists five states in which *manovijñāna* is lacking: birth among *asaṁjñidevas*, two meditation states (*asaṁjñisamāpatti* and *nirodha-samāpatti*), mindless stupor *(middha),* and unconsciousness *(mūrcchā)* (480–492).

18. According to Kōitsu Yokoyama's observation:

> The view that all *bīja*s were planted by linguistic activities has always been the common understanding in the Yogācāra thought since *Saṃdhivir-mocana Sūtra.* . . . Later in the *CWSL,* the terminology was simplified to habitual energy of naming *(ming yan xi qi)* or seeds of naming *(ming yan zhong zi)* and this became the general term for *bīja.* However, what is *bīja?* It is the potential energy planted into *ālayavijñāna* through linguistic activities, and conversely the driving force giving rise to our linguistic activities. (142)

What is striking is the prominence of linguistic activity in defining *bīja* in that linguistic activities plant some potential energy into the storehouse consciousness, which in turn generates our linguistic activities. In other words, *bīja* is essentially linguistic. However, Xuan Zang's definition of *bīja* in the *CWSL* is broader.

19. The *CWSL* lists two kinds of *nāma:* "There are those that express mean-ings: They can explain the differences in meanings and sounds. Others reveal their objects: They are the mind and its concomitant activities that perceive their objects" (582). Xuan Zang is very brief in his explanation and does not give any rationale as to why linguistic activity is singled out.

20. As Lambert Schmithausen observes, this seems to be case in the *Basic Section* of the *Yogācārabhūmi* concerning the relation between *ālayavijñāna* and seeds in the "Initial Passage" identified by him:

> It admits of being understood not only in the sense that *ālayavijñāna* possesses or contains the Seeds, implying that it is, itself, something more, but also in the sense that *ālayavijñāna* merely comprises them, being hardly anything else but their sum or totality. In other words: There does not seem to exist, in the Initial Passage, any reliable clue for assuming that it did anything else but hypostatize the Seeds of mind lying hidden in corpo-real matter to a new form of mind proper, this new form of mind hardly, or, at best, but dimly, acquiring as yet an essence of its own, not to speak of the character of a veritable *vijñāna.* (30)

Xuan Zang seems to be trying to strike a balance between substantializing *ālayavijñāna* and making it simply the collection of *bīja*s. He appears to be cau-tious in making it an entity of some sort, aware of the risk involved.

21. This is somewhat reminiscent of the Kantian argument that causality is a form of human subjectivity because it is the way human consciousness organizes the world.

22. In another somewhat cryptic passage, Xuan Zang writes, "The eight con-sciousnesses cannot be said to be definitely one in their nature. . . . Nor are they definitely different. . . . Thus, they are like illusory beings that have no definite nature. What was previously said with regard to the distinct characteristics of consciousnesses is the result of convention, not the ultimate truth. In the ultimate truth, there is neither the mind nor word" (498).

23. According to the *CWSL*, *ālayavijñāna* is the perfumable and the seven consciousnesses are the perfumers. Xuan Zang stipulates that the perfumable has to be durable, meaning that it has to be an uninterrupted series; it has to be non-defined, hence able to be perfumed; it has to be perfumable; and it has to be in intimate and harmonious relation with the perfumer. Consequently, "Only *vipākavijñāna* has all four characteristics. *Vipākavijñāna* is perfumable, not its five *caittas*" (130). On the other hand, the perfumer has to have the following characteristics: not eternal; capable of activity; able to create and nourish *bījas*; endowed with eminent activity that rules out the eighth consciousness; and capable of increase and decrease (which rules out the fruits of Buddha); in intimate and harmonious relation with the perfumed (which rules out physical bodies of other persons and earlier and subsequent moments) (130–132): "Only the seven *pravṛttivijñānas*, with their concomitant mental activities, are conspicuous and can increase and decrease. They have these four characteristics and are thus capable of perfuming" (132).

24. I am taking Wei Tat's interpretation of "one's own *bījas*" as "one's *indriyas*" (545).

25. The ten *hetu*s refer to the following:

1) Things, names, and ideas that are the basis upon which the speech depends; 2) sensation; 3) the perfuming energy that can attract its own fruit indirectly; 4) direct cause, namely matured *bījas*; 5) complementary cause; 6) adductive cause; 7) special cause: each *dharma* generating its own fruit; 8) a combination of conditions; 9) obstacles to the generation of fruit; 10) non-impeding conditions (Xuan Zang, 552–556).

26. As Xuan Zang explains, there are two theories regarding the manifestation of consciousnesses: first, that of Dharmapāla and Sthiramati, which maintains that consciousness manifests itself in two functional divisions, image and perception, out of the self-witness division; and second, that of Nanda and Bandhuśrī, which contends that inner consciousness manifests itself in what seems to be an external sphere of objects (Wei Tat, 11). It is clear that Xuan Zang incorporates both views into his scheme in the *CWSL*. It is even conceivable that Xuan Zang's account of the collectivity of our experience might have been influenced by the latter view, but because Nanda's and Bandhuśrī's works are now lost there is no way to verify such a hypothesis.

27. There are two approaches to the question of how consciousness alone can account for the collective dimension of our experience. We can regard *ālayavijñāna* either as a universal consciousness and the individual consciousness as the result of its individuation or as essentially individualistic but having a universal dimension. M. J. Larrabee summarizes the two possibilities well:

First, the *ālaya* is one, but "materializes" at many points as individual consciousnesses which are empirically but erroneously viewed as individual ego-centered persons. Second, the *ālaya* is many, that is, each individual person has an *ālaya* as one of the eight consciousnesses which make up that individual. As we can see, the latter interpretation emphasizes the psychological descriptive aspect of the Yogācāra doctrine, while the former highlights the metaphysical or ontological aspect. (4)

Larrabee rightly points out that Xuan Zang takes the view that *ālayavijñāna* is individualistic, which "militates against any monistic tendencies of the doctrine of consciousness-only, which at times seems to posit some single ultimate reality" (6). Larrabee chooses the other alternative, which interprets *ālayavijñāna* as the ground for the individual ego-centers and, consequently, as a common ground for the consistency of world-experience undergone by the majority of individual human subjects, specifically the continuous yet (for Buddhists) illusory belief engendered by the *manas*-consciousness that a substantial world with substantially enduring ego-subjects exists (ibid.).

Such a monistic interpretation of *ālayavijñāna* betrays a clear Advaitin influence on the part of Larrabee. Xuan Zang's individualistic interpretation of *ālayavijñāna* is more in accord with the general Buddhist tenet.

28. As Dan Lusthaus observes:

Eventually Buddhist epistemology would accept only perception (*pratyakṣa*) and inferential reasoning *(anumāna)* as valid means for acquiring knowledge (*pramāṇa*), and these changes were only beginning in India while Hsüan-tsang [Xuan Zang] was there. They were not yet institutionalized. Prior to that shift the two acceptable means were scriptural testimony (*śruti*) and reasoning (*yukti, anumāna*). It was Vasubandhu's disciple, Dignāga, after all, who firmly established perception and inference as the two valid *pramāṇas*, and undermined the status of scripture. (1989, 321)

Because the scriptural support Xuan Zang cites does not have a direct bearing on the philosophical argument, I will not go into it here.

29. Unlike Hindu philosophers, Buddhists do not seem to be interested in the so-called "dreamless" state.

Chapter 3: The Unconscious

1. I am not suggesting that Freud and Jung belong to the same school, but rather that there is a definite continuity between their theoretical endeavors given their personal and professional connections. I will deal with the similarities and differences between the two later in the chapter.

2. Freud did not, rightly, credit himself with the discovery of the unconscious, but he is undoubtedly the one who made the unconscious the center of his psychoanalytic theory and practice, and he is the one instrumental in popularizing it. As Peter Gay puts it, "His particular contribution was to take a shadowy, as it were poetic, notion, lend it precision, and make it into the foundation of a psychology by specifying the origins and contents of the unconscious and its imperious ways of pressing toward expression. 'Psychoanalysis was forced, through the study of pathological repression,' Freud observed later, to 'take the concept of the 'unconscious' seriously'" (128).

3. Freud thinks that this critical agent is a later development acquired in the course of growing up; when a child dreams the fulfillment of a wish is apparent.

4. Here Freud is referring to the psychical apparatus, the components of which are called the "ψ-systems," that he sets up to explain the relationship between different agents or systems operative in our minds:

The first thing that strikes us is that this apparatus, compounded of ψ-systems, has a sense of direction. All our psychical activity starts from stimuli (whether internal or external) and ends in innervations [the transmission of energy into an efferent system to indicate a process tending towards discharge]. Accordingly, we shall ascribe a sensory and a motor end to the apparatus. At the sensory end there lies a system which receives perception; at the motor end there lies another, which opens the gateway to motor activity. Psychical processes advance in general from the perceptual end to the motor end. (1965, 575–576)

5. In a footnote added in 1919, Freud writes, "If we attempted to proceed further with this schematic picture, in which the systems are set out in linear succession, we should have to reckon with the fact that the system next beyond the *Pcs.* is the one to which consciousness must be ascribed—in other words, that *Pcpt. = Cs.*" (1965, 580).

6. "Cathexis" means investment of mental or emotional energy in a person, object, or idea.

7. This is nicely summarized by James Strachey in his introduction to Freud's *The Ego and the Id* (1960, xxx), using Freud's famous words from the work: "[I]n the descriptive sense there are two kinds of unconscious, but in the dynamic sense only one" (6).

8. Malcolm Macmillan presents an interesting account of Freud's move from the topographical system to the structural system. He sees it as an effort by Freud to accommodate the death instinct in his theoretical scheme while Freud himself claims the move was based on terminological difficulties and new discoveries. Given the nature of the current work, I will not go into the merits of such a dispute and accept Freud's own explanation.

9. This is from James Strachey's introduction to *The Ego and the Id.*

10. In his *New Introductory Lectures on Psycho-Analysis,* Freud summarizes the difference between the topographical and the structural systems: Conscious, preconscious, and unconscious are qualities of what is mental; superego, ego, and id are mental provinces (89–90).

11. "It is filled with energy reaching it from the instincts, but it has no organization, produces no collective will, but only a striving to bring about the satisfaction of the instinctual needs subject to the observance of the pleasure principle. The logical laws of thought do not apply in the id, and this is true above all of the law of contradiction. Contrary impulses exist side by side, without canceling each other out or diminishing each other. . . . There is nothing in the id that could be compared with negation; and we perceive with surprise an exception to the philosophical theorem that space and time are necessary forms of our mental acts. There is nothing in the id that corresponds to the idea of time; there is no recognition of the passage of time, and . . . no alteration in its mental processes is produced by the passage of time. . . [A]fter the passage of decades they [wishful impulses] behave as though they had just occurred. They can only be recognized as belonging to the past, can only lose their impotence and be deprived of their cathexis of energy, when they have been made conscious by the work of analysis. . . . The id of course knows no judgements of value: no good and evil, no morality. . . . Instinctual cathexes seeking discharge—that, in our view, is all there is in the id" (Freud 1964, 92–93).

12. Although Jung is an original thinker in his own right, the influence of Freud is unmistakable. Hence, in this book I take the view that Jung's theory of the unconscious is a development of Freud's. This does not mean that Jung simply accepts Freud's theory and builds his own theory on it—far from it. It is widely known that Jung differs from Freud on several crucial points that I will discuss later in the chapter. However, it is probably fair to say that if there were no Freudian theory of the unconscious, there would not have been a Jungian theory, at least not the one we know today. This is what I mean by Jung's development of Freud's theory of the unconscious.

13. According to Liliane Frey-Rohn, there are three phases in the development of the concept of the unconscious in Jung's psychology:

Jung's first phase was connected with the opposition of personal and impersonal memory traces; the second phase was founded on the recognition of archetypal dominants as the structural elements of the background of the psyche. Because of this Jung was able to distinguish the personal and the collective unconscious, a finding which was extremely important for understanding his psychology. Finally, a third phase led to the discovery of the archetype-as-such. Under this term Jung understood a structural framework which culminated in the idea of a basic form of the unconscious psyche which was non-representable, that is, psychoid. (117)

14. "By psyche I understand the totality of all psychic process, conscious as well as unconscious" (Jung 1971, 463).

15. This excerpt is from the essay "Spirit and Life" in Volume 8 of Jung's collected works.

16. Immediately following the above definition, Jung states, "Hence I also speak of an *ego-complex*. The ego-complex is as much a content as a condition of *consciousness*, for a psychic element is conscious to me only in so far as it is related to my ego complex. But inasmuch as the ego is only the centre of my field of consciousness, it is not identical with the totality of my psyche, being merely one complex among other complexes" (1971, 425, original italics). "Complex" is defined by Jung as the phenomenon of the "feeling-toned groups of representations" in the unconscious (Jacobi 1959, 6) that are of "an intrapsychic nature and originate in a realm which is beyond the objective control of the conscious mind and which manifests itself only when the threshold of attention is lowered" (7). This means that ego is *essentially* unconscious, which is contrary to Jung's earlier definition of the ego that basically equates it with consciousness. This apparent inconsistency in Jung's theories can be smoothed out by interpreting ego as an organizing principle providing a coherent structure of continuity and identity, but such an organizing principle is essentially unconscious although the coherence it creates is consciousness. However, Jung does not seem to differentiate the ego from consciousness in most of his writings.

17. This point is echoed in Jung's essay "Spirit and Life": "The ego is a complex that does not comprise the total human being" (1969a, 324). It is only a fragmentary complex.

18. This extract is from Jung's essay "The Structure of the Psyche" in Volume 8 of his collected works.

19. Many Jungian scholars insist that the personal unconscious correlates with Freud's notion of the unconscious as an equivalent to the repressed and only an epiphenomenon of consciousness (Franz, 6; Yuasa, 145). It seems to me that this prevailing view amongst Jungians about Freud's notion of the unconscious primarily focuses on Freud's topographical system; in his structural system the unconscious becomes a quality of a mental process and not a mental region, as the Jungian personal unconscious is. Such a view is hardly justified when Freud's structural system is taken into consideration. The id and the superego are largely unconscious; they cannot be regarded as epiphenomena of consciousness; rather they are independent mental regions that have autonomous functions in themselves. It is important to distinguish the three ways Freud uses the term "unconscious" in his two systems. He explicitly points out in his structural system that

phylogenetically the id is prior to the emergence of the ego, resulting from the id's contact with the external world. This means that the unconsciousness of the id is a necessary precondition for the emergence of the consciousness of the ego. Of course, the ego can also be unconscious as we have seen.

20. Even though Jacobi insists that "according to Jung, it is not dreams (as Freud believed) but complexes that provide the royal road to the unconscious" (1959, 6), this observation seems to be more of a partisan move intended to highlight the differences between Jung and Freud; it only points to Jung's experiments with word association in his early career. It is doubtful, at least in my reading of Jung, that after he became associated with Freud he still relied more on complexes than on dreams in approaching the unconscious.

21. "Knowledge of its existence seems futile; its harmful action will continue until we succeed in 'discharging' it, or until the excess of psychic energy stored up in it is transferred to another gradient, i.e., until we succeed in assimilating it emotionally" (Jacobi 1959, 10).

22. Jung does put together a list of definitions of the key concepts of his psychology at the end of *Psychological Types,* but often his usage of the concepts does not follow these definitions. A good example is his use of the concept of instinct, which varies wildly from place to place; his definition at the end of *Psychological Types* does not provide much clarification at all. This wide variation in Jung's use of concepts represents the continuous evolution of his conceptualization of key notions.

23. This is very different from Freud's formulation of the ego, which is more aligned with the external world through perception, as is evident in Malcolm Macmillan's observation, "[T]he cathexis of an object or its introjection or projection requires connections to be formed between the 'traces' or 'mnemic residues' constituting a structure like the ego and those making up the representation of the object itself" (367). I will deal with this point at some length later in the chapter.

24. Instincts are also referred to as instinctive actions by Jung: "We speak of 'instinctive actions,' meaning by that a mode of behaviour of which neither the motive nor the aim is fully conscious and which is prompted only by obscure inner necessity. . . . Thus instinctive action is characterized by an unconsciousness of the psychological motive behind it. . . . Only those unconscious processes which are inherited, and occur uniformly and regularly, can be called instinctive" (1969a, 130–31). This is from the article "Instinct and the Unconscious" in Volume 8 of Jung's collected works.

25. This is from the essay "Psychological Factors Determining Human Behaviour" in Volume 8 of Jung's collected works.

26. Jung has tried to defend himself against accusations that he regards ideas as hereditary in his concept of archetype: "It is not . . . a question of inherited *ideas* but of inherited *possibilities* of ideas" (1969b, 66, original italics). "The archetype in itself is empty and purely formal, . . . a possibility of representation which is given a priori. The representations themselves are not inherited, only the forms, and in that respect they correspond in every way to the instincts, which are also determined in form only" (79).

27. Jung himself does not always pay attention to the distinction he makes between the two.

Chapter 4: Three Paradigms of the Subliminal Mind

1. In this chapter, "self" is used in the most general sense, whereas "Self" is used specifically in the Jungian sense.

2. This means that Xuan Zang does not dispute the empirical self as a continuum but rejects the metaphysical self as a substance.

3. This more or less correlates with Jung's own characterization in *Aion*: "Psychologically the self is a union of conscious (masculine) and unconscious (feminine). It stands for the psychic totality. So formulated, it is a psychological concept. Empirically, however, the self appears spontaneously in the shape of specific symbols, and its totality is discernible above all in the mandala and its countless variants. Historically, these symbols are authenticated as God-images" (Jung 1969, 268). The symbolic expression of the Self is regarded as an empirical phenomenon whereas in Jung's other characterizations it is usually regarded as the archetypal aspect of the Self. This can be explained by resorting to the context wherein the archetypal nature of the Self is assumed in the cited text and the psychological, empirical, and historical aspects are deemed as manifestations of the archetypal Self in different aspects.

4. When Jung talks about the Self as the whole or totality of the consciousness and the unconscious, he is using the term in the structural sense, meaning the psyche in the course of individuation forms a structure around the central archetype of the Self. The psyche as the conscious-unconscious totality is used only in a descriptive sense. This means that the psyche is a chaotic whole and it becomes organized in the course of individuation. I will talk about this point later in the book.

5. "By 'totality' Jung means more than unity or wholeness. The term implies a kind of integration, a unification of the parts, a creative synthesis, comprising an active force. It is a concept that should be identified with the 'self-regulating system'" (Jacobi 1973, 10, n3).

6. There is a clear resonance between *ātman* and *Brahman* as taught in the *Upaniṣads* and Jung's conceptualization of the archetype of the Self.

7. This refers to the often unrecognized and neglected psychic qualities in a man that are normally associated with a (stereotyped) woman, such as sentimentality, tenderness, and so forth.

8. This is the collection of masculine qualities in a woman, the counterpart of the anima in a man. It is associated with power, resoluteness, and so forth. It is needless to point out that both anima and animus are based upon stereotypical images of man and woman, but if we can ignore their gender associations and instead focus on their compensatory function to the dominant pattern in a personality, they can still have certain validity.

9. This refers to Jung's psychological typology (Jung 1971), which distinguishes the two attitude types (extraversion and introversion) and the four function types (thinking, feeling, sensation, and intuition) in the operation of the psyche. Usually, there is a dominant type, attitudinal and functional, within an individual, and this becomes the superior function of her psyche. The rest become the inferior function. The individuation process aims at restoring the balance between these different types and their functions within the psyche.

10. The essay "The Transcendent Function" explains this concept in detail: "The psychological 'transcendent function' arises from the union of conscious

and unconscious content" (1969a, 69). It is essentially a process that expands the conscious content by incorporating the unconscious content, and although it can revitalize the consciousness through the canalization of the previously disconnected energy hidden in the unconscious into the consciousness, the ego still ends up retaining its authority over the unconscious. In other words, the standpoint of the ego, though expanded, is not transformed onto a higher plain, as it were, where both the conscious and the unconscious are its integral parts. This theme is picked up later on and evolves into Jung's notion of the individuation process aimed at placing the Self as the new center while rendering the ego a passive observing agency within the transformed psyche.

11. Even though Jung's official position is that "[f]or Freud . . . the unconscious is of an exclusively personal nature" (1969b, 3), he does point out that Freud's notion of superego "denotes the collective consciousness" (ibid., n2).

12. James Dicenso observes:

The psychoanalytic distinction between *illusion* and *delusion* is crucial, yet it is one that Freud does not consistently maintain. This inconsistency also reflects differentiations within Freud's object of inquiry; that is, religion actually falls into both categories. Thus Freud notes that religious forms often lapse into the realm of delusion. Religious statements concerning reality sometimes contradict what has been collectively and empirically established to be the case, especially by the culturally dominant methods and paradigms of science. (33–34, original italics)

13. This is from the article "On the Nature of the Psyche" in Volume 8 of Jung's collected works.

14. I am using the term "spiritual" in its broadest sense in my book. I will not engage myself in comparing the spiritual goals schematized by these three philosophers because the discussion is not entirely clear in the writings of Freud and Jung on this topic. Furthermore, any study of such a nature involves detailed empirical investigations that go far beyond my expertise.

15. However, there seems to be an implicit presupposition in this assertion, namely the pure *bīja*s will never be destroyed by any power, while the defiled ones will be destroyed by the power of pure *dharma*s. This is necessary in order to accommodate the possibility of both *saṃsāra* and *nirvāṇa*.

16. As we have seen in Chapter Two, one of the characteristics of *bīja*s is that they must belong to a definite moral species; this rules out the doctrine that a cause of one species can engender a fruit of another species (Xuan Zang, 126).

17. Wei Tat, in his translation of *CWSL*, defines this pure *dharmadhātu* as

[f]ree from the impurities of *klesavarana* and *jneyavarana*; the true and non-erroneous nature of all *dharma*s; the cause which brings to birth, nourishes and supports the *aryadharma*s; the true nature of all *Tathagatas*; pure in itself from the beginningless past; possessed of diverse qualities more numerous than the atoms of the universes of the ten regions; without birth or destruction, like space; penetrating all *dharma*s and all beings; neither identical with *dharma*s, nor different from them; neither *bhava* nor *abhava*; free from all distinguishing marks, conceptions, cogitation; which is only realized by the pure *aryajnana*; having as its nature the *tathata* which the two voids reveal; which the *arya*s realize partially; which the Buddhas realize completely; that is what is called the pure *dharmadhātu* (Wei Tat, 783–785).

18. Here the direct preaching of the Buddha from the pure *dharmadhātu* has a "mystical" element to it because it cannot refer to the teaching of the historical Buddha.

19. As Paul Williams points out with regard to the production of Mahāyāna *sūtras*, which were claimed to be the words of the Buddha himself: "In some cases the followers may have felt themselves in direct contact with a Buddha who inspired them in meditation or in dreams" (33). As a result, all the Mahāyāna *sūtras* have been attributed to the Buddha himself within the Mahāyāna Buddhist tradition.

20. This can be explained by the fact that Xuan Zang, being a devout Buddhist, has to leave room for the Buddha in his theory and that Jung, being a psychologist, does not have such a concern. This explanation, however, does not necessarily exhaust other possibilities that I will not elaborate on here.

21. *Nirvāṇa* cannot be regarded as an archetype in the strict Jungian sense because archetypes as defined by Jung are purely formal, and as such the archetype-per-se can never be realized. Hence for Jung the individuation process is a never-ending one, whereas in Buddhism *nirvāṇa* is by no means formal and can be reached through the meditation practice prescribed in the tradition.

22. It can also be argued that for Freud spirituality is an inherent possibility in order for it to happen at all and for Xuan Zang it is a forced necessity because it is not a natural course of human development. But this does not appear to be the way Xuan Zang and Freud theorize spirituality in their respective systems. In other words, they have different concerns in their theorizations of spirituality: Freud emphasizes the aspect of its being forced upon individuals—hence civilization is deemed the enemy of individuals—whereas Xuan Zang stresses the aspect of its inherent possibility due to the religious orientation of his theory. Furthermore, Freud puts emphasis on the necessity of spiritual transformation simply because it is a necessary condition for our very survival in the social world, and Xuan Zang only talks about its possibility because for him spiritual transformation, in the Buddhist sense of the term, is not a necessary condition for everyday human living.

23. According to Britannica Online (2003):

> Neuroses are characterized by anxiety, depression, or other feelings of unhappiness or distress that are out of proportion to the circumstances of a person's life. They may impair a person's functioning in virtually any area of his life, relationships, or external affairs, but they are not severe enough to incapacitate the person. Neurotic patients generally do not suffer from the loss of the sense of reality seen in persons with psychoses. An influential view held by the psychoanalytic tradition is that neuroses arise from intrapsychic conflict (conflict between different drives, impulses, and motives held within various components of the mind). Central to psychoanalytic theory, which is based on the work of Sigmund Freud, is the postulated existence of an unconscious part of the mind which, among other functions, acts as a repository for repressed thoughts, feelings, and memories that are disturbing or otherwise unacceptable to the conscious mind. These repressed mental contents are typically sexual or aggressive urges or painful memories of an emotional loss or an unsatisfied longing dating from childhood. Anxiety arises when these unacceptable and repressed drives threaten to enter consciousness; prompted by anxiety, the conscious part of the mind (the ego) tries to deflect the emergence into consciousness

of the repressed mental contents through the use of defense mechanisms such as repression, denial, or reaction formation. Neurotic symptoms often begin when a previously impermeable defense mechanism breaks down and a forbidden drive or impulse threatens to enter consciousness.

24. Their different concerns also shape the way the body is schematized in regard to the ego. For Freud, "[t]he ego is first and foremost a bodily ego; it is not merely a surface entity, but is itself the projection of a surface" (1960, 20). The primary importance of the body in the scheme of an ego for Freud is due to its dual nature: It is both internal and external; it is where the internal comes in contact with the external. Xuan Zang shares Freud's view that the ego has a dual nature, internal and external, or personal and collective. We have already dealt with its collective aspect in the previous chapter. As to its personal nature, it is the bodily sense of self that arises out of the attachment of the sixth consciousness to the five aggregates: form/body, sensation, perception, volition, and consciousness (Xuan Zang, 20). For Xuan Zang the bodily self is an interrupted self, and it is not as tenacious as the one that is born of *manas'* attachment to the storehouse consciousness. Xuan Zang's view is justified if we take into consideration the self in a dream wherein the body is not directly involved, or the dreamless state wherein the self does not appear at all. In the Yogācāra scheme, dreams are a higher reality than the physical world. This is evident in the way the self is argued against. The self that is involved in the physical world is one that is subject to interruption—by a dream state, for example. The highest sense of self is, of course, encountered in the dreamless state wherein the self that appears in a dream also disappears. Simply put, for Freud the concern in schematizing the body with regard to the ego is the issue of internality/externality, whereas for Xuan Zang it is the issue of continuity.

25. According to Britannica Online (2003), psychosis is

any of several major mental illnesses that can cause delusions, hallucinations, serious defects in judgment and insight, defects in the thinking process, and the inability to objectively evaluate reality. It is difficult to clearly demarcate psychoses from the class of less severe mental disorders known as psychoneuroses (commonly called neuroses) because a neurosis may be so severe, disabling, or disorganizing in its effects that it actually constitutes a psychosis. But, in general, patients suffering from the recognized psychotic illnesses exhibit a disturbed sense of reality and a disorganization of personality that sets them apart from neurotics. Such patients also frequently believe that nothing is wrong with them, despite the palpable evidence to the contrary as evinced by their confused or bizarre behaviour. Psychotics may require hospitalization because they cannot take care of themselves or because they may constitute a danger to themselves or to others.

26. As J. N. Mohanty notes, "While the question of why the Indian thinkers were indifferent to history remains, one must, while doing comparative philosophy, also keep in mind that Western thought came to take history seriously only in modern times (despite the nascent historicity of Judaeo-Christian self-understanding)" (188). The observation is also applicable to Xuan Zang because his theory is grounded in the work of his Indian predecessors.

27. "Natural" is used here in the sense that it is necessarily possible in the Kantian sense.

28. "Archetype and instinct are the most polar opposites imaginable. . . . They belong together as correspondences, which is not to say that the one is derivable

from the other, but that they subsist side by side as reflections in our own minds of the opposition that underlies all psychic energy. Man finds himself simultaneously driven to act and free to reflect. This contrariety in his nature has no moral significance, for instinct is not in itself bad any more than spirit is good. Both can be both" (Jung 1969a, 206).

29. "A man in the first half of life with its biological orientation can usually, thanks to the youthfulness of his whole organism, afford to expand his life and make something of value out of it. But the man in the second half of life is oriented towards culture, the diminishing powers of his organism allowing him to subordinate his instincts to cultural goals" (Jung 1969a, 60).

30. The solution to making the archetypes into a hierarchical system, suggested by Jolande Jacobi, seems to be more indicative of the problem than a solution that is consistent with the formal aspects of the archetypes:

In the world of the archetypes we can accordingly establish a certain hierarchical order. We designate as "primary" those archetypes which are not susceptible of further reduction, which represent, as it were, the "first parents"; we term the next in line, their "children," "secondary," their "grandchildren" "tertiary," etc., until we arrive at those highly diversified archetypes which stand closest to the familiar domain of our consciousness and hence possess the least richness of meaning and numinosity or energy charge. Such a hierarchical chain might, for example, be formed of those archetypes which manifest the basic traits of the entire human family, of the feminine sex alone, of the white race, of Europeans, of Nordics, of the British, of the citizens of London, of the Brown family, etc. (Jacobi 1959, 56–57)

31. Indeed, Jung himself in his later career developed the idea of the psychoid archetype that is transcendent (1969a, 213). This is a step in the right direction, but because it is formulated to connect the psychic and the physical worlds, its objective in serving as the goal of spiritual transformation seems to have changed. This shows that Jung is probably not fully aware of the problem involved here; nevertheless his continuing theoretical endeavors point in a promising direction, albeit only a direction because the idea was never fully fleshed out.

Chapter 5: Accessibility of the Subliminal Mind

1. My definition of transcendence combines those given by David Hall and Roger Ames (13) and their critic, Robert Neville (151), in their exchanges on the problematic of transcendence in mainstream Western philosophy and traditional Confucian philosophy. I will not discuss their debate here as it is irrelevant to our discussion, but it did inspire my approach to the subliminal consciousness.

2. In fact Jung claims that philosophical and rational concepts are archetypes in disguise (1969a, 136).

3. Jung's theoretical ambiguity reveals a tension that resembles the dispute between rationalism and empiricism that Kant faced, namely whether our knowledge comes from reason or experience. Jung's solution in certain ways echoes Kant's approach. That is, Jung shares Kant's view that "though all our knowledge begins with experience, it does not follow that it all arises out of experience" (Kant, B1). One might point out that Kant's focus differs from the knowledge Jung is concerned with, namely unconscious apprehension: "Just as conscious apprehension gives our actions form and direction, so unconscious apprehension through the archetype determines the form and direction of instinct" (Jung 1969a, 137). The Kantian categories are obviously concerned with the forms of conscious

cognition, although Kant did not think in these terms. Jungian archetypes are forms of the collective unconscious, even though Jung sometimes blurs the distinction between the concept of collective unconscious to which Jungian archetypes are applied and the concept of collective consciousness to which the Kantian categories are more applicable. For Kant, knowledge requires cooperation between the two faculties of the mind, intuition and understanding. For Jung, archetypes are forms of unconscious representation just like categories are forms of conscious cognition.

4. Even though Jung claims that he is an empiricist (1969b, 75), his formulation of the concept of archetype is sufficient to put such a label in question, to say the least.

5. Jung has tried to defend himself against accusations that he regards ideas as hereditary in his concept of archetype: "It is not . . . a question of inherited *ideas* but of inherited *possibilities* of ideas" (1969b, 66). "The archetype in itself is empty and purely formal, . . . a possibility of representation which is given a priori. The representations themselves are not inherited, only the forms, and in that respect they correspond in every way to the instincts, which are also determined in form only" (79).

6. We saw in Chapter Three that these two purposes of Jung's archetype are not fully compatible. However, there is no need to bring up that argument here as it is not immediately relevant to our discussion.

7. Brian Brown's work *The Buddha Nature: A Study of the Tathāgatagarbha and Ālayavijñāna* is an important contribution to modern scholarship on Xuan Zang's conceptualization of *ālayavijñāna*. However, I have several important disagreements with Brown, despite sharing some of his understanding of Xuan Zang. Firstly, I disagree with his interpretation of Xuan Zang's *CWSL* as a case of absolute or metaphysical idealism. As we discussed in Chapter Three, Xuan Zang's philosophy should be understood as qualified metaphysical idealism. To interpret it as metaphysical idealism might be the result of its being too closely allied with *tathāgatagarbha* (Buddha nature) thought; the convergence between the two is the theme of Brown's work. Excluding the insights it sheds on the common ground between *tathāgatagarbha* and *ālayavijñāna*, Brown appears to have somewhat forced his interpretation of *tathāgatagarbha* upon Xuan Zang's conceptualization of *ālayavijñāna*. Secondly, I disagree with Brown's interpretation of Xuan Zang's formulation of *ālayavijñāna* as the universal consciousness, "as that integral wholeness of reality, the processive self-determination of substance to subject," (273) which is the demonstration of "the principle of active self-emergence from latent, abstract universality to perfect self-explicit awareness of" (ibid.). As the author himself reveals in his conclusion, the interpretation shows too strong an influence of the Hegelian Absolute Spirit, which is primarily historical and social.

8. It is, however, not my intention to claim that Xuan Zang's conception of *ālayavijñāna* is purely a description of the meditative experience. As we have seen in Chapter Three, where the storehouse consciousness was discussed in detail, the conceptualization of *ālayavijñāna* is very much doctrinally oriented. That is, Xuan Zang's effort to formulate *ālayavijñāna* is restricted by various orthodox Buddhist doctrines. The point I am trying to make here is that, given the prominent role meditation plays in the theorization of *ālayavijñāna*, it is natural for Xuan Zang to turn to meditation to solve the problem of access.

BIBLIOGRAPHY

Anacker, Stefan. 1998. *Seven Works of Vasubandhu: The Buddhist Psychological Doctor*. Delhi: Motilal Banarsidass.

———. 1999. Vasubandhu, Bhāṣya on his *Abhidharmakośam*. In *Encyclopedia of Indian Philosophies*, edited by Karl H. Potter. Vol. 8, *Buddhist Philosophy from 100 to 350 A.D.* Delhi: Motilal Banarsidass.

Aronson, Harvey B. 2004. *Buddhist Practice on Western Ground: Reconciling Eastern Ideals and Western Psychology*. Boston: Shambhala.

Bishop, Peter. 1992. Jung, Eastern Religion, and the Language of Imagination. In *Self and Liberation: The Jung-Buddhism Dialogue*, edited by Daniel J. Meckel and Robert L. Moore. New York: Paulist Press.

Bhikkhu Bodhi, trans. 2000. *The Connected Discourses of the Buddha: A New Translation of the Saṃyutta Nikāya*. Somerville, Mass.: Wisdom Publications.

Bhikkhu Ñāṇamoli, trans. 2001. *The Life of the Buddha According to the Pali Canon*. Seattle: BPS Pariyatti Editions.

Brown, Brian Edward. 1991. *The Buddha Nature: A Study of the Tathāgatagarbha and Ālayavijñāna*. Delhi: Motilal Banarsidass.

Clarke, J. J. 1994. *Jung and Eastern Thought: A Dialogue with the Orient*. London: Routledge.

———. 1997. *Oriental Enlightenment: The Encounter between Asian and Western Thought*. London: Routledge.

———. 2002. *The Tao of the West: Western Transformation of Taoist Thought*. London: Routledge.

Claxton, Guy, ed. 1986. *Beyond Therapy: The Impact of Eastern Religions on Psychological Theory and Practice*. London: Wisdom Publications.

Coleman, James William. 2001. *The New Buddhism: The Western Transformation of an Ancient Tradition*. Oxford: Oxford University Press.

Collins, Steven. 1982. *Selfless Persons: Imagery and Thought in Theravāda Buddhism*. Cambridge: Cambridge University Press.

Colman, Warren. 2000. Models of the Self. In *Jungian Thought in the Mod-

ern World, edited by Elphis Christopher and Hester McFarland Solomon. London: Free Association Books.

Davids, C. Rhys, and F. L. Woodward, trans. 1995. *The Book of the Kindred Sayings*. London: Pali Text Society.

Davidson, Richard J., and Anne Harrington, eds. 2002. *Visions of Compassion: Western Scientists and Tibetan Buddhists Examine Human Nature*. Oxford: Oxford University Press.

De Silva, Padmasiri, M.W. 1973. *Buddhist and Freudian Psychology*. Colombo: Lake House Investments.

———. 1979. *An Introduction to Buddhist Psychology*. London: Macmillan.

Dicenso, James J. 1999. *The Other Freud: Religion, Culture and Psychoanalysis*. London: Routledge.

Dilman, Ilham. 1972. "Is the Unconscious a Theoretical Construct?" *The Monist: An International Quarterly Journal of General Inquiry* 56, no. 3: 313–342.

Douglas, Claire. 1997. The Historical Context of Analytical Psychology. In *The Cambridge Companion to Jung*, edited by Polly Young-Eisendrath and Terence Dawson. Cambridge: Cambridge University Press.

Engler, Jack. 1984. "Therapeutic Aims in Psychotherapy and Meditation: Developmental Stages in the Representation of Self." *Journal of Transpersonal Psychology* 16, no.1: 25–61.

———. 1998. Buddhist Psychology: Contributions to Western Psychological Theory. In *The Couch and the Tree: Dialogues in Psychoanalysis and Buddhism*, edited by Anthony Molino. New York: North Point.

———. 2003. Being Somebody and Being Nobody: A Reexamination of the Understanding of Self in Psychoanalysis and Buddhism. In *Psychoanalysis and Buddhism: An Unfolding Dialogue*, edited by Jeremy Safran. Boston: Wisdom Publications.

Epstein, Mark. 1995. *Thoughts Without a Thinker: Psychotherapy from a Buddhist Perspective*. New York: Basic Books.

———. 1998. Beyond the Oceanic Feeling: Psychoanalytic Study of Buddhist Meditation. In *The Couch and the Tree: Dialogues in Psychoanalysis and Buddhism*, edited by Anthony Molino. New York: North Point.

Faure, Bernard. 1993. *Chan Insights and Oversights: An Epistemological Critique of the Chan Tradition*. Princeton: Princeton University Press.

Finn, Mark. 1998. Tibetan Buddhism and Comparative Psychoanalysis. In *The Couch and the Tree: Dialogues in Psychoanalysis and Buddhism*, edited by Anthony Molino. New York: North Point.

Franz, Marie-Louise Von. 1998. *C. G. Jung: His Myth of Our Time*. Translated by William H. Kennedy. Toronto: Inner City Books.

Frauwallner, Erich. 1995. *Studies in Abhidharma Literature and the Origins of Buddhist Philosophical Systems*. Translated by Sophie Francis Kidd under the supervision of Ernst Steinkellner. Albany, N.Y.: State University of New York Press.

Freud, Sigmund. 1957. The Unconscious. In *On the History of the Psycho-Analytic Movement, Papers on Metapsychology and Other Works*, edited by James Strachey. Vol. 14, The Standard Edition of the Complete Psychological Works of Sigmund Freud. London: Hogarth Press and the Institute of Psycho-Analysis.

————. 1960. *The Ego and the Id.* Edited and translated by James Strachey. New York: W. W. Norton.

————. 1961a. *Civilization and Its Discontents.* Edited and translated by James Strachey. New York: W. W. Norton.

————. 1961b. *The Future of an Illusion.* Edited and translated by James Strachey. New York: W. W. Norton.

————. 1964. *New Introductory Lectures on Psycho-Analysis.* Edited and translated by James Strachey. New York: W. W. Norton.

————. 1965. *The Interpretation of Dreams.* Edited and translated by James Strachey. New York: Avon Books.

Frey-Rohn, Liliane. 1974. *From Freud to Jung: A Comparative Study of the Psychology of the Unconscious.* Translated by Fred E. Engreen and Evelyn K. Engreen. New York: G. P. Putnam's Sons.

Fromm, Erich, D. T. Suzuki, and Richard De Martino, eds. 1960. *Zen Buddhism and Psychoanalysis.* New York: Harper and Row.

Fukaura, Seibun. 1968. *Yuishikigaku Kenkyū* (A study of Yogācāra). 2 vols. Kyoto: Nagata Bunshōdō.

Funabashi, Issai. 1954. *Gō no Kenkyū* (The study of karma). Kyoto: Hōzōkan.

Gay, Peter. 1988. *Freud: A Life for Our Time.* New York: W. W. Norton.

Griffiths, Paul. 1986. *On Being Mindless: Buddhist Meditation And the Mind-Body Problem.* La Salle, Ill.: Open Court.

Griffiths, Paul, Noriaki Hakamaya, John Keenan, and Paul Swanson, trans. and eds. 1989. *The Realm of Awakening: A Translation and Study of the Tenth Chapter of Asaṅga's* Mahāyānasaṃgraha. New York: Oxford University Press.

Guenther, Herbert. 1997. Basic Features of Buddhist Psychology. In *The Authority of Experience: Essays on Buddhism and Psychology*, edited by John Pickering. Surrey, England: Curzon Press.

Gupta, Bina. 1998. *The Disinterested Witness: A Fragment of Advaita Vedanta Phenomenology.* Evanston, Ill.: Northwestern University Press.

Hall, David, and Roger Ames. 1987. *Thinking Through Confucius.* Albany, N.Y.: State University of New York Press.

Harrington, Anne. 2002. A Science of Compassion or a Compassionate Science? What Do We Expect from a Cross-Cultural Dialogue with Buddhism. In *Visions of Compassion: Western Scientists and Tibetan Buddhists Examine Human Nature*, edited by Richard J. Davidson and Anne Harrington. Oxford: Oxford University Press.

Harvey, Peter. 1995. *The Selfless Mind: Personality, Consciousness and Nirvana in Early Buddhism.* Surrey, England: Curzon Press.

Hirakawa, Akira. 1990. *A History of Indian Buddhism: From Śākyamuni to Early Mahāyāna.* Edited and translated by Paul Groner. Honolulu: University of Hawai'i Press.

Hiriyanna, M. 1993. *Outlines of Indian Philosophy.* Delhi: M/S Kavyalaya.

Husserl, Edmund. 1931. *Ideas: General Introduction to Pure Phenomenology.* Translated by W. R. Boyce Gibson. New York: Collier Books.

Inada, Kenneth K. 1993. *Nāgārjuna: A Translation of His Mūlamadhyamakakārikā with an Introductory Essay.* Delhi: Sri Satguru Publications.

Jacobi, Jolande. 1959. *Complex, Archetype, Symbol in the Psychology of Jung*. Translated by Ralph Manheim. Princeton: Princeton University Press.

———. 1973. *The Psychology of C. G. Jung*. New Haven: Yale University Press.

Jaini, Padmanabh S. 1959. "The Sautrāntika Theory of *Bīja*." *Bulletin of the School of Oriental and African Studies* 22: 236–249.

Jung, C. G. 1966. *Two Essays on Analytical Psychology*. 2d ed. Vol. 7, *The Collected Works of C. G. Jung*, edited by Michael Fordham, Sir Herbert Read, and Gerhard Adler. Translated by R. F. C. Hull. Bollingen Series 20. Princeton: Princeton University Press.

———. 1969a. *The Structure and Dynamics of the Psyche*. 2d ed. Vol. 8, *The Collected Works of C. G. Jung*, edited by Michael Fordham, Sir Herbert Read, and Gerhard Adler. Translated by R. F. C. Hull. Bollingen Series 20. Princeton: Princeton University Press.

———. 1969b. *The Archetype and The Collective Unconscious*. 2d ed. Vol. 9, part 1, *The Collected Works of C. G. Jung*, edited by Michael Fordham, Sir Herbert Read, and Gerhard Adler. Translated by R. F. C. Hull. Bollingen Series 20. Princeton: Princeton University Press.

———. 1969c. *Aion: Researches into the Phenomenology of the Self*. 2d ed. Vol. 9, part 2, *The Collected Works of C. G. Jung*, edited by Michael Fordham, Sir Herbert Read, and Gerhard Adler. Translated by R. F. C. Hull. Bollingen Series 20. Princeton: Princeton University Press.

———. 1971. *Psychological Types*. Vol. 6, *The Collected Works of C. G. Jung*, edited by Michael Fordham, Sir Herbert Read, and Gerhard Adler. Translated by R. F. C. Hull. Bollingen Series 20. Princeton: Princeton University Press.

Kajiyama, Yuichi. 1977. Realism of the Sarvāstivāda School. In *Buddhist Thought and Asian Civilization: Essays in Honor of Herbert V. Guenther on His Sixtieth Birthday*, edited by Leslie S. Kawamura and Keith Scott Kawamura. Emeryville, Calif.: Dharma Press.

Kalupahana, David J. 1975. *Causality: The Central Philosophy of Buddhism*. Honolulu: University of Hawai'i Press.

———. 1987. *The Principles of Buddhist Psychology*. Albany, N.Y.: State University of New York Press.

———. 1992. *A History of Buddhist Philosophy: Continuities and Discontinuities*. Honolulu: University of Hawai'i Press.

Kant, Immanuel. 1929. *Critique of Pure Reason*. Translated by Norman Kemp Smith. New York: St. Martin's Press.

Kasulis, Thomas P. 2002. *Intimacy or Integrity: Philosophical and Cultural Difference*. Honolulu: University of Hawai'i Press.

Katsumata, Shunkyō. 1969. *Bukkyō ni okeru Shinshikisetsu no Kenkyū* (A study of *citta-vijñāna* thought in Buddhism). Tokyo: Sankibō Busshorin.

Katz, Nathan, ed. 1983. *Buddhist and Western Psychology*. Boulder, Colo.: Prajñā Press.

Kochumuttom, Thomas A. 1989. *A Buddhist Doctrine of Experience: A*

New Translation and Interpretation of the Works of Vasubandhu the Yogācārin. Delhi: Motilal Banarsidass.

Kuhn, Thomas S. 1962. *The Structure of Scientific Revolutions*. Chicago: University of Chicago Press.

Larrabee, M. J. 1981. "The One and the Many: Yogācāra Buddhism and Husserl." *Philosophy East and West* 31 (January): 3–15.

Levine, Marvin. 2000. *The Positive Psychology of Buddhism and Yoga: Paths to a Mature Happiness with a Special Application to Handling Anger*. Mahwah, N.J.: Lawrence Erlbaum Associates.

Levy, Donald. 1996. *Freud Among the Philosophers: The Psychoanalytic Unconscious and Its Philosophical Critics*. New Haven: Yale University Press.

Loy, David R. 2002. *A Buddhist History of the West: Studies in Lack*. Albany, N.Y.: State University of New York Press.

Lusthaus, Dan. 1989. "A Philosophical Investigation of the *Ch'eng Wei-Shih Lun:* Vasubandhu, Hsüan Tsang and the Transmission of Vijñapti-Mātra (Yogācāra) from India to China." Ph.D. diss., Temple University.

———. 2002. *Buddhist Phenomenology: A Philosophical Investigation of Yogācāra Buddhism and the Ch'eng Wei-shih Lun*. London: Routledge Curzon.

Macmillan, Malcolm. 1997. *Freud Evaluated: The Completed Arc*. Cambridge, Mass.: MIT Press.

Magid, Barry. 2002. *Ordinary Mind: Exploring the Common Ground of Zen and Psychotherapy*. Boston: Wisdom Publications.

Manné, Joy. 1997. Creating a Contemporary Buddhist Psychotherapy. In *The Authority of Experience: Essays on Buddhism and Psychology*, edited by John Pickering. Surrey, England: Curzon Press.

Matilal, Bimal Krishna. 1986. *Perception: An Essay on Classical Indian Theories of Knowledge*. Oxford: Clarendon Press.

Meckel, Daniel J., and Robert L. Moore, eds. 1992. *Self and Liberation: The Jung-Buddhism Dialogue*. New York: Paulist Press.

Mimaki, Katsumi. 1972. "Shoki Yuishiki Shoronsho ni Okeru Sautrāntika Setsu" (The thoughts of the Sautrāntikas as revealed in the works of early Vijñānavādins). *Tōhōgaku* 43 (January): 77–92.

Miyuki, Mokusen. 1980. "A Jungian Approach to the Pure Land Practice of Nien-fo." *Journal of Analytical Psychology* 24, no. 3 (July): 265–274.

———. 1992. Self-Realization in the Ten Oxherding Pictures. In *Self and Liberation: The Jung-Buddhism Dialogue*, edited by Daniel J. Meckel and Robert L. Moore. New York: Paulist Press.

Mohanty, J. N. 1992. *Reason and Tradition in Indian Thought: An Essay on the Nature of Indian Philosophical Thinking*. New York: Oxford University Press.

Molino, Anthony, ed. 1998. *The Couch and the Tree: Dialogues in Psychoanalysis and Buddhism*. New York: North Point.

Nagao, Gadjin M. 1991. *Madhyamika and Yogācāra*. Edited and translated by L. S. Kawamura. Albany, N.Y.: State University of New York Press.

Nagatomo, Shigenori. 1992. *Attunement Through the Body*. Albany, N.Y.: State University of New York Press.

Nakamura, Hajime. 1980. *Indian Buddhism*. Delhi: Motilal Banarsidass.

Neville, Robert Cummings. 2000. *Boston Confucianism: Portable Tradition in the Late-Modern World*. Albany, N.Y.: State University of New York Press.

Osaki, Akiko. 1978. "What Is Meant by Destroying the *Ālayavijñāna*." *Journal of Indian and Buddhist Studies* 26 (March): 1064–1069.

Pande, G. C. 1993. Time in Buddhism. In *Religion and Time*, edited by Anindita Niyogi Balslev and J. N. Mohanty. Vol. 54, *Studies in the History of Religion*. Leiden: E. J. Brill.

Parsons, William B. 1999. *The Enigma of the Oceanic Feeling: Revisioning the Psychoanalytic Theory of Mysticism*. Oxford: Oxford University Press.

Paul, Diana Y. 1984. *Philosophy of Mind in Sixth-Century China: Paramārtha's 'Evolution of Consciousness.'* Stanford: Stanford University Press.

Pickering, John. 1997. *The Authority of Experience: Essays on Buddhism and Psychology*. Surrey, England: Curzon Press.

Pruett, Gordon. 1987. *The Meaning and End of Suffering for Freud and the Buddhist Tradition*. Lanham, Md.: University Press of America.

Radhakrishnan, Sarvepalli, and Charles A. Moore, eds. 1957. *A Sourcebook in Indian Philosophy*. Princeton: Princeton University Press.

Ricoeur, Paul. 1970. *Freud & Philosophy: An Essay on Interpretation*. Translated by Denis Savage. New Haven: Yale University Press.

Robinson, Paul. 1992. *Freud and His Critics*. Berkeley: University of California Press.

Rospatt, Alexander von. 1995. *The Buddhist Doctrine of Momentariness: A Survey of the Origins and Early Phase of This Doctrine Up to Vasubandhu*. Stuttgart: Franz Steiner Verlag.

Rubin, Jeffrey. 1996. *Psychotherapy and Buddhism: Toward an Integration*. New York: Plenum Press.

———. 2003. A Well-Lived Life: Psychoanalytic and Buddhist Contributions. In *Psychoanalysis and Buddhism: An Unfolding Dialogue*, edited by Jeremy Safran. Boston: Wisdom Publications.

Russell, Elbert. 1986. "Consciousness and the Unconscious: Eastern Meditative and Western Psychotherapeutic Approaches." *Journal of Transpersonal Psychology* 18, no. 1: 51–72.

Sachs, David. 1991. In Fairness to Freud: A Critical Notice of *The Foundations of Psychoanalysis* by Adolf Grünbaum. In *The Cambridge Companion to Freud*, edited by Jerome Neu. Cambridge: Cambridge University Press.

Safran, Jeremy, ed. 2003a. *Psychoanalysis and Buddhism: An Unfolding Dialogue*. Boston: Wisdom Publications.

———. 2003b. Psychoanalysis and Buddhism as Cultural Institutions. In *Psychoanalysis and Buddhism: An Unfolding Dialogue*, edited by Jeremy Safran. Boston: Wisdom Publications.

Said, Edward. 1978. *Orientalism*. London: Penguin Books.

Sasaki, Genjun H. 1986. *Linguistic Approach to Buddhist Thought*. Delhi: Motilal Banarsidass.

Schmithausen, Lambert. 1987. *Ālayavijñāna: On the Origin and the Early*

Development of a Central Concept of Yogācāra Philosophy. Tokyo: International Institute for Buddhist Studies.

Schweizer, Paul. 1994. "Momentary Consciousness and Buddhist Epistemology." *Journal of Indian Philosophy* 22: 81–91.

Scott, Charles. 1977. "Archetypes and Consciousness." *Idealist Studies: International Philosophical Journal* 7, no. 1: 28–49.

Segall, Seth Robert, ed. 2003. *Encountering Buddhism: Western Psychology and Buddhist Teachings.* Albany, N.Y.: State University of New York Press.

Smart, Ninian. 1964. *Doctrine and Argument in Indian Philosophy.* London: Allen and Unwin.

Stcherbatsky, Th. 1993. *Buddhist Logic.* 2 vols. Dehli: Motilal Banarsidass.

Streng, Frederick J. 1992. Mechanisms of Self-Deception and True Awareness. In *Self and Liberation: The Jung-Buddhism Dialogue,* edited by Daniel J. Meckel and Robert L. Moore. New York: Paulist Press.

Suler, John. 1993. *Contemporary Psychoanalysis and Eastern Thought.* Albany, N.Y.: State University of New York Press.

Sulloway, Frank J. 1979. *Freud, Biologist of the Mind.* New York: Basic Books.

Tanaka, Junshō. 1968. *Kūkan to Yuishikikan: Sono genri to hatten* (Emptiness and consciousness-only: Their doctrines and developments). Kyoto: Nagata Bunshōdō.

Ueda, Yoshifumi. 1967. "Two Main Streams of Thought in Yogācāra Philosophy." *Philosophy East and West* 17: 155–165.

Varela, Francisco. 1998. Is There an Unconscious in Buddhist Teaching? A Conversation between Joyce McDougall and His Holiness the Dalai Lama. In *The Couch and the Tree: Dialogues in Psychoanalysis and Buddhism,* edited by Anthony Molino. New York: North Point.

Vasubandhu. 1988. *Abhidharmakośabhāṣyam.* Translated into French by Louis de La Vallée Poussin and translated into English by Leo M. Pruden. Berkeley: Asian Humanities Press.

Waldron, William Stone. 1990. "The Ālayavijñāna in the Context of Indian Buddhist Thought: The Yogācāra Conception of an Unconscious." Ph.D. diss., University of Wisconsin-Madison.

———. 1994. "How Innovative Is the Ālayavijñāna? The Ālayavijñāna in the Context of Canonical and Abhidharma vijñāna Theory. Part 1." *Journal of Indian Philosophy* 22: 199–258.

———. 2003. *The Buddhist Unconscious: The Ālaya-vijñāna in the Context of Indian Buddhist Thought.* London: RoutledgeCurzon.

Watson, Gay. 1998. *The Resonance of Emptiness: A Buddhist Inspiration for a Contemporary Psychotherapy.* Surrey, England: Curzon Press.

Welwood, John. 2000. *Toward a Psychology of Awakening: Buddhism, Psychotherapy, and the Path of Personal and Spiritual Transformation.* Boston: Shambhala.

Werner, Karel. 1988. "Indian Concepts of Human Personality in Relation to the Doctrine of the Soul." *Journal of the Royal Asiatic Society of Great Britain and Ireland* no.1: 73–97.

Williams, Paul. 1989. *Mahāyāna Buddhism: The Doctrinal Foundations.* London: Routledge.

Williams, Paul, and Anthony Tribe. 2000. *Buddhist Thought: A Complete Introduction to the Indian Tradition*. London: Routledge.

Wriggins, Sally Hovey. 1996. *Xuanzang: A Buddhist Pilgrim on the Silk Road*. Boulder, Colo.: Westview Press.

Wu, Rujun. 1978. *Wei-Shi Zhe Xue: Guan Yu Zhuan Shi Cheng Zhi Li Lun Wen Ti Zi Yan Jiu* (Yogācāra philosophy: A study of *āśraya-parāvṛtti*). Kao Hsiung, Taiwan: Fo Kuang Publishing House.

Xuan Zang. 1973. *Ch'eng Wei-Shih Lun: The Doctrine of Mere-Consciousness*. Translated by Wei Tat. Hong Kong: Ch'eng Wei-Shih Lun Publishing Committee.

Yokoyama, Kōitsu. 1979. *Yuishiki no Tetsugaku* (Yogācāra philosophy). Kyoto: Heirakuji Shoten.

Yuasa, Yasuo. 1989. *Yongu to Tōyō* (Jung and the east). Tokyo: Jinbun Shuen. īūś

INDEX

Abhidharma Buddhism, 21–22, 32, 60, 161n.33

access to subliminal mind, 17, 19–20, 128–144, 148; direct (*ālaya-vijñāna* of Xuan Zang), 20, 128–129, 130, 138–144, 148, 176n.8; indirect (unconscious of Freud and Jung), 20, 128–135, 138, 140, 143–144, 148

action: bodily, 28, 30; instincts, 106, 170n.24; *karma*, 28–30; speech, 28, 158n.15

actuality: potentiality and, 60–63, 71, 77. *See also* reality

adhipatipratyaya/condition *qua* contributory factor, 71, 75–78, 84, 139

ālambanapratyaya/condition *qua* perceived object, 71, 73–78, 80, 139; close and remote, 73–75, 80

ālayavijñāna/storehouse consciousness, 14–16, 18–19, 44, 47, 48–86, 107, 138–149, 159n.18, 162–167; attachment of *manas* to, 59, 64, 83–85, 108–109, 122–123, 174n.24; and *bījas*/seeds, 33, 44–46, 49, 55, 59–60, 64–71, 77, 79–82, 118–121, 143, 165nn.18, 20, 166n.23; Brown

on, 139, 140, 176n.7; continuity and, 18, 43, 45, 49–50, 59, 64–65, 68, 76–77, 82–87, 109, 110, 123, 138, 146–147; corporeal character, 46, 165n.20; direct access to, 20, 128–129, 130, 138–144, 148, 176n.8; as *mūla-vijñāna*/root consciousness, 59, 60, 65, 119; as new form of mind, 46, 48, 58–86, 165n.20; origin/early development of concept of, 21–47, 155n.1; perceived aspect, 51–54, 65, 73, 74; perceiving aspect, 51–52, 54, 65, 73–76, 84–85, 109; self-corroboratory aspect, 54–55, 65, 66, 84, 109; and seven consciousnesses, 59, 66, 68–86, 139, 166n.23; three meanings of, 82; transformation of, 46, 66–67, 77, 118–121; and unconscious, 7–16, 86, 109–110, 128, 146–149; as *vipākavijñāna*/ripening consciousness, 59, 69, 79, 81, 166n.23

analysis, 157n.11; causal, 34, 73–74, 75; of consciousness, 34, 58, 70–76, 85–86; intentional, 74–75; synchronic and diachronic (of *dharmas*), 32. *See also* psychoanalysis

ABOUT THE AUTHOR

Tao Jiang is an assistant professor in the Department of Religion at Rutgers University, New Brunswick, where he teaches Mahāyāna Buddhism, classical Chinese philosophy, and comparative philosophy. After receiving his Ph.D. from the Department of Religion at Temple University in 2001, Jiang taught as an assistant professor in the Philosophy Department at Southern Illinois University Carbondale from 2001 to 2005. His articles have appeared in *Philosophy East & West*, *Journal of the American Academy of Religion*, *Journal of Chinese Philosophy*, *Journal of Indian Philosophy*, *Continental Philosophy Review*, *Dao*, and in several edited volumes. He co-chairs a new program unit under the American Academy of Religion, "Religions in Chinese and Indian Cultures: A Comparative Perspective."

SOCIETY FOR ASIAN AND COMPARATIVE PHILOSOPHY MONOGRAPH SERIES

John W. Schroeder, *Editor*

Orders should be directed to University of Hawai'i Press, 2840 Kolowalu Street, Honolulu, Hawai'i 96822, via e-mail to <uhpbooks@hawaii.edu>, or online at <www.uhpress.hawaii.edu>. Manuscripts should be directed to John W. Schroeder, Department of Philosophy and Religious Studies, St. Mary's College, St. Mary's City, Maryland 20686.